AF598002

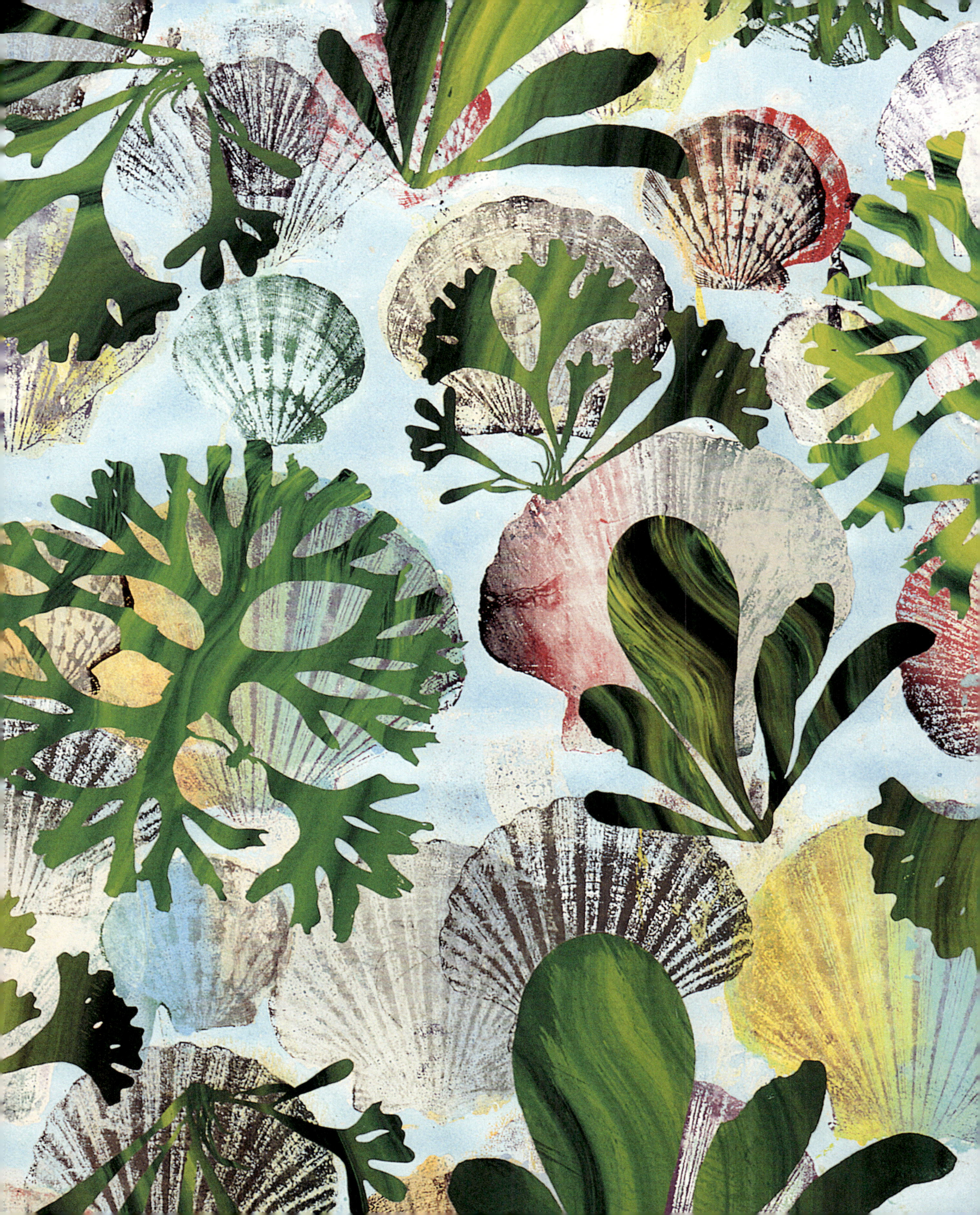

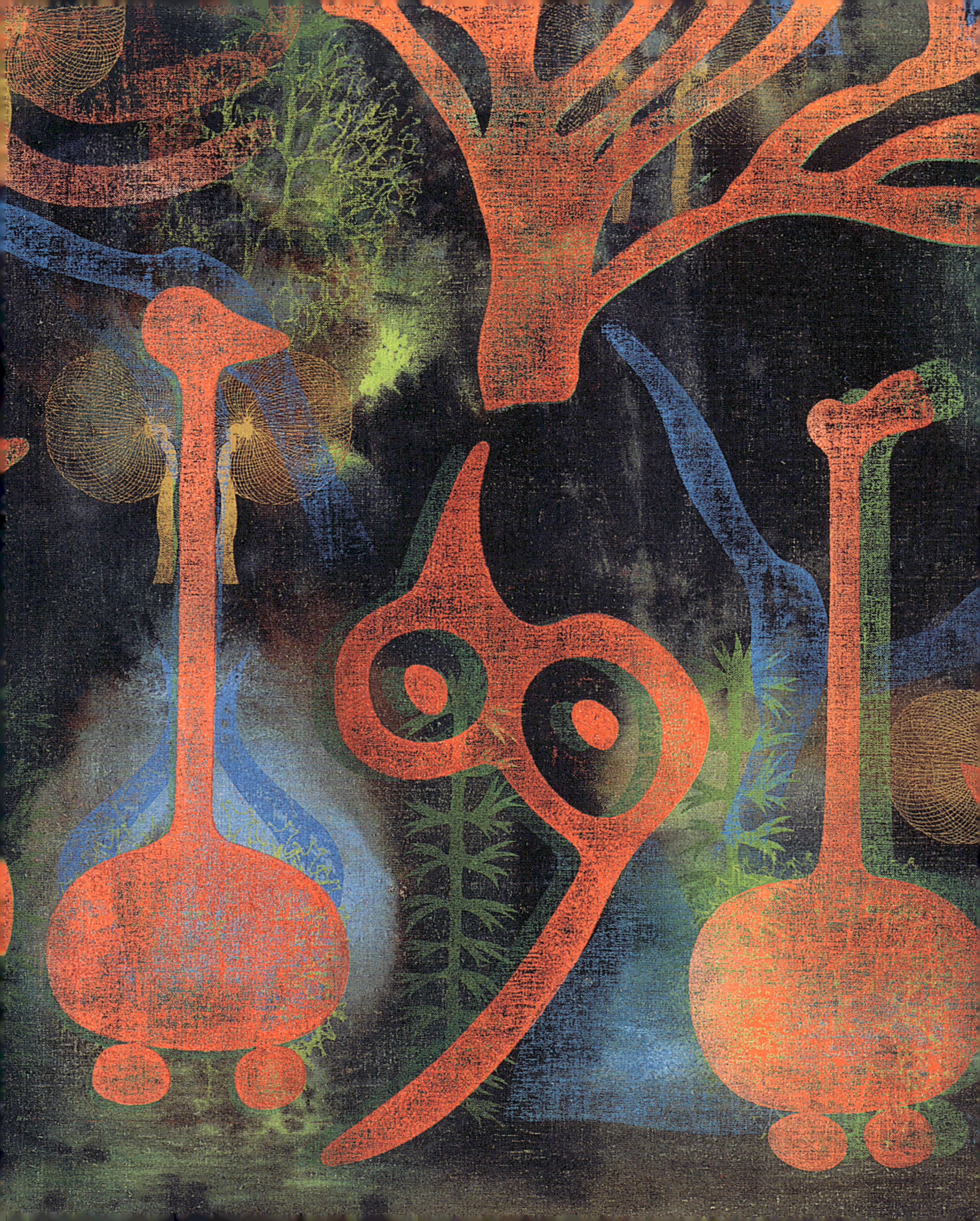

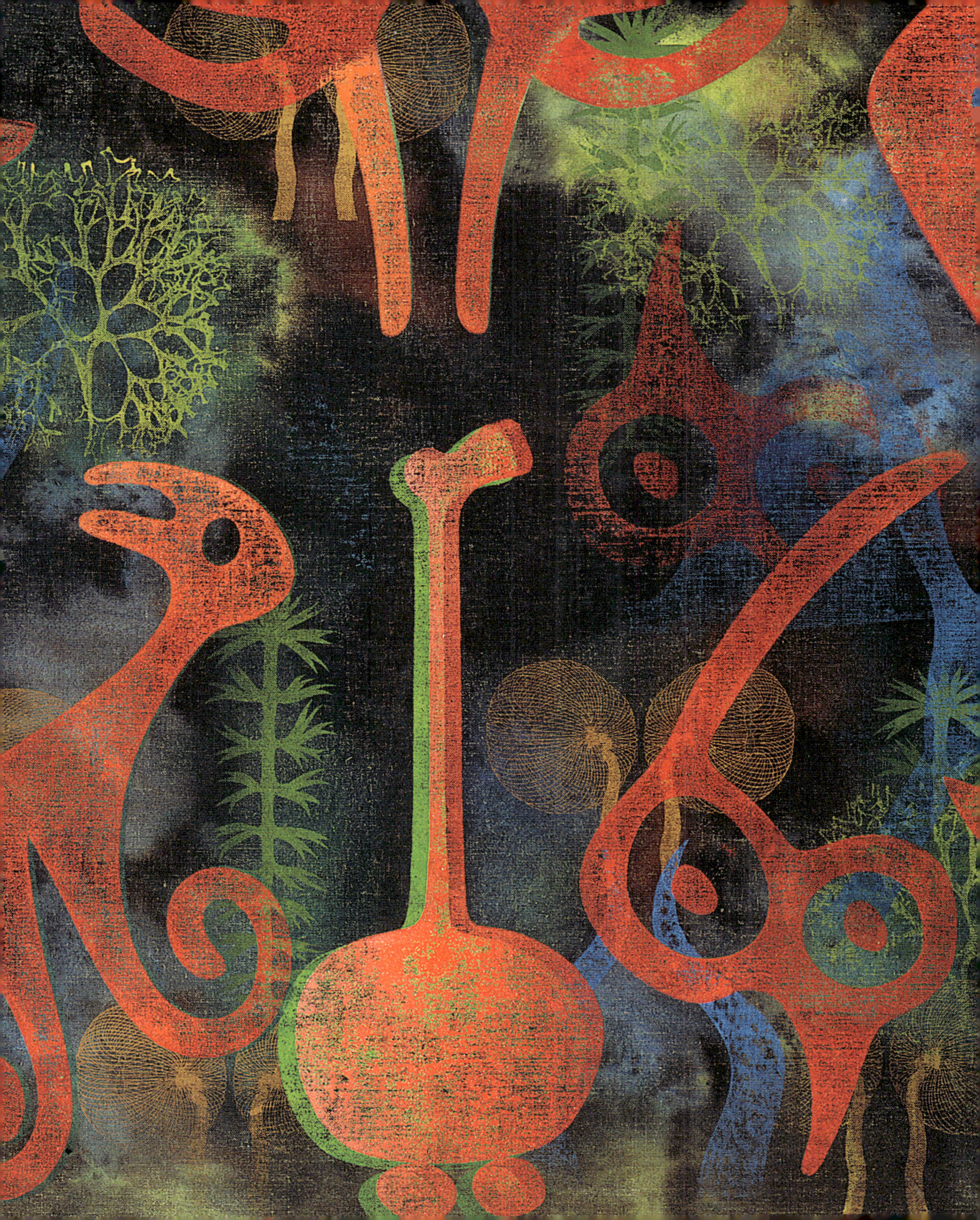

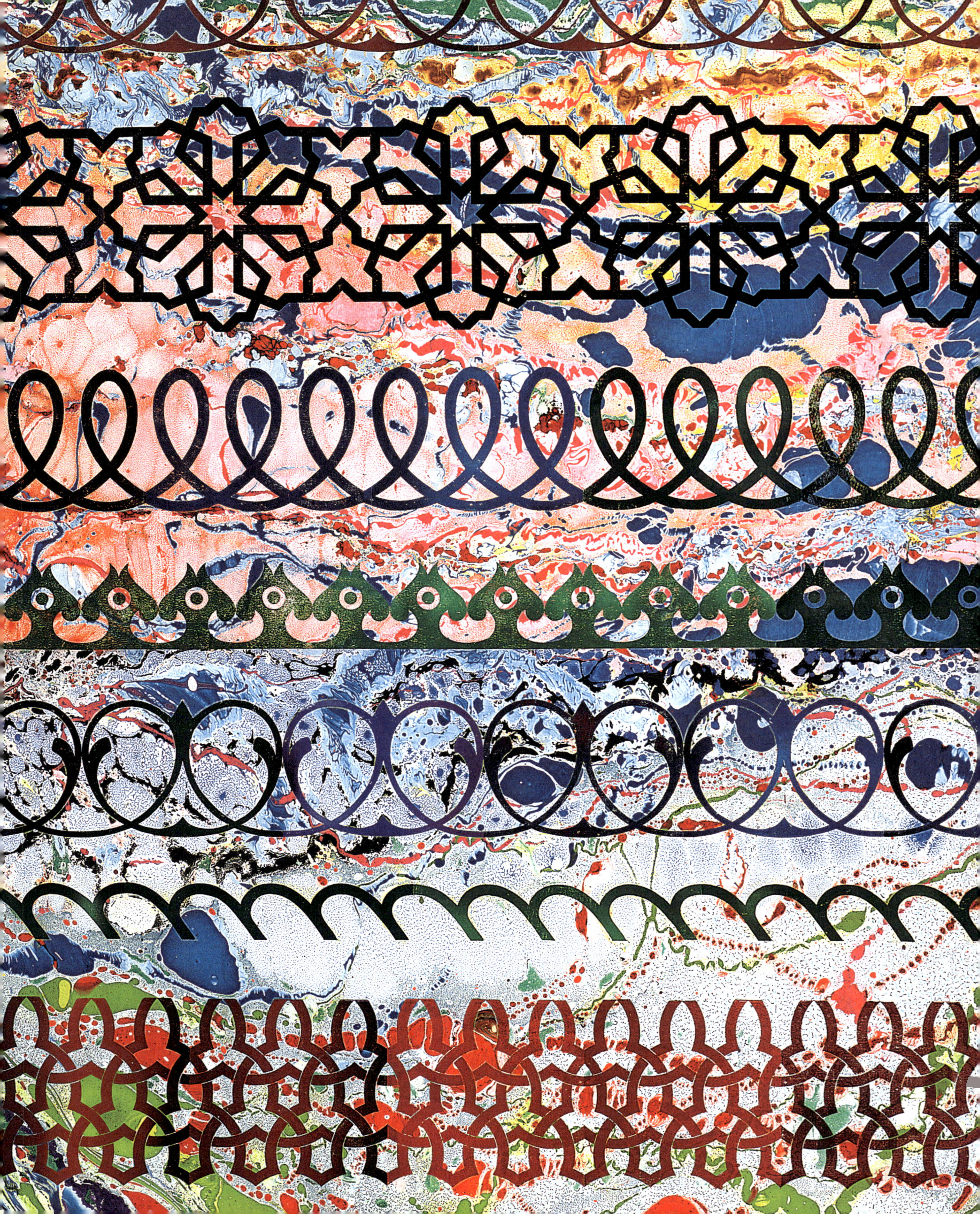

Philip Taaffe

Anima Mundi

Irish Museum of Modern Art

2011

Contents

Foreword

The Irish Museum of Modern Art is delighted to present this survey of paintings made during the last ten years by Irish-American artist Philip Taaffe. He is no doubt one of the most significant painters working in America today and he is certainly responsible, with a handful of other artists, for the renewed interest in abstraction which has been ongoing internationally since the 1990s. These artists include fellow American Terry Winters and Spaniard Juan Uslé, who have recently shown at IMMA. We hope that this inaugural exhibition of Taaffe's work in Ireland will make his work known to an Irish audience, particularly following the acquisition of a major work of his, *Cape Siren* (2008), which was donated to us by Lochlann Quinn using the Section 1003 scheme.

The exhibition presented at IMMA focuses exclusively on his paintings. Taaffe's work has evolved during the years but he developed his distinctive style quite early in his career. Multiple cultural references from present and past times appear in his work creating multilayered final images of great complexity and extraordinary beauty. Taaffe's work goes well beyond formalism. Acknowledging the great tradition of Abstract Art initiated by Wassily Kandinsky, František Kupka and Piet Mondrian, Taaffe does not consider form as an end in itself. His paintings are equally well rooted in the present time, and somehow could not have been imagined before the world we now live in, bombarded as we are by information technology.

I wish to convey my deep appreciation to all those who have made this exhibition possible. Meriting particular mention and without whom this project could not have been accomplished is Philip Taaffe, for his ever-exciting vision and practice. I curated his first retrospective show at IVAM in Valencia about ten years ago and have been following his work with great enthusiasm for quite a number of years now. Special thanks are also due to Raymond Foye in New York for his deep knowledge of the artist's work and his tremendous commitment and always pertinent suggestions to realising this exhibition and its accompanying book. It has also been a pleasure to cultivate an enjoyable working relationship with all at Gagosian Gallery, Jablonka Galerie, Studio d'Arte Raffaelli and Thomas Ammann Fine Art. Further thanks are due to all my staff at IMMA, notably Seán Kissane, Head of Exhibitions and Eimear O'Raw, Curatorial Coordinator, Exhibitions. Thanks also to Gale Scanlan, Operations Manager; Cillian Hayes, Head Technical Supervisor and Edmund Kiely, Technical Supervisor, for their technical support and skills throughout this installation and the duration of the show.

For their contribution to and faith in this significant catalogue I would like to thank its designer Herman Lelie, with whom IMMA has already a long and fruitful relationship; Colm Tóibín for his evocative text and David Brody for his revealing interview. We received invaluable assistance from Gagosian Gallery to produce this catalogue and for this we express gratitude.

Last but not least, I wish to thank all those who contributed to this project in any way. Their skills, inquisitiveness and motivation have been a continual source of inspiration throughout the project.

Enrique Juncosa
Director, Irish Museum of Modern Art

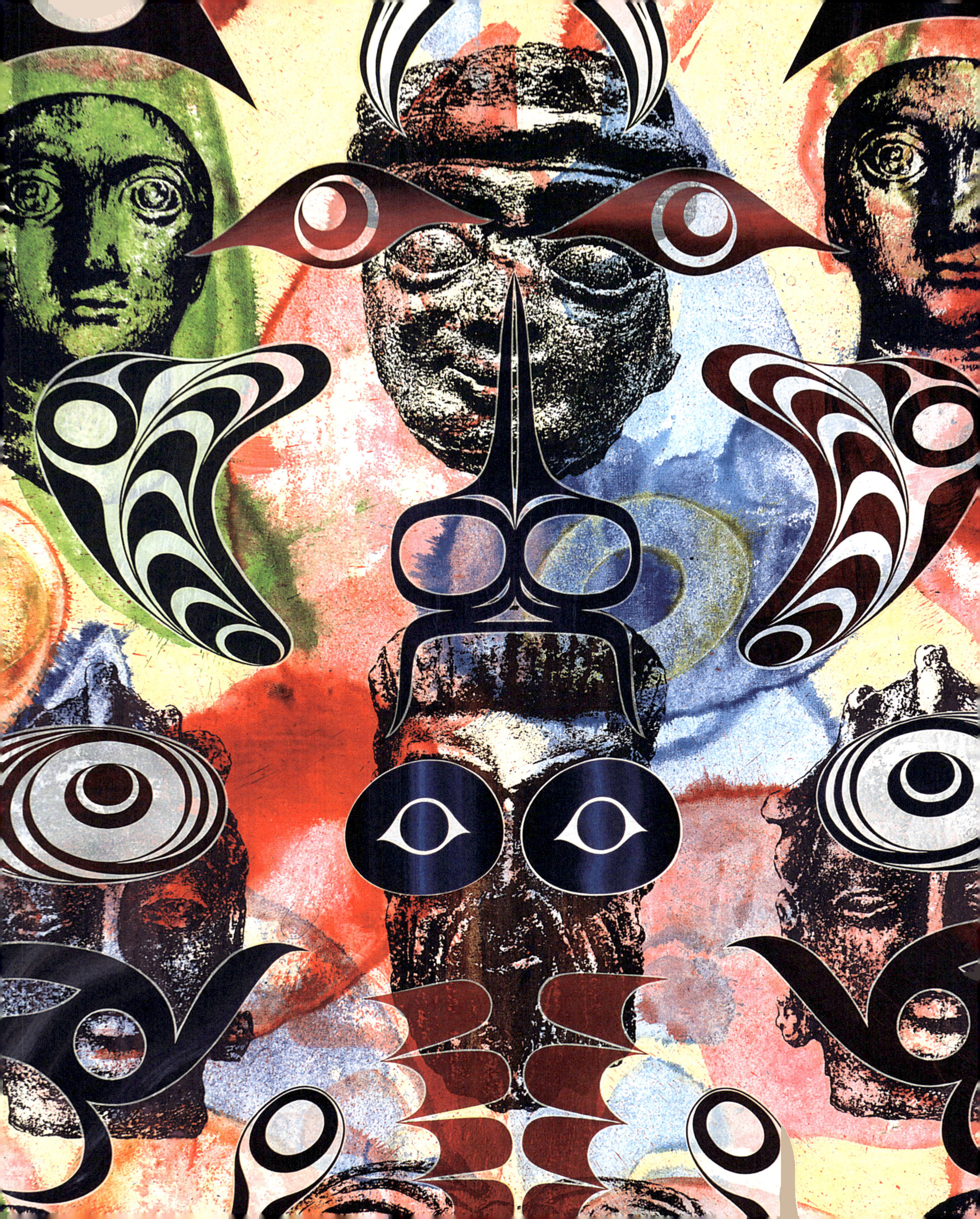

Anima Mundi

Enrique Juncosa

I.

> A single vision would have come to him again and again, a vision of a boat drifting down a broad river between high hills where there were caves and towers, and following the light of one Star; and that voices would have told him how there is for every man some one scene, some one adventure, some one picture that is the image of his secret life, for wisdom first speaks in images…
>
> W. B. Yeats [1]

Philip Taaffe, whose first solo exhibition took place in 1982, belongs to a generation of artists who in the eighties succeeded in restoring credibility to abstraction after the suicide of sorts it suffered under the theorising of Minimalism, with its drive to reduce painting to a mere index of formal characteristics. From Kazimir Malevich and Wassily Kandinsky to Robert Ryman and Brice Marden, via many other artists of the last century such as Piet Mondrian, Jean Arp, Joan Miró, František Kupka, Jackson Pollock and Mark Rothko, abstract art had, up until this point, been emblematic of Modernism, constructing a space where stylistic revolution was ever possible. In the sixties, however, the most advanced theoretical debates migrated towards the realm of sculpture, and from there to art forms centred on the creative process and its conceptual formulation, which some (Thomas McEvilley, for example) have called anti-artistic.[2] This period also sees the discovery of video as a medium, followed by other forms of digital technology, and the development of a multi-disciplinary art scene. Some two decades passed before painters such as Philip Taaffe, alongside Terry Winters, David Reed, Jonathan Lasker, Juan Uslé, Olav Christopher Jenssen, Bernard Frize, and Helmut Dorner, succeeded in reinvigorating abstract painting, and painting in general, by steering the theoretical debate away from syntax and towards semantics. All of these artists have demonstrated that painting continues to be a valid language in an increasingly multicultural world dominated by information technology.

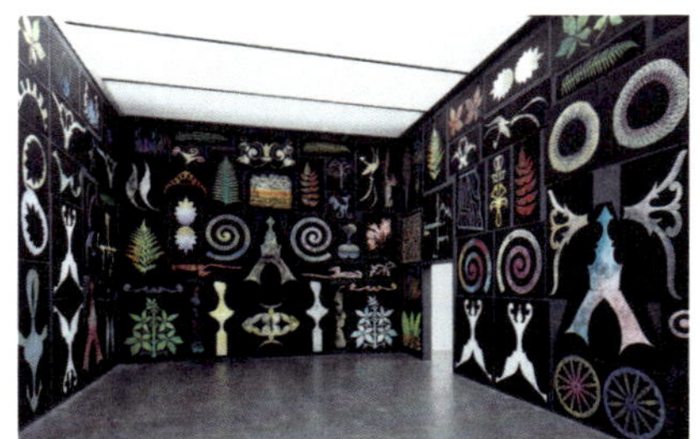

Philip Taaffe, *Sanctuarium*, 2010.
Installation, Kunstmuseum Luzern

In the eighties and nineties, various international group shows explored these questions from a range of viewpoints.[3] Philip Taaffe's work appeared in some of these exhibitions. Soon after, solo exhibitions were organised in art institutions featuring the artists involved in these shows, with Taaffe's first retrospective taking place in Valencia's IVAM in 2000.[4] Subsequently, a new group of painters began to emerge that included such influential figures as Luc Tuymans, Franz Ackermann, Ellen Gallagher, Chris Ofili, Udomsak Krisanamis, Thomas Scheibitz, Julie Mehretu, Fergus Feehily, Francis Alÿs, and Amy Sillman, who, in some ways, follow in the footsteps of the first generation of postmodern painters leaving old arguments, e.g. whether painting is merely for bourgeois consumption, far behind. For some of these more recent artists, painting is but one facet of their artistic output. Even Taaffe has created spaces which could be described as installations – rooms completely covered in monotype prints – in recent museum shows in Wolfsburg and Luzern.

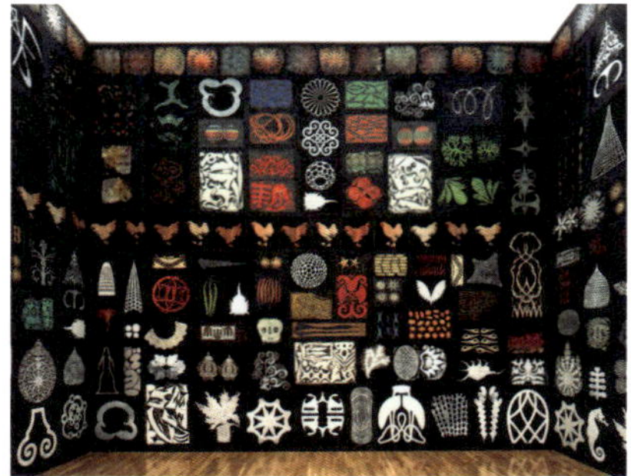

Philip Taaffe, *Lalibela Kabinett*, 2008.
Installation, Kunstmuseum Wolfsburg

Over a thirty-year career we can analyse not only Taaffe's evolution within a wider artistic milieu, but also examine the defining characteristics of his work as an individual outside the context of his artistic generation. While the present exhibition at the Irish Museum of Modern Art looks exclusively at work over the past ten years, I would like to begin by discussing his work prior to this period, and in so doing refer to some developments that are fundamental to a proper understanding of it.

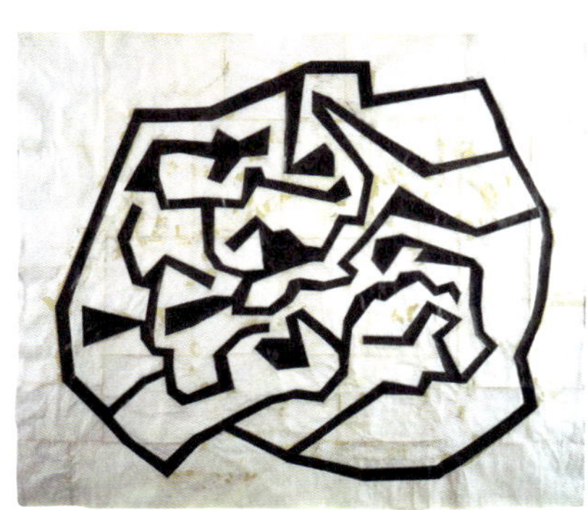

Philip Taaffe, *Glyphic Brain*, 1980–81

The artist's earliest surviving paintings were completed between 1980 and 1982. They belong to a group of works known as the *Picture Binding* series, a group of collages that employ black, blue, or red adhesive tape (of the type used for mounting photographs in photo albums), composed on white backgrounds of collaged paper or masonite panels. *Glyphic Brain* (1980–81) belongs to this series. Taaffe builds imaginary architectural spaces closed in on themselves – the artist explained that he was thinking of medieval walled cities as he created them. These works are generally small and employ one colour on a white background. Formally, they are linked to the Constructivist tradition, but already show some enduring characteristics of the artist's mature work. First, he uses collage as an organising principle. Second, he constructs an abstract image that is both representational and emblematic, presaging his later work, where ornamental motifs are often repeated. Clearly for Taaffe, painting has already become a means of depicting a distinct space, which is simultaneously idealised, imaginal, and intellectual. Lastly, we see the ritualised repetition of a specific way of working, particularly laborious and rigorous, which, despite the level of concentration it demands, nevertheless leaves room for chance and improvisation.

In 1983, Taaffe's work changes scale. His first large format collage, *Martyr Group* (1983), took its inspiration from twelfth century frescoes from the Moldavian region of Romania. The work was made using police target-practice figures that Taaffe found outside one of the printing plants he frequented in search of discarded materials, in the vast industrial parks near his studio in Jersey City, New Jersey. The resulting image presents a contemporary reality: the targets allude to those by Jasper Johns, while the martyred figures refer indirectly to AIDS, which was devastating the artist's friends and society at the time. These themes are placed side by side with a medieval mode of composition and a frontal arrangement of figures. This juxtaposition of forms and ideas from heterogeneous sources becomes a defining characteristic of his work.

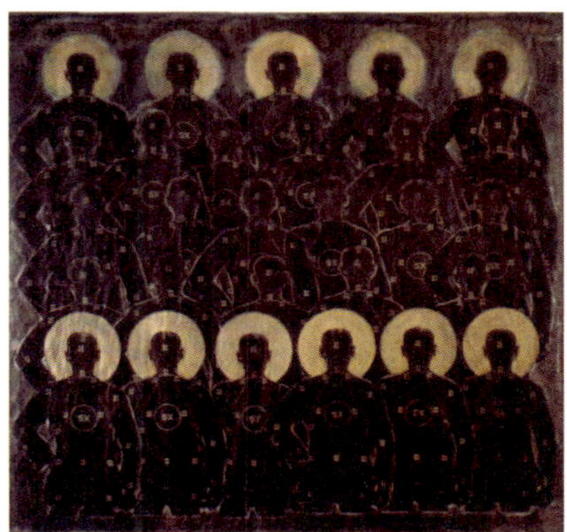

Philip Taaffe, *Martyr Group*, 1983

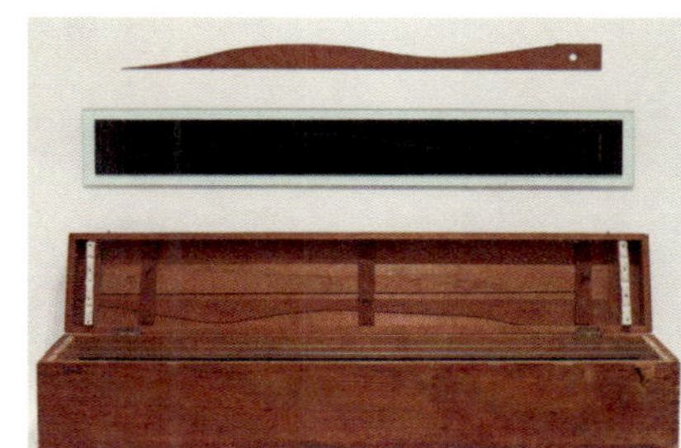

Marcel Duchamp (1887–1968): *Three Standard Stoppages* (3 Stoppages Etalon). Paris, 1913–14. New York, Museum of Modern Art (MoMA)

From 1983 until more or less the beginning of the nineties, Taaffe frequently although not exclusively made works in homage to other artists from the modern period, especially Bridget Riley, Ellsworth Kelly, and Barnett Newman, but also to Marcel Duchamp (see *Green/White Stoppages*, 1984), Jean Arp, Clyfford Still, Mark Rothko, Adolph Gottlieb, Ad Reinhardt (see *Chi-Chi Meets the Death of Painting*, 1985) or the less well-known Paul Feeley, Charles Shaw, and Myron Stout. Throughout this period, he became associated with other 'appropriationist' artists such as Mike Bidlo and Sherrie Levine, and also with so-called Neo-Geo painting, a group that included artists such as Peter Halley, Peter Schuyff, and Ross Bleckner (who wrote the introduction to the first Taaffe exhibition catalogue).[5] At the time these Taaffe works that incorporated specific references to others received significant attention and sparked quite a bit of controversy – naturally, considering Bridget Riley and Ellsworth Kelly are alive and, indeed, still working today. It is understandable how the use of their art as sources for decorative motifs, treating them as works from the past, could be provocative, even if the op-art paintings of Bridget Riley, which reached their peak during the 1960s, were of declining interest by the 1980s.

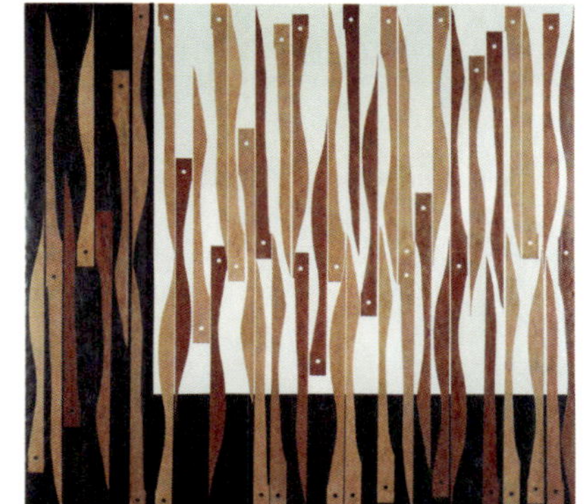

Philip Taaffe, *Green/White Stoppages*, 1984

It should be pointed out that Philip Taaffe's so-called 'appropriationism' is in no way cynical, nor is it an act of artistic necrophilia. It does not play conceptual or theoretical games. Taaffe recreates these canvases from pioneering periods of the recent past without questioning or ridiculing them, but rather he taps into a tradition that he wishes to be a part of, invoking these works as in a magic ritual. Taaffe specifically used Riley's paintings as models to create his own, and gave them new titles, for example: *Overtone* (1983) or *Brest* (1983–84), the latter a reference to Jean Genet's novel *Querelle de Brest*. Importantly, one should note these are also collages. Taaffe made linocut prints, imitating the British painter's curves and waves, which he later pasted onto thick paper (likewise discarded print runs, this time of light bulb packaging).

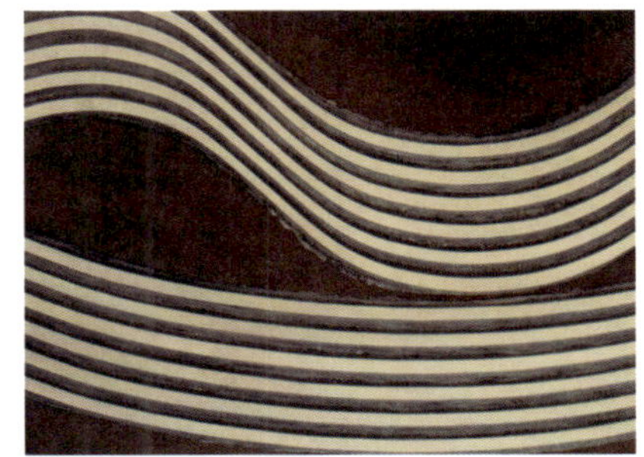

Philip Taaffe, linocut, 1983

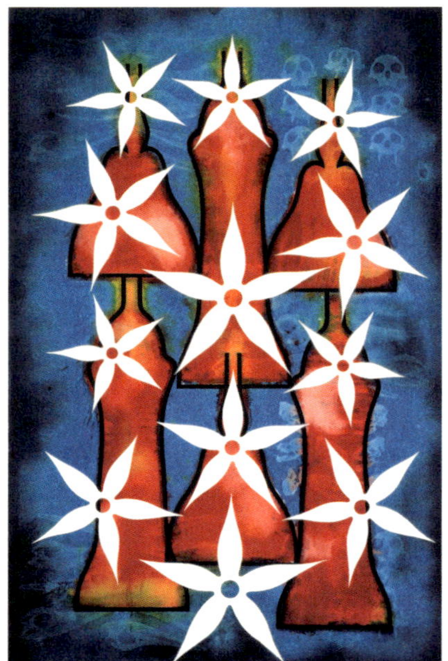
Philip Taaffe, *Ghost Still Life*, 2000

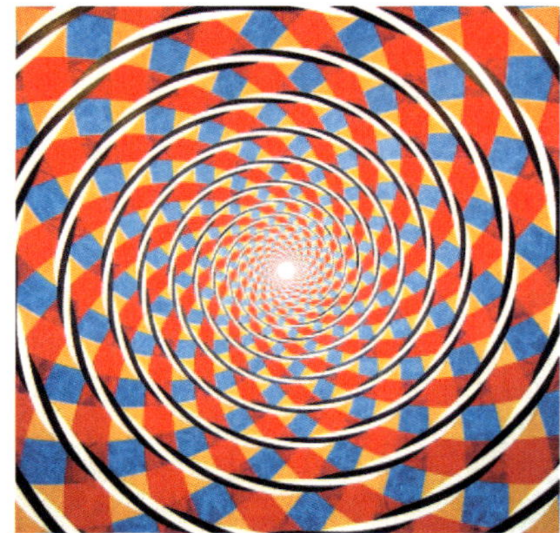
Philip Taaffe, *Unit of Direction*, 2003

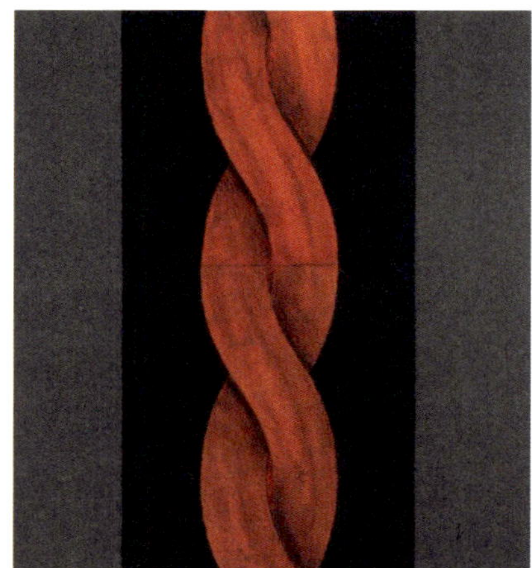
Philip Taaffe, *Abraham and Isaac*, 1986 (detail)

The result is texturally rich and fragile and has little to do with the highly finished, almost industrial perfection of the works that inspired them. Taaffe's originality, or authorship, comes through the process of conceptualising the final images (which are no longer ends in themselves) and constructing them in a way that can be described as at once verisimilitudinous and hand crafted. The artist does not treat these models of inspiration as banal or obsolete; on the contrary, he reconstructs them in order to celebrate them and explore their meaning, offering us a kind of romantic reverberation or echo. Furthermore, this reconstruction of space, in the act of painting itself, becomes the representation of a pulsating world of unquenchable metaphors. This interpretation is supported by many later works that show extremely dense rhythmic spaces which at times approach psychedelia. The psychedelic aspect of Taaffe's painting appears in more recent works such as *Cairene Window II*, *Damascene Triangle I* (both from 2008) or *Flag* (2009), which we will return to later. *Ghost Still Life* (2000) is in fact dominated by a Mexican species of morning glory whose seeds are ingested in Mesoamerican civilisations for their hallucinogenic effects.

Looking again at the paintings inspired by Bridget Riley, we can see how, over time, Taaffe's use of waveforms prefigures an interest in optical spaces as metaphors for the ecstatic/meditative power of the image. After the eighties, paintings such as *Inner City* (1993), *Reef* (1999–2000), *Chasm* and *Rose Nocturne* (both from 2002), and *Unit of Direction* (2003), continue to explore these rhythmic, compositional, and symbolic ideas towards metaphorical, rather than appropriationist, ends. In all of these works, Taaffe transforms metaphors into visual images, and this becomes one of the defining aspects of his work.

Paintings such as *We Are Not Afraid*, *Queen of the Night*, or *Homo Fortissimus Excelsus* (all from 1985), reference Barnett Newman. One of the best examples of this can be seen in Taaffe's 1986 painting *Abraham and Isaac*. In these works and *Abraham and Isaac*, (1986), Taaffe transforms into ornamental twists the line that runs vertically through Newman's canvases (referred to as the 'zip' by the artist and, for a while, something of an emblem of abstract modernism). The intention behind this act has been much debated but clearly contains elements of both irony and homage. In relation to this, Taaffe himself declared: *"I am interested in a sublimity which encourages laughter and delight in the face of profound uncertainty"*.[6] Looking back, however, I think it is even more relevant to highlight another aspect of the artist's versions of Newman's work, and that is the will to *read* abstract images. These paintings are, after all, representations of other paintings, only now the 'zips' have been transformed into garlands. Kay Heymer explains how Newman's *Who's Afraid of Red, Yellow and Blue* (1967), which led to Taaffe's *We Are Not Afraid* (1985), may have been inspired by a scene in Mike Nichols' film of Edward Albee's play *Who's Afraid of Virginia Woolf?* (1966), in which the protagonist, played by Elizabeth Taylor, is sitting on a swing. The division of space is very similar to Newman's composition, and Heymer suggests that in some way Taaffe is representing the rope that holds up the swing.[7] Also shared with Newman are the triangular formats that of late appear in Taaffe's works.

Taaffe has come to consider Abstract Expressionism as a repository of pictorial forms and ideas, which he uses in much the same way as he uses visual sources from diverse periods in history and diverse places around the world. For example in his snake paintings (*Snake Totem* or *Painting with King Snakes* from 1998), in which the reptiles are transformed into calligraphic forms, Taaffe refers to the drippings of Jackson Pollock's 'all-over' works, as well as to Arabic calligraphy. In another work, *Ahmed Mohamed* (1989), he superimposes Arabic calligraphy on an Adolph Gottlieb background. And *Old Cairo* (also from 1989) refers as much to Rothko as it does to Islamic ornamentation. One might add that Taaffe also carries on a number of Joan Miró's ideas, for example his constellation compositions, but transports them to the monumental formats of Abstract Expressionism. Taaffe's work can be seen as a continuation of Abstract Expressionism and not merely for the appropriation of some of its formal characteristics. This is certainly the case for Taaffe as regards Rothko and Newman, whose works are full of religious and transcendental connotations. Their great monochromatic expanses evoke the abstract sublime, continuing a Romantic tradition which includes Caspar David Friedrich and J. M. W. Turner.

Taaffe has also made versions of Ellsworth Kelly paintings where he fills the flat areas of colour with repeated ornamental motifs, e.g. *Nativity (Red/White)* (1986), and *Blue/Green* (1987). In so doing, Taaffe 'colonises' Kelly's spaces. In clearly suggesting an intention not merely concerned with form, the ornamental shapes grow like a coral reef, giving Kelly's forms a new life beyond the limits of formalism. The use of ornament soon becomes the most conspicuous aspect of Taaffe's work, as he developes his mature style towards the end of the eighties with works like *Intersecting Balustrades* (1987), a scaled rendering of a section of a wrought iron balustrade from the Jersey City Public Library. Although Taaffe has created other works inspired by wrought iron railings, e.g. *Onement* (1987) – a motif that also inspired Paul Klee when he visited Tunisia – he more often finds his subjects in old illustrated books. His library is certainly spectacular, almost Borgesian.

In 1989, having been invited to exhibit in Naples by the legendary gallery owner Lucio Amelio, Taaffe relocated to this city at the centre of Mediterranean culture, where one can observe the influence of many civilisations stacked on top of each other – a condition that undoubtedly interested him. Taaffe resided in Naples for almost four years. From Italy, he travelled to Egypt, Syria, Tunisia, Morocco, India, and other places, developing a profound interest in Islamic art.

The beginning of the nineties saw a major new development: Taaffe started to introduce zoological and botanical motifs regularly into his work, with images that traced the development of natural history illustration from the fifteenth to the twentieth centuries, as much a subject for Taaffe as the imagery depicted. These images were often interwoven with other decorative and architectural elements, reflecting the interrelation between nature and art. At this point the basis of his visual language was consolidated, and ever since that time he has been adding further layers of complexity.

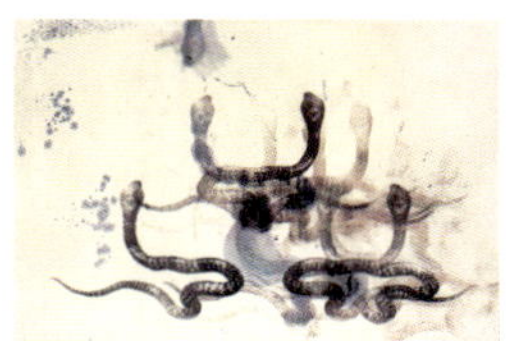

Philip Taaffe, *Calligraphic Study I*, 1996

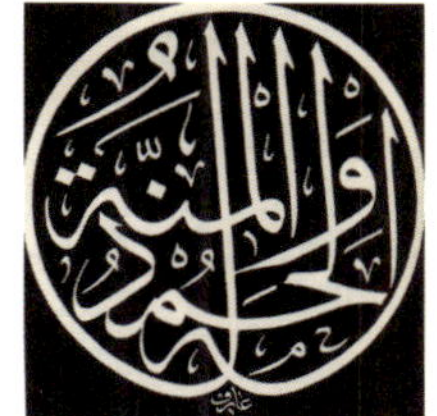

Calligraphy, Ottoman, 19th century

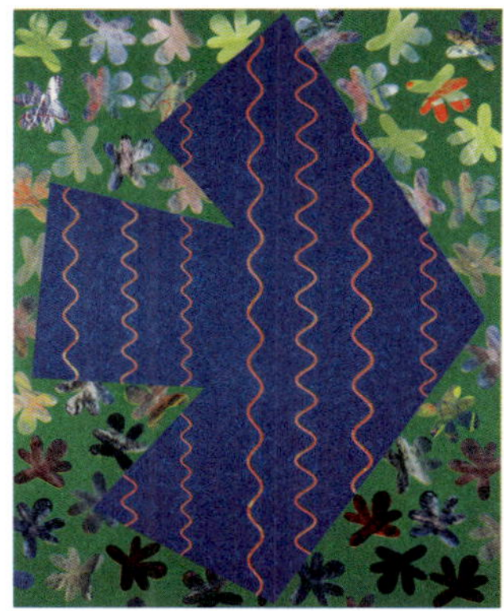

Philip Taaffe, *Blue/Green*, 1987

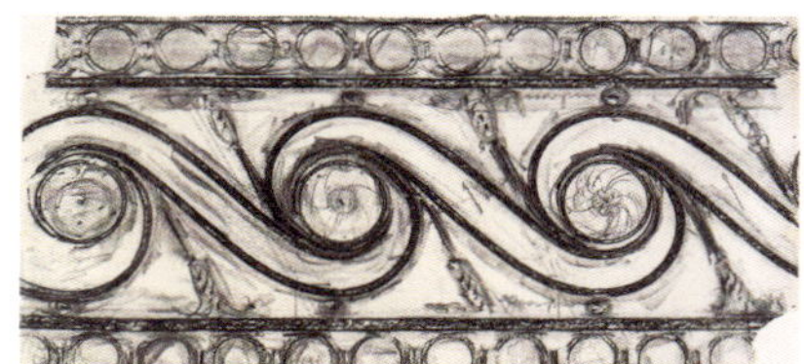

Philip Taaffe, drawing for *Intersecting Balustrades*, 1987

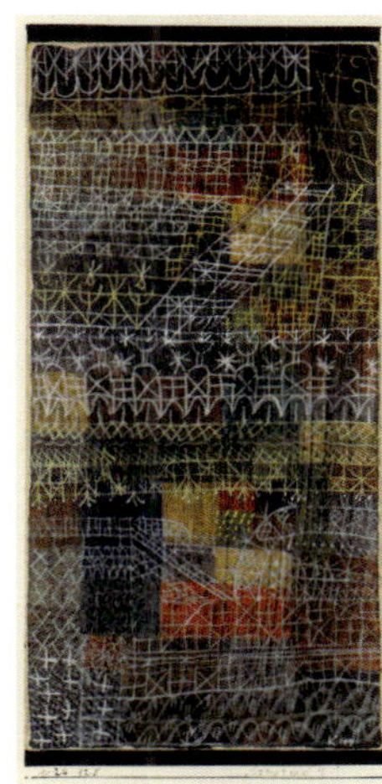

Paul Klee (1879–1940), *Structural I*, 1924. New York, Metropolitan Museum of Art

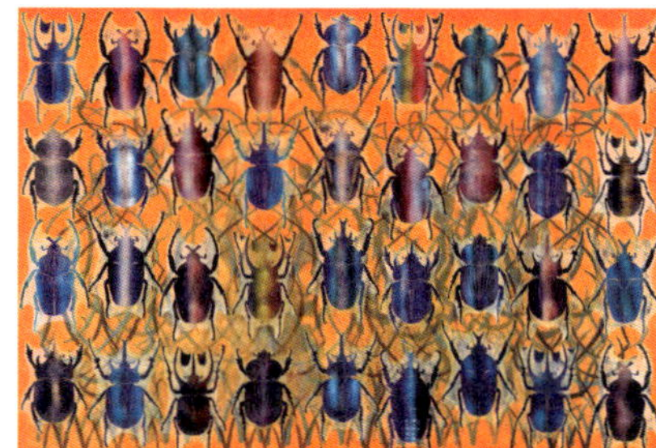

Philip Taaffe, *Scarabesque*, 1993–94

The first of these more complexly layered paintings was *Scarabesque* (1993–94), a large horizontal frieze of images of Scarab beetles – the Egyptian symbol of resurrection and eternal life. In terms of its use of figurative elements, this has a precedent in the dogs depicted in *Chi-Chi Meets the Death of Painting* (1985).

Taaffe's interests are broad and his knowledge of the history of image making is encyclopaedic. His methods have allowed him to develop a body of work that is visually extremely rich and highly individual. He is capable of harmoniously intermingling diverse ideas and cultural phenomena in a very open, inclusive, and seductive way, that leaves room for irony and political commentary while remaining open to interpretation by the viewer.

On one occasion Taaffe spoke about his work as having a healing aspect, coming after a century of continual aesthetic ruptures. Yet for him style is not an end in itself. In a text published in 1998, shortly before the first works in the current exhibition were painted the artist explains:

> I would say that to look at a painting means one is taken up with another reality, a pictorial fictive reality, and as such that picture represents an imaginary location. So if one is fed up with the mundane and pedestrian experiences of life, and instead stands in front of a painting, that is a place, an imaginary construction to inhabit with one's sensory being. To be lost inside of a painting is the crucial experience here, as an alternative to other places in the world. [8]

The often superimposed ornamental motifs that populate his canvases are a mechanism to transport us to another place, which is not necessarily a physical space, a characteristic shared by Islamic art and the art of Thailand, to give two examples. Raymond Foye wrote that Taaffe: "uses the decorative to inspire an awareness of the divine order behind the world of appearances."[9]

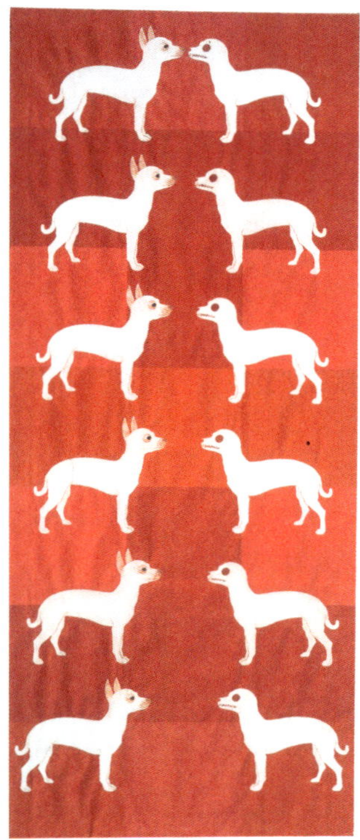

Philip Taaffe, *Chi-Chi Meets the Death of Painting*, 1985

In early December 2010, I visited the artist at his New York studio and also attended a public conversation with the poet and art critic John Yau at Rutgers University (New Jersey). During this time I had the opportunity to speak to him in person about the selection of paintings for this exhibition; our conversation forms the basis for the following exploration of the semantic implications they convey.

II.

Between voice and echo infinite rains and crystals float
José Lezama Lima [10]

Philip Taaffe's paintings carry immediate references to other regions of space and time, yet in the same breath construct a language which is perfectly contemporary. In describing some of the artist's works one might start with those titles that refer to places – a regular occurrence with Taaffe. Words such as 'port', 'cape', 'passage', 'strait', in the titles of works in the present exhibition (and others such as 'canyon', 'archipelago', 'city', 'garden', 'megapolis') refer to the history of travel and the circulation of people, ideas, goods, and other cultural phenomena. Words such as 'sanctuary', 'reliquary', or 'cappella' refer to sacred places, and others, such as 'field station', to isolated places dedicated to scientific research. Bearing in mind these facts alone, it is not difficult to see Taaffe's work as a kind of universal quest, even though the locations described are sometimes imaginary.

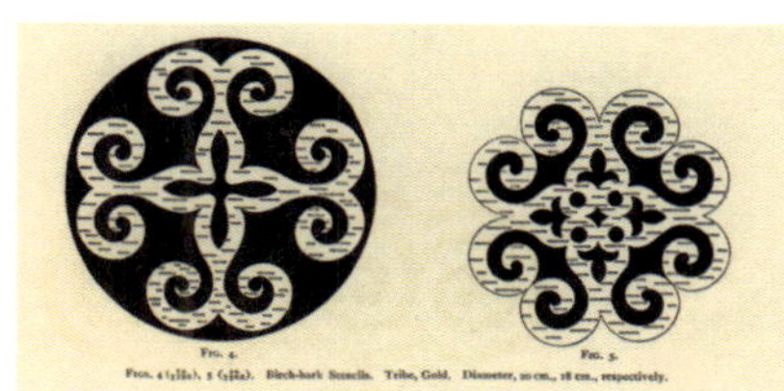

Laufer, *Decorative Art of the Amur Tribes*, 1902

Let us begin with *Porte Amur* (2001) (p. 51), which takes its name from the white shapes that dominate the composition. These ornamental motifs are patterns inspired by bark stencilling used by the people of the Amur River in Mongolia, one of the most northerly locations where Buddhism became established. The central pattern, which appears a further four times, in two instances inverted, looks something like the head of a deer, while the others are abstract. These white shapes cover almost the entire surface of the canvas with the exception of the upper section, which features a line of stylised vine leaves, giving the work a festive or Bacchic feel. The vine leaves and the Amur decorative patterns appear on different layers, the lower layers in darker colours. The effect of superimposing colours and forms is vibratory, like falling snow, and accentuates the rhythm of a composition based on repeated shapes, whose orientation occasionally changes. The background of the upper section is dark blue, giving it a vespertine air, and the warm red of the lower part suggests, perhaps, fire in a grate. As with many of Taaffe's works, everything is balanced symmetrically and has an architectural quality. It is as if we were looking at the elaborate door of an ancient temple built by a sophisticated civilisation now lost in the mists of time.

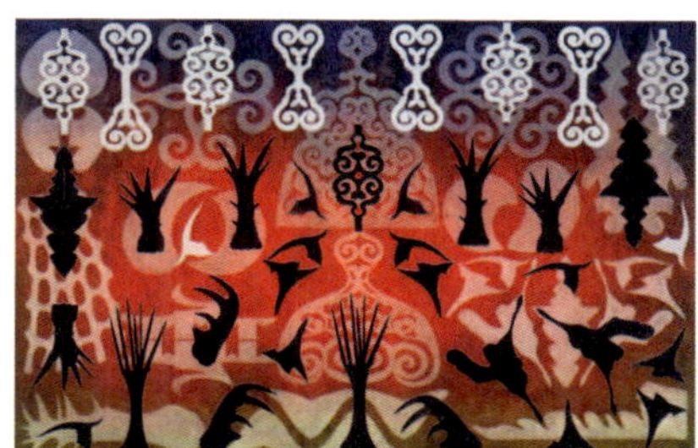

Philip Taaffe, *Amur Field*, 2009

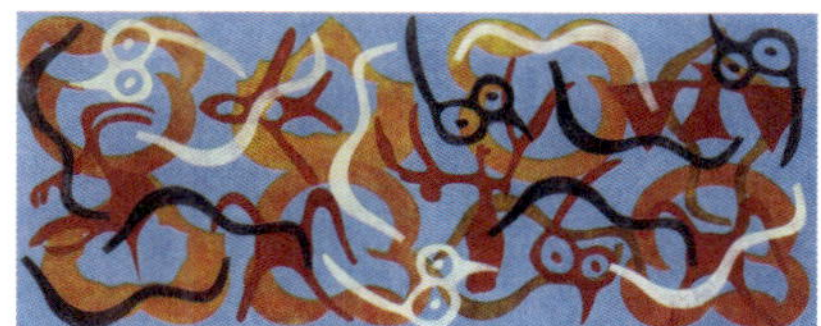

Philip Taaffe, *Glyphic Frieze*, 2003

The composition of *Sanctuary* (2002) is dominated by petroglyph images (also known as rock engravings), some of which were used earlier in *Glyphic Field* (1998–99). Petroglyphs are found in distinct locations across the globe and some may be precursors to writing. They are considered symbolic and have profound cultural and religious significance. Some interpretations indicate that they were most likely made by shamans working in altered states of mind, although there is as yet no consensus on how certain geometric forms could have recurred in civilisations that had no contact with each other. The great Romanian historian of religions, Mircea Eliade, believed that coincidences in shamanic phenomena

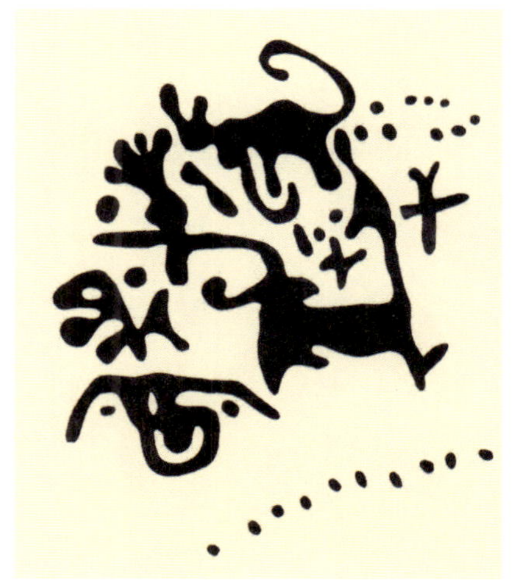

Antonio Núñez Jiménez, *Petroglifos del Peru*, Havana, 1986

have to do with primordial and even genetic realities and "belong to man as such and not to man as a historical being." [11]

Some of the predominant forms in *Sanctuary* are stylised images of birds and women with elongated arms. Beneath these reddish and earthy coloured forms there are other more abstract blue shapes, and on a level lower still one can make out mosses and ferns. The whole ensemble is dark with muted and humid tones and is clearly evocative of a sacred cave, with the symbolic suggestion that caves form passages and entrances to other subterranean worlds. The rectangular format and large scale of the work gives it an enveloping quality. The curved forms seem to move slowly, and the different layers suggest depth. Everything is ritualised and secret.

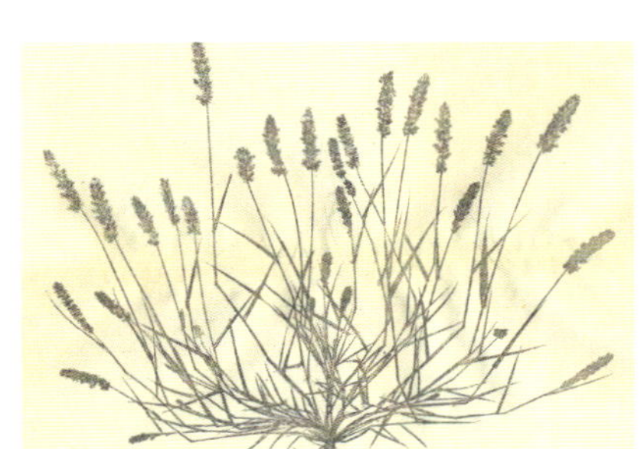

Illustration of the Indigenous Fodder Grasses of the Plains of North-Western India. Nature-Printed at the Thomason Civil Engineering College Press. Roorkee, 1886. Plate XXXIX

Field Station (2003) takes its name from the places where botanists and naturalists set up camp out of doors while doing research. The background of charcoal lines drawn directly on the canvas and oil paint in muted primary colours is overprinted in green with images of Indian fodder grasses pressed against the coloured background. The upper layer is a lattice of bands of ornamental black and white shapes that suggest an observation station set up to examine the vegetation in the background. The lattice is made up of four bands. The lower one comprises three elements and the three upper bands two. In the second and third, the forms are black or white; on the upper level they are both black and white. It is a mysterious work that both reveals and conceals. Once again, the metaphor of looking into the depths of things, through the lattice is made visual.

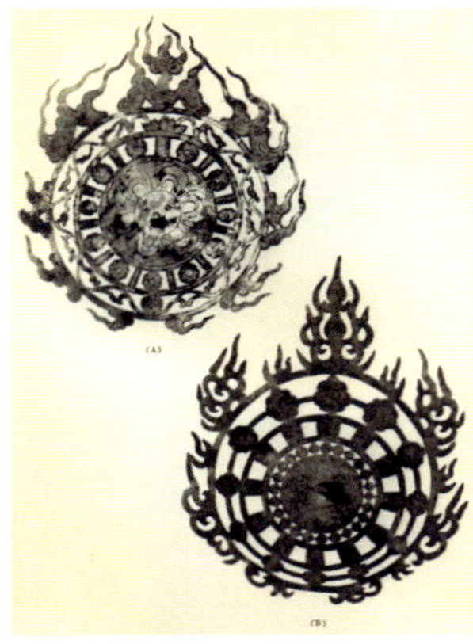

Seiroku Noma: *Ancient Japanese Gilt Bronze Buddhas Formerly in the Imperial Collection*. Benrido Co., Ltd., Kyoto, 1952. Plate 116

Asuka Passage (2006) refers to the site in Japan of the oldest surviving wooden constructions in the world – some very early Buddhist temples. The largest shapes in this work are a series of flaming Buddhist aureoles of perforated bronze. These appear over and beneath a rhythmic series of curved forms which, in combination with the yellow and orange tones, give the whole a fiery appearance, suggesting Buddhist illumination.

Cape Siren (2007) is the fourth in a series of paintings that have fictive capes in their titles. All of them feature decorative motifs used by the natives of western Canada, a zone full of capes. Forms from this shamanic culture are alternated with Chinese heads and mermaid and siren heads (hence the title) of Greco-Roman origin. The whole has a totemic feel to it – the thin, vertical totem format is one which appears regularly throughout the artist's work.

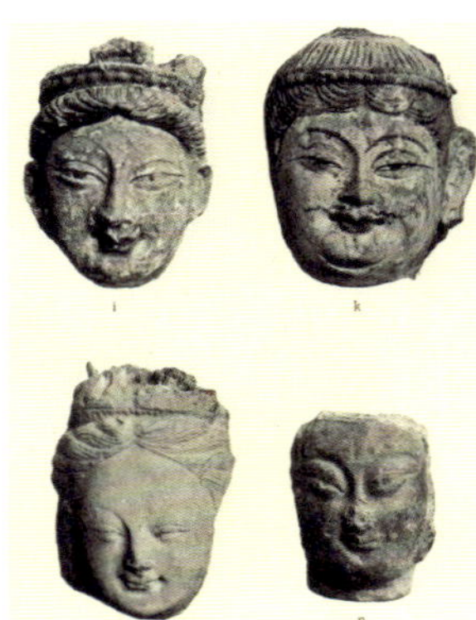

Cape Siren Figure illustration, Dietrich Reimer (Ernst Vohsen), Berlin, 1913

Port of Saints (2007) takes its title from a book by William S. Burroughs, and is dominated by gold leaf lino carvings of curves borrowed from Islamic decoration. The painting has a cosmic dimension depicting a sky filled with Islamic stars, with decorative work below taken from the *mihrab*, or prayer niche, of a mosque. The gilded curves undulate and shimmer, making the work dynamic and Dionysian. The Burroughs reference is not by chance, nor simply a result of their collaborating on a catalogue.[12] The 'cut-up' technique invented by the author whereby texts are cut up and later strung together again to exploit the expressive possibilities of chance and unforeseen juxtapositions, has a clear connection with Taaffe's work.

The painting *Artificial Paradise (Loculus)* (2008) refers to the French poet Charles Baudelaire's book on the use of mind-altering substances. Images of seeds, ferns, corals, cacti, and echinoderms float over a black background, reminiscent of Miró's constellation compositions and also, more obliquely, of his spiritual *Self-Portrait II* (1938) in Detroit. The colours used are almost fluorescent, bringing to mind fireworks or pulsing energy points. While making it, the artist was thinking of the atmospheric electrical phenomenon known as Saint Elmo's fire that sometimes occurs on ships during storms. Normally it blazes violet and blue and appears on masts accompanied by a buzzing sound. Originally the phenomenon was considered mysterious and of divine origin.

In summary, all of the works mentioned above emphasise the concept of painting as a mechanism or point of entry to another dimension. This is achieved through decorative motifs which are themselves crystallisations of energies and modes of thought and metaphors for ecstatic trance.

There is a further large body of work that contains botanical references. *Devonian Leaves* (2004) is a floating, constellation-like arrangement of images of fossilised leaves from extinct plants of another geological epoch. The enamel marbled background gives the work a magma-like quality, bringing to mind the Big Bang and the origins of the universe. In some ways it is also an ecological work, in that the leaves depicted are already victims of history and evolution. The irregular white band in the upper part of the painting gives the work a glacial appearance, suggesting the conditions for how these plants might have become extinct.

Composition with Shells and Algae (2005) depicts exactly what its name suggests: superimposed shells and seaweed in a celebration of the possibilities of abundance. The artist explains how he made this work after seeing some photographs of the Covento de Cristo of Diogo Arruda in Tomar, Portugal, built in the Manueline style. This particularly exuberant Baroque style evolved with a knowledge of the architecture of South Indian temples, the Portuguese having taken Goa not long before. Both Indian and Portuguese temples exhibit something of the exuberance of tropical vegetation.

The botanical references continue with *Dryadic Figures* (2006). The dryads referred to in the title are tree nymphs. Dryads were said to live inside trees and risk death if they strayed too far from them. The five nymphs suggested by the vertical shapes in the work are made of bark patterns from the giant Douglas fir, trees being symbolic of life and growth in many cultures. These bark columns are decorated with motifs taken from a German cabinet-making manual and with distaffs from ancient looms. The lower part of the work, which we can read as the earth, is green, as are the grasses growing on it, while the blue starry sky employs star shapes from Egyptian funerary paintings on tomb ceilings in the spectacular Valley of the Kings.

Other paintings have more abstract titles that merely refer to the pictorial elements in each composition. For example, in *Abstract Painting (Vipera russelli)* (2002), the motifs that Taaffe uses (nine times) are the snakes referred to in the title, a particularly venomous specimen.

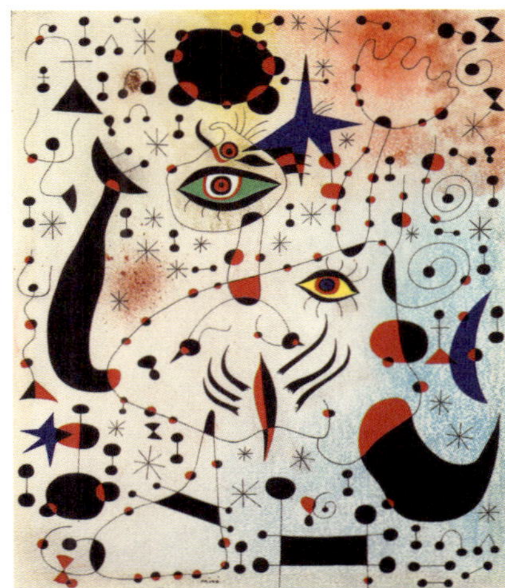

Joan Miró, (1893–1983), *Ciphers and Constellations in Love with a Woman*, 1941. Gift of Mrs. Gilbert W. Chapman, 1953.338, The Art Institute of Chicago

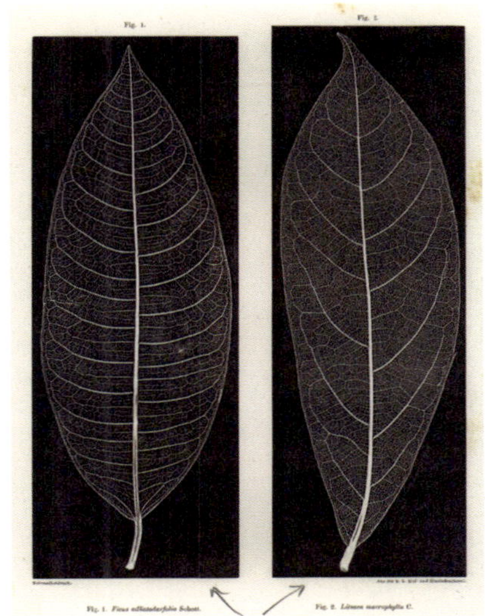

Constantin Ritter von Ettingshausen, *Leaf-Skeletons of Dicotyledons*, Vienna, 1861

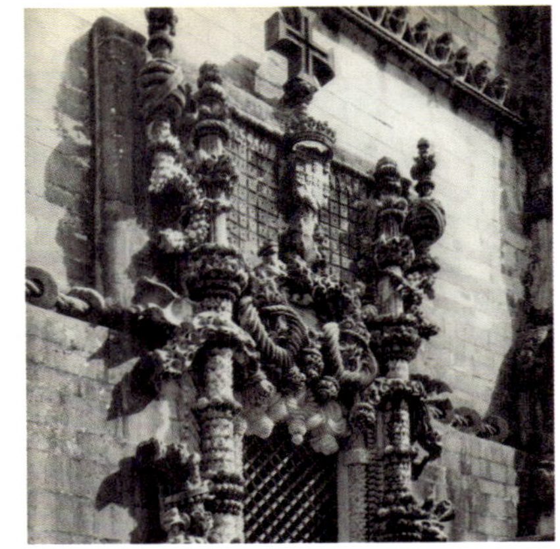

Diogo de Arruda, Convento de Cristo, Tomar, Portugal, c. 1510

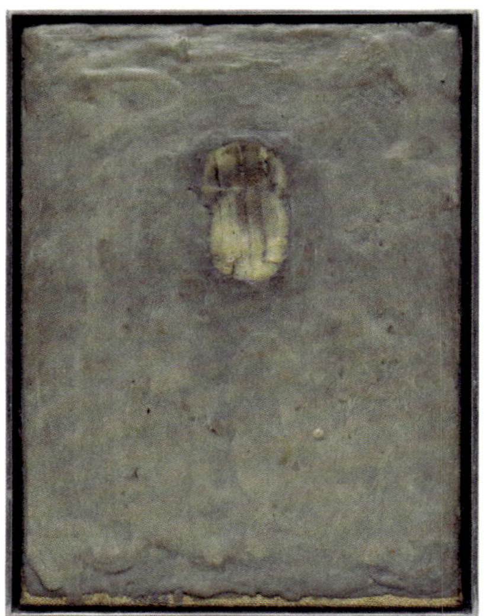

Jasper Johns (b. 1930), *Painting Bitten by a Man*, 1961. New York, Museum of Modern Art (MoMA)

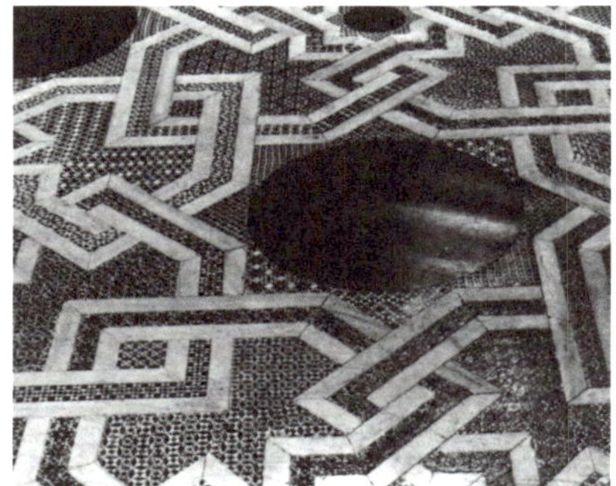

Cosmati work, Monreale Cathedral

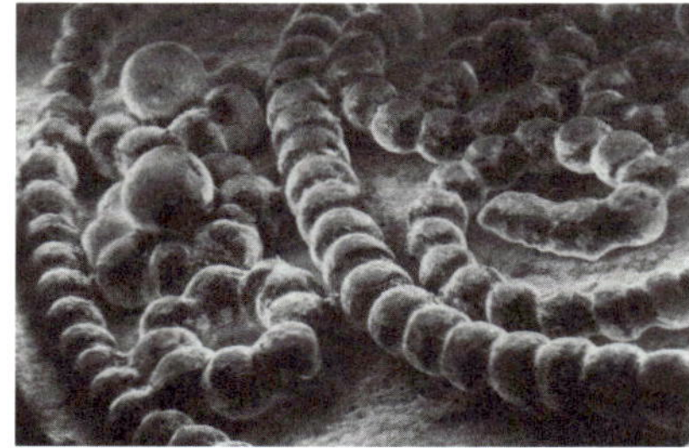

Detail from Wladyslaw Duczko, *The Filigree and Granulation Work of the Viking Period*, Stockholm, 1985

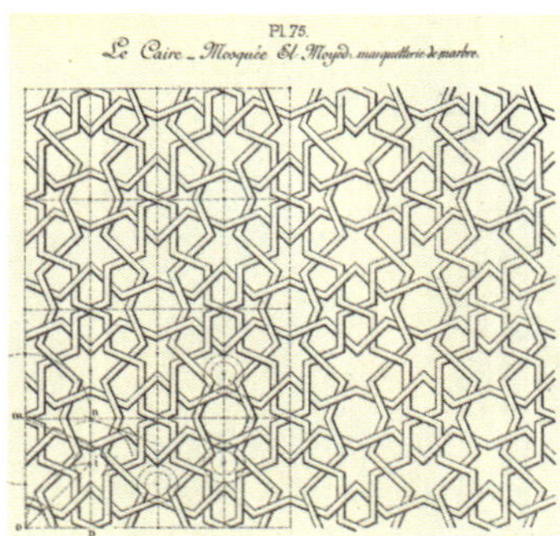

J. Collin, *Étude Pratique de la Décoration Polygonale Arabe*, Paris, c.1920

The background is made using lithographic ink on glass transferred to paper sheets that are collaged to the canvas. A tension is produced in the work between the celestial, i.e. the blue, and the earthly, and also between the calligraphic snakes and the lithographic marks in the background.

Painting with Teeth (2002), by contrast, shows six vertical, decorated columns composed of representations of neatly ordered teeth that, again, refer clearly to tribal totem poles. Teeth (and skulls) are a motif Taaffe had already used in *The Sorcerer's Apron* (1998–99), a work that, according to the artist, was inspired by a short story by Georges Bataille, which refers to a painting comprised entirely of teeth. Later, the artist noted an unintended reference to Jasper Johns' *Painting Bitten by a Man* (1961) in the MoMA collection. The title of the earlier teeth painting also refers to magical Tibetan aprons worn by shamans during a wrathful dance, as part of a Tantric initiation ceremony. Again there are parallels here between Taaffe and Johns, the latter painting a series of works entitled *Tantric Detail* at the beginning of the eighties in which skulls and scrota appear over a decorative background.

The titles of other works refer to different forms of decoration. *Cosmati* (2007) is the name of a Roman family who, in the twelfth and thirteenth centuries, invented decorative, geometric designs for church floor mosaics using tiny triangular and rectangular pieces of stone and coloured glass. The painting has a varnished, shiny surface. *Viking Filigree Totem* (2008) belongs to a large series of works that use a vertical format in the form of a totem pole, although in this case the painting is much wider. Once again, these works lead us to think immediately of primitive and tribal art. The imagery in this canvas comes from a book about Viking filigree work. The book includes detailed close-ups reminiscent of bacteria or other biological specimens. Taaffe uses these here for the background. The dark tones give it a medical or scientific quality like images seen through a microscope.

Painting with Byzantine Fragments (2008) is an unusually monochromatic work. In making it the artist took images from books on the archaeology of early Christianity and its architecture in Asia Minor, Syria, and Egypt. The artist re-sized and carefully re-drew these elements using an antiquated and labour-intensive resist technique of stopping-out, using grease crayon and shellac, on silkscreens that were later printed.

Lastly, the works *Damascene Triangle I, Cairene Window II* (both from 2008), and *Flag* (2009), belong to a recent series where Islamic decorative elements from a French book entitled *Étude Pratique de la Décoration Polygonale Arabe* are superimposed on backgrounds of saturated colours made using *orizomegami*, a Japanese craft of folding and dying paper. Taaffe was fascinated by the fact that both techniques originate in the eleventh century, a time when pre-geometricised Islamic art still retained a closeness to imagery from nature. These works are not about mixing styles and cultures freely, but are the product of patient observation of historical instances where visual epiphanies are brought into concrete existence – all viewed and recombined by the artist through the lens of the Western tradition of abstraction. As we have seen, superimposing geometric structures over unbridled multicoloured backgrounds is a method that Taaffe uses often, exemplifying the contrast between Classical and Romantic and between Apollo and Dionysus. Both the ordered geometry of the surface and the luminous chaos of the background are composed of motifs that could extend to infinity, suggesting a tension that cannot be resolved. With regard to his use of decorative elements, Taaffe has said:

> Decoration is usually derived from a local natural situation; it can epitomize the lush quality of, let's say, palms or lotus flowers or jungle overgrowth. Decoration in this sense is a kind of culturalized representation of nature. It's closest to the raw elements that reflect a very specific geographical situation in historical time. The importance of it for me is that I can have these circumstances of time and place in a crystalline form, and I can feel those realities, feel the history that they inevitably speak about in this natural cultural sense (...). I primarily want to feel the living reality of these elements, and to respond to them in a personal way by making a composition that allows these other voices to speak again in a way that I've understood and responded to. These voices are part of this lived experience represented by decoration, and I would like those voices to share a dialogue with the formulations that I produce. The fact that one can repeat something in order to achieve a dynamic synthesis, a sort of crescendo of decoration – having this possibility of tempo, change and restructuring – means that these voices can be amplified and joined together in a way that I couldn't have anticipated. And I want to see, I want to hear, I want to experience this .... I don't use them [these images and decorative fragments] only because they are interesting or exotic forms, or because they can be used in a certain way structurally or formally. It's always a matter of feeling ... and shaping something out of that enthusiasm, that passion.[13]

In recent years the artist developed two important series on paper using the specific techniques (that reflect the use of the traditional to form something altogether new) of paper marbling and decalcomania. Marbling was most likely invented in China during the Tang dynasty before passing to Japan. In both countries marbling was associated with divination, and later, in Europe, it had links to alchemy. The backgrounds of paintings such as *Devonian Leaves* (2004), *Porte Amur* (2004), and *Plinth* (2006) use marbling on paper collaged onto canvas. It is easy to imagine why Taaffe is interested in this manner of working. With it the artist is able to attain visually rich effects, bringing to life the conflict between order and chaos and the tension between what is visible and what is hidden. Decalcomania was used especially by Spanish surrealist painter Óscar Domínguez in the beginning of the twentieth century. Taaffe used decalcomania to produce a great number of works on paper during the summers of 2007, 2008, and 2009. The resulting images are complex and mysterious and feature symmetrical frameworks with skulls, spirals, and vegetation, suggesting dreamlike, hermetic, and psychedelic ideas.

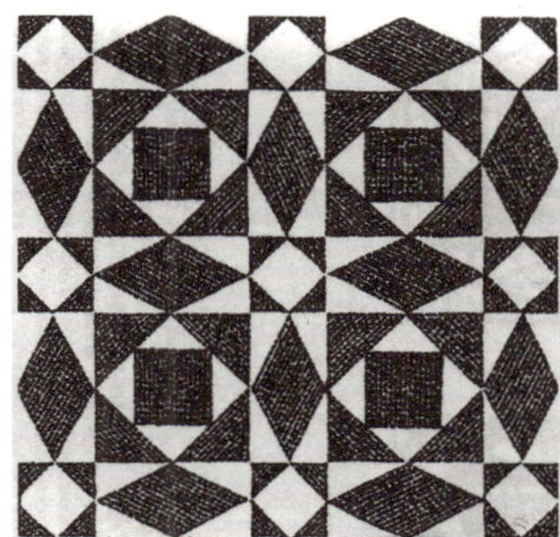
Cosmati mosaic pattern, *Le Décor Géométrique de la Mosaïque Romaine*, Paris, 1985

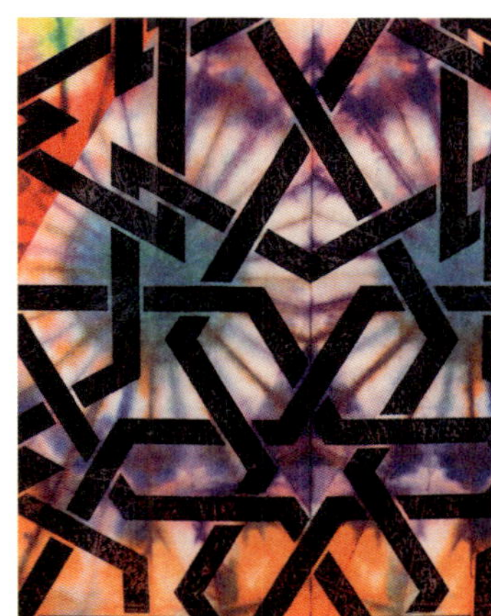
Philip Taaffe, *Orizomegami* drawing with linocut overprinting, (detail)

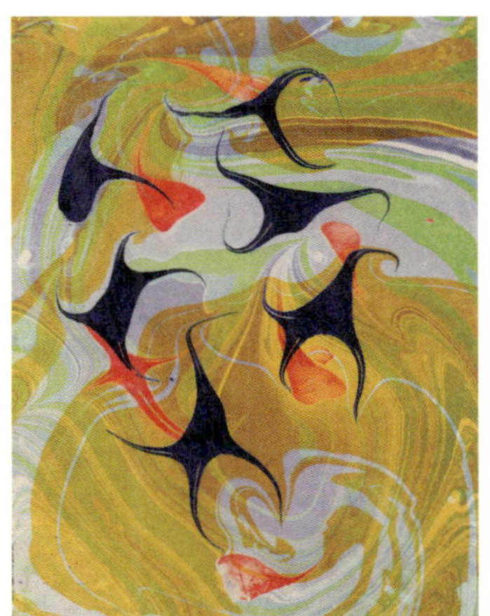
Philip Taaffe, *Untitled*, 2003

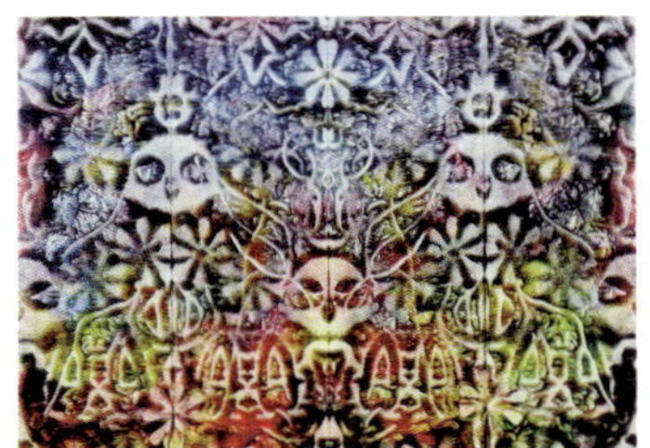
Philip Taaffe, *Gravinia*, 2008

III.

In this rite the Great Magician stirs in His dream,
and the magician dreaming murmurs to his beloved:
thou art so near to me
thou art a phantom that the heart
would see –
and now the great river of their feeling grows so wide
its shores grow distant and unreal.
Robert Duncan [14]

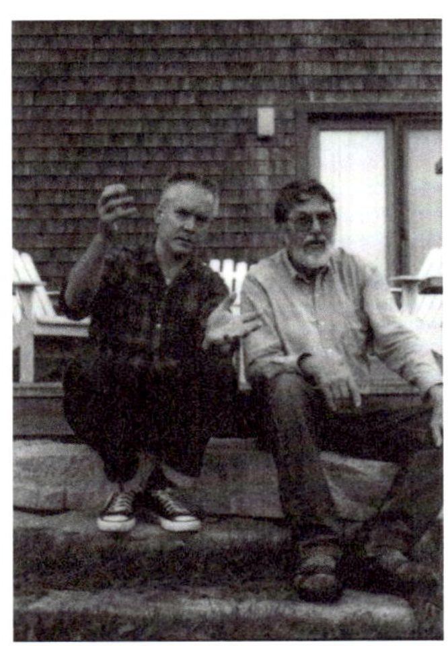
Philip Taaffe and Robert Creeley, Waldoboro, Maine, 1999

William Butler Yeats is perhaps the most famous poet from the previous century to be associated with esoteric traditions. Alongside a rich lode of Celtic myths (the texts of which had been translated into English not long before his birth), this spiritual ancestry served the development of his original visionary poetry. In the words of Daniel Albright:

> As a poet, Yeats hoped to subvert a language created for the description of the everyday world, in order to embody visions of the extraterrestrial …Yeats's poetry shows a lifelong search for such images, images that were not reflections but illuminations … he came to the conclusion that there was in fact one source, a universal warehouse of images that he called the Anima Mundi, the Soul of the World. [15]

I believe this text has particular resonance with the painting of Philip Taaffe, an artist who seeks the radiant points of energy in decorative motifs from all epochs to create hypnotic and pulsating images that invite us to enter meditative trances and the gateway to paradise.

DRAWING DIALOGUE

WILLIAM S. BURROUGHS
PHILIP TAAFFE

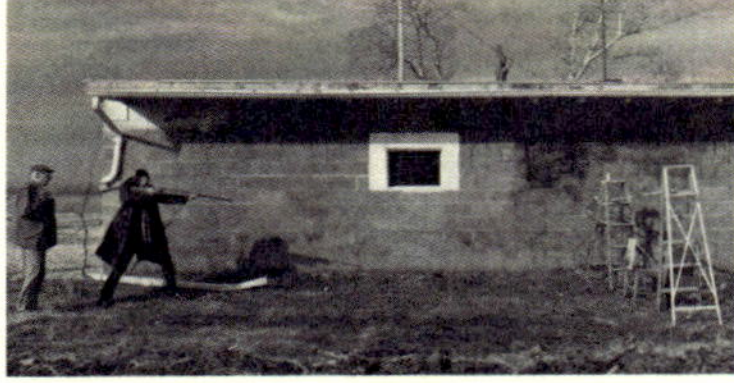

EXCERPTS FROM A DIALOGUE MADE DURING A DRAWING COLLABORATION RECORDED IN LAWRENCE, KANSAS, ON 1 FEBRUARY 1987

EDITED BY DIEGO CORTEZ AND JAMES GRAUERHOLZ

PUBLISHED ON THE OCCASION OF AN EXHIBITION OF NEW PAINTINGS BY PHILIP TAAFFE AT THE

PAT HEARN GALLERY
NEW YORK 1987

Drawing Dialogue, William S. Burroughs and Philip Taaffe, 1987

Taaffe's art also brings to my mind the work of the great Cuban writer José Lezama Lima. He was one of the greatest twentieth-century poets writing in Spanish, yet his work is relatively unknown in the English-speaking world (although perhaps it is worth noting that he maintained an important correspondence with Wallace Stevens). Lezama cultivated a language – a poetic system – to understand the world in which everything must be invented anew through imagery. These poetic images are the manifestations of an invisible world, and grant us access to what Lezama called "the imaginary eras", a universe of signs and possible meanings. For him, culture was not an historical moment but rather the coexistence of images in a landscape. The manifestation of these images creates opportunities for chance, coincidence, and unexpected connections rather than historically located meaning. In transporting the culture of our time to an imaginary era, Western teleology and European time/logic are made redundant and a new version of history yields to the poetry of his Latin-American roots. Here poetry is a magical act that allows one to enter into the flux of things, into all eternity simultaneously. Thus the poet becomes a shaman whose body is transformed into an eternal flow of imagery that transcends physical constraints. For Lezama poiesis is an act of release. In *Confluencias*, one of his most renowned essays, Lezama describes the poet as a being who waits for the night to cover him completely. The night is black, vast like the sea and full of voices. Gradually, the sea and the night become one, indistinguishable from the breathing and concentration of the poet, who becomes transformed into an organic flow of imagery. All of this I see in a painting such as *Artificial Paradise (Loculus)* (2008).

This year an unusual book by another poet has been published in full for the first time: *The H.D. Book* (2011) by the American, Robert Duncan.[16] Like Yeats and Taaffe, Duncan was interested in obscure traditions. The book in question is a reflection on the work of H.D. and other modern poets that develops into an extensive treatise on poetry. Duncan maintains that *"the poet's craft is to bring what is hidden to our attention while honoring its hiddenness"*.[17] For Duncan, whose own poetry is not only a vivid representation of sensations but also evocatively scratches beneath the surface, the poet's craft is completely bound up with the sense that craft itself is something that emerges from the work as a permanent fact, albeit obliquely at times. Every artist must find his or her own way of making meaning visible. Contemplating Philip Taaffe's work, I feel that these notions resonate with the artist, who (to mention one final literary reference) has expressed an interest in Charles Olson.[18] Also a poet, Olson is credited with coining the term postmodern; his tremendously ambitious work is very dense in cultural and historical references. Taaffe's open work has always attracted the attention of writers. William S. Burroughs, Robert Creeley, Vincent Katz, Rene Ricard, Mohammed Mrabet, Gore Vidal, Marina Warner, Edmund White, Peter Lamborn Wilson, and John Yau have all written about or collaborated with him. This is due to the fact that his work is complex and suggestive in an artistic scene where the critical essay – theoretical and sociological – has asserted its authority over poetry.

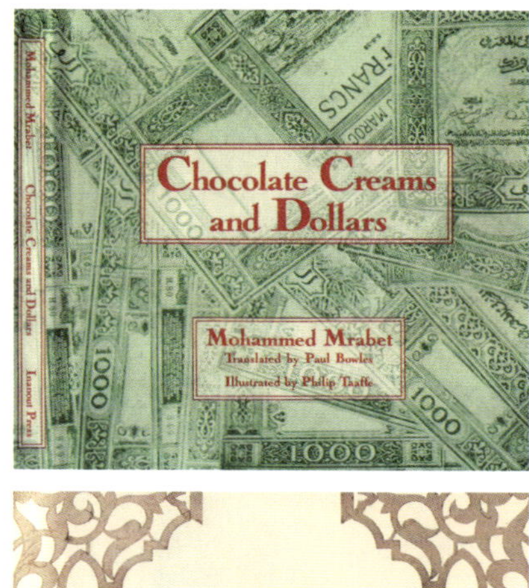

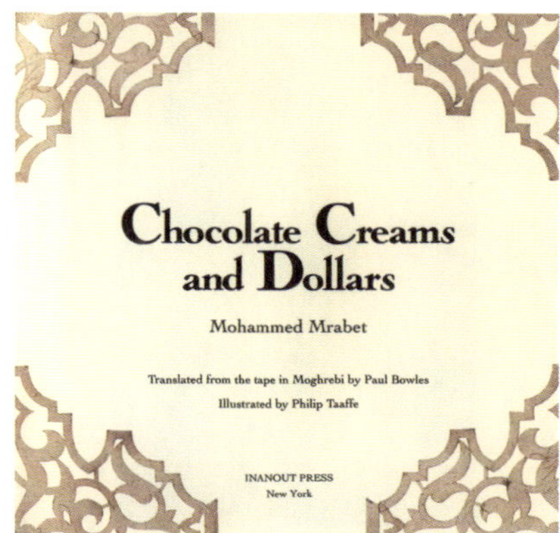

Mohammed Mrabet, *Chocolate Creams and Dollars*, New York, 1992

Some days before I began writing this text, I had the opportunity to see *Film Socialism*, the most recent film by French-Swiss director Jean-Luc Godard. The work feels like a testament of sorts, and in fact Godard has announced that it will be his final picture. The film is shot entirely in digital and features stunning images and colours as well as a moving soundtrack. The narrative is non-linear, portraying a series of interconnected stories. Despite there being no clear plot, the film deals with some of Godard's constant obsessions, e.g. the Spanish Civil War, the concentration camps, and Palestine, as well as with cinema itself. Godard tasks himself with inventing a language capable of developing all of these themes in a precise way, in a historical period characterized by information overload and the impossibility of knowing or including everything. *Film Socialism* is also a very intimate, calm, and reflective film. Among its innovations is the decorative and aesthetic treatment of the subtitles in the English version. The overall effect is hypnotic and filled with references to history, culture, and political conflict, in Europe especially but also throughout the Mediterranean. Contemplating this film, with its rhythmic editing and metalinguistic references, I could not help thinking of the work of Philip Taaffe, its way of being historical and outside history at the same time, its radical will to discover a unique language capable of incorporating the personal and the political. His respect and love for the medium in which he works sets him apart from much of today's anti-artistic and cynical art practice, exhausted by the impossibility of doing anything new, beyond dragging old ideas from the archives. To my mind, both artists, as well as Yeats, Lezama, Duncan, and Olson – and of course all of the tradition of abstraction referred to throughout this text – remain radically moving and absolutely essential.

1
William B. Yeats, "The Philosophy of Shelley's Poetry" (1900) from *Essays and Introductions* (London: Macmillan, 1961), 94–95.

2
Thomas McEvilley, *The Triumph of Anti-Art* (New York: McPherson & Company, 2005).

3
Post Abstract Abstraction, Aldrich Museum of Contemporary Art, Ridgefield (1987); *Similia/Disimilia: Modes of Abstraction in Painting, Sculpture and Photography Today*, Kunsthalle Düsseldorf (1987); *Psychological Abstraction*, Deste Foundation, Athens (1989); *Strange Abstraction*, Touko Museum of Contemporary Art, Tokyo (1991); *The Broken Mirror*, Kunsthalle, Vienna (1993); *Italia/America: Abstraction Redefined*, Galleria Nazionale d'Arte Moderna, San Marino (1993); *Unbound: Possibilities in Painting*, Hayward Gallery, London (1994); *The Adventure of Painting*, Kunstverein für Rheinlande, Düsseldorf (1995); and *New Abstractions*, Museo Nacional Centro de Arte Reina Sofia, Madrid (1996).

4
I curated both Taaffe's retrospective at the IVAM and the "New Abstractions" group exhibition in Madrid. The latter show traveled to Bielefeld, Germany, and Barcelona.

5
Ross Bleckner, *Philip Taaffe* (New York: Pat Hearn Gallery, 1986).

6
Philip Taaffe, "Sublimity Now and Forever, Amen," *Arts Magazine* (March 1986), 19.

7
Kay Heymer, "On the Development of the Pictorial Work of Philip Taaffe," in *Philip Taaffe. The Life of Forms, Works 1980–2008*, (Wolfsburg: Kunstmuseum Wolfsburg, 2008), 17.

8
Philip Taaffe, "A Conversation with Stan Brakhage," in *Philip Taaffe: Composite Nature* (New York: Peter Blum Edition, 1998),110.

9
Raymond Foye, "The Alchemical Image," in *The Heavenly Tree Grows Downward* (New York: James Cohan Gallery, 2002), 47.

10
José Lezama Lima, "Cuadernos Americanos," Issue 53/54, Mexico, 246.

11
Mircea Eliade, *Shamanism: Archaic Techniques of Ecstasy*, translated by Willard R. Trask (London: Routledge and Kegan Paul, 1964).

12
William S. Burroughs and Philip Taaffe, *Drawing Dialogue* (New York: Pat Hearn Gallery, 1987).

13
Shirley Kaneda, "Interview with Philip Taaffe," *Bomb* (Spring 1991).

14
Robert Duncan, "Transgressing the Real," passages 27, in *Bending the Bow* (New York: New Directions, 1968), 121.

15
Daniel Albright, Introduction to William B. Yeats, *The Poems* (London: Everyman's Library, 1992), XXI–XXIII, XLI.

> ...Each human soul could attune itself to revelation, to miracle, because each partook in the world's general soul ... Yeats tried to discipline his imagination to cultivate a detachment from the normal world, to smooth and empty his mind until it could flame with images from the world beyond our own ... he favoured images of extravagance ... All the mind's eye needs is a slight adjustment of focus, and paradise is right there ... Yeats was equally excited by the notion that amazing energies, at once artistic and sexual, could be whirled into tight focus, brought to bear on one small spot. Yeats's poetry continually strives to embody the processes through which the imagination receives images, as if a poem could be a funnel delivering symbols from the Anima Mundi.

16
Robert Duncan, *The H.D. Book* (Berkeley: University of California Press, 2011). An extensive reflection on the work of the American poet, novelist and memoirist Hilda Doolittle, better known as H.D., and other modern poets which develops into a broader thesis on poetry, hermeticism, and modernism.

17
Michael Boughn and Victor Coleman, Introduction to ibid., 7.

18
Robert Creeley and Philip Taaffe, "Conversation," in *Philip Taaffe* (Valencia: IVAM, 2000), 158–161.

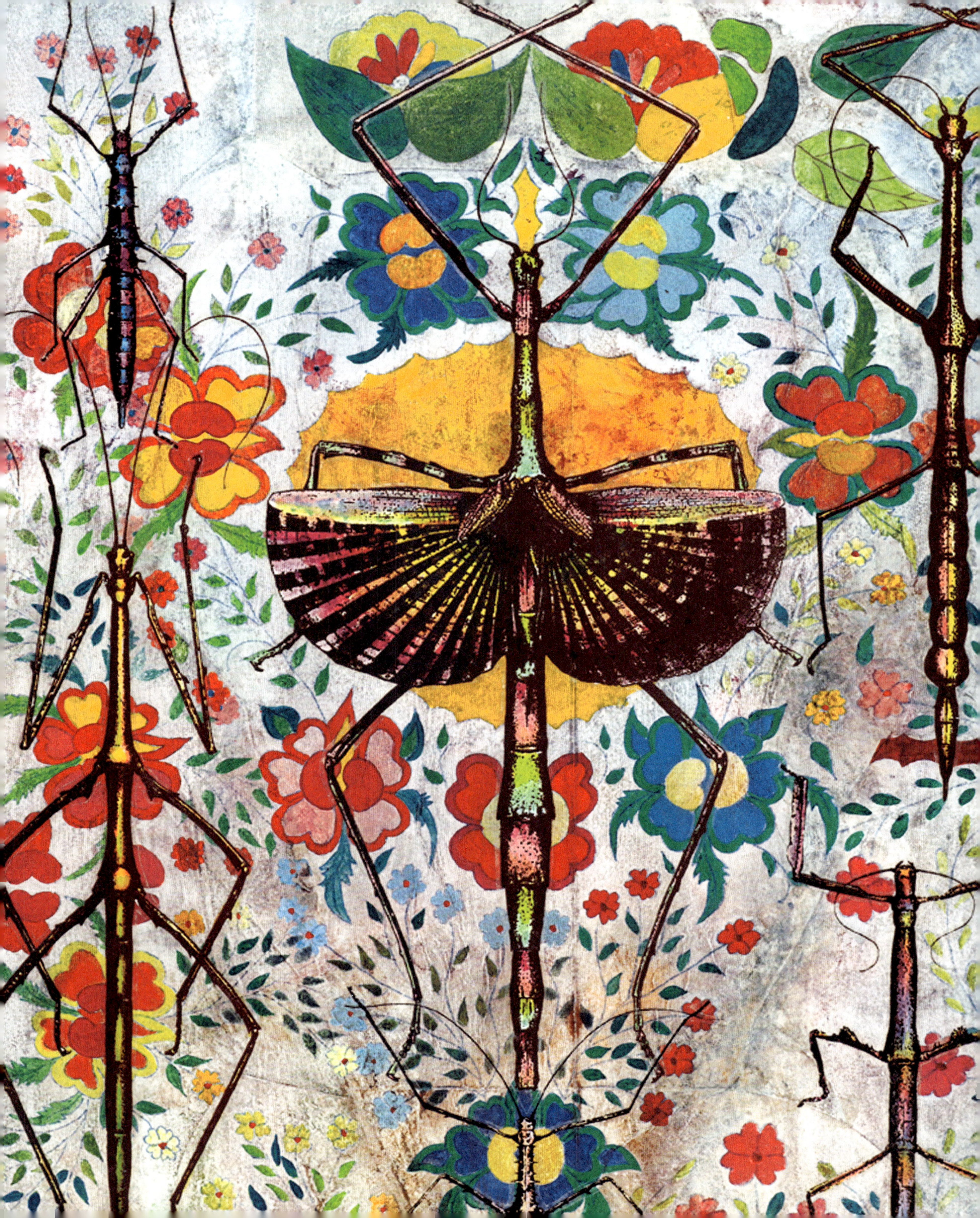

Philip Taaffe

Colm Tóibín

*

I have in mind a dream-time in a dream-city. The city is on water and may once have been a great port; there is a wide, slow-flowing river and there may be old disused canals and perhaps in the distance cranes and gantries. The port may be still busy, or the trade may have gone elsewhere; it may have been rebuilt after a war, or even had its name changed as history moved. Ismir, Gdansk. It is probably in Europe, but it could also have elements of Buenos Aires, Tangiers, Calcutta, Wellington. I imagine winding streets and a hill, perhaps a military outpost of some sort, a wide-spanning bridge and old stone warehouse buildings, and a great square with an equestrian statue and a plaque commemorating a colonial war. And a covered market or bazaar. And nineteenth century buildings that housed great banks and insurance companies and shipping companies. And a sense of islands, maybe, in the distance to which pleasure boats, or tourist boats still go, islands which have resisted the lure of the city's culture, with towns, once walled, heavily fortified, which still stand alone and apart from Naples, Genoa, Barcelona. If the dream city were in Europe it could also be Cork, Lisbon, Hamburg, Trieste.

An historian of the city could explain things that are both mysterious and clear. The layers and patterns which made their way into streetscape, for example, or into ceramics, or earthenware pots, or iron works, into how stone was cut or wood painted or glazes created.

Or how certain words are still in use, or how certain street names came into being. Or how the narrow streets on one side were once Jewish or Arab, or Byzantine or African; how the wider streets and boulevards were made by the French or the English. How the railway system was built by the English, but the canals were created by French engineers. How the city's wealth came first from salt or spices, wine or cotton, cod or cloth, plunder and war. How the city was bombed or burned and then rebuilt.

How the Greeks were here, or the Romans, or the Moors, or the Vikings, or the Normans, or the Visigoths or the English or the Germans. How certain dishes still cooked have elements which came from elsewhere; how flowers, or plants, or vegetables were brought to the city at a certain time, the same time as a new-shaped coffee pot, or a way of brewing tea. Or musical instruments, or certain tones and systems in music. Or a type of art deco or art nouveau.

The dream-cities are filled with cafes and churches, mosques and synagogues; the dream-cities are filled too with long empty mornings and shadowy afternoons when the light lurks and lingers and nothing seems to move much. Some of the churches are permanently locked; others on display because of the layers within – the Romanesque side chapel, or the Moorish arch, or the Baroque statues, or the Byzantine cupola, or the onion-dome, or the coffin in a vault, or the vast brave Gothic battlefield of a central nave. The mosques are busy. In some of the dream-cities the synagogues are part of the dream, and those who once went to them haunt the dead streets on the Sabbath.

In the market, food is on display as though it were a sort of fabric you might weave or wear. The spices piled up could easily be dyes, their colour beguiling, fascinating to the eye. The fruit and vegetables are displayed as though beautifully and intricately manufactured – the black-purple of the aubergine skin could easily have been made to order by a specialist, and so too the porous orange of the tangerine. The seafood curls in elemental shapes, dark patterns, like something which had emerged from the imagination itself after a long gestation in its cavernous dream-time. The skin of each fish has been stencilled, the colours muted and exact, almost worn down; the surface of each fish has come to look like a silkscreen print of itself.

At the edge of the market there are shops which sell fabric. It is rolled to make a sort of pillar, and stored standing up or on its side. The patterns are pure repetition, abstract shapes, lines and angles, some adapted maybe from Islamic art, or shapes from nature, from clouds, or flowers, or plants or birds in flight. And close by are the shops that sell tiles, some of them austere in their single glaze, others with swirling shapes or angled patterns, some of the patterns burned into the tile, others standing out in relief. They are waiting to be placed beside each other, the pattern of each becoming part of the larger pattern.

These seem now like designs, work done to decorate and delight the eye, distract the mind. But, in the ambiguous hour which comes to these dream cities with sombre memories of a time when large questions loomed, it is easy to remember that these patterns and colours and designs and hints of calligraphy once had a sort of sanctity.

In the Christian world, god could be painted or sculpted or set in mosaic; he could have eyes and a face; his son could have a bruised body and outstretched arms; his son's mother a blue gown. In the Islamic world it was the job of artists to suggest rather than portray or depict; the tiles in mosques in their intricate angles and intimations of infinity and eternity, movement and intersection, natural forms and flows, roots and branches, managed to prepare the mind for life moving inexorably towards the end of life, the body moving towards air and emptiness. Using line and colour, ornament and decoration, relief and exquisite carving and patterning, there is a suggestion of a beauty that came before earthly beauty, and a beauty which will survive beyond it.

There are museums and antiquarian book-shops in the old city, open maybe only in the morning, or closed during the long shadowy time after the bright noon. The city and the land around are havens for archaeologists and geologists, and the first rooms of the museums have glass cases that seem themselves to have been found and preserved. In them are stored the flints and fossils, insects and shells, early shapes in culture and nature which curl or end in sharpness. Other museums specialise in natural history – underwater life and strange stuffed animals. Still other museums display cloth and fabric, old tiles and wall hangings.

In some of the cities there is a bright new building, like a bunker; or an old market building that has been restored. And this is the Museum of Contemporary Art where a new set of dreams, all sleek and expensive, adorn the high concrete walls or are hung in the inner sanctum, the white cube. Here there are flashes of sheer colour, or fearless patterns using primary colours. Or rooms where the exotic has been given tame space. There is much whiteness too, and black and grey. And shiny steel. It would be easy to tell the students of the future that these high rooms became the churches of the contemporary, places to visit on Sunday for easy contemplation, with a café on the top floor offering the best view of the old port, the plate glass windows pulling in the light from the sea. This also is part of the dream, although it might look too new to belong fully to the dream's dark rules. But this work on display by contemporary dreamers has its own rules, its own purity, its own hybrid connection to ancient sources. It belongs to the city as much as the tiled roof, or the cut stone, or the skinny cats that skulk and flit, or the ironwork on the roof of the market, or the glazed pots with plants in them, or the figure of a woman in a bright patterned apron standing on the balcony staring down into the street.

She is watching the old bookseller on his way to open his shop. If it is Calcutta the old bookseller remembers Tagore; if it is Buenos Aires he remembers Borges; if it is Cork he remembers Corkery; if it is Lisbon he remembers Pessoa; if it is Hamburg or Gdansk he remembers the bombing; if it is Ismir, he remembers the fire; if it is Tangiers he remembers Paul Bowles; if it is Trieste he remembers Svevo. His shop is piled high with things. He still buys whole collections from nieces and grand-children. On Sundays in some cities he used to have a stall, but he does not like competing with cheap DVDs and remaindered books. He knows what he has.

From floor to ceiling, on one whole wall, he has large-size books about art, about pottery and ceramics and architecture and jewellery, about famous gardens and great old cities. Many of the plates in these books are in black and white and he has little time for browsers who want everything to be in colour. On another wall, he has books about nature and science, with reproductions of photographs of fossils and fish, wild animals, plants, flowers, seeds. There are medical books with diagrams of what the body looked like in a time before x-rays. And manuals of early dentistry, or early surgery or early printing. And old postcards and early pornography and old advertisements for Bacardi and old packets of cigarette papers. He is in touch with collectors, and is a secret sharer in an old pre-internet world of stamps, timetables for ships and trains, letters written in ink, colour plates, signed black and white photographs in old frames, dust jackets, coins, share certificates, Baedeker guides.

**

This idea of the word or the phrase as palimpsest, as something which comes to us bearing the hallmarks of many layers and much travelling is an essential element in the poetry of the twentieth century. This idea of a dream life nurtured gloriously by what is hybrid and impure came to poetry in the early part of the twentieth century as something new and essential and modern as much as it came in painting and music. In these years also a poem came as pure, unfettered, unadorned statement, or as a vast reference library, packed with images, layered with borrowings and rubbings and quotations. The poem was as pure as a single note from a tuning-fork or as chaotic and dynamic as a port city in the first hours of business. For some poets, the single image in all its fierce eastern mystery was enough if it could be rendered with sufficient articulate energy. In his two-line 'In a Station of the Metro', Ezra Pound wrote:

> 'The apparition of these faces in the crowd;
> Petals on a wet, black bough.'

In 'Spring and All', William Carlos Williams wrote:

> 'so much depends
> upon
>
> a red wheel
> barrow

glazed with rain
water

beside the white
chickens.'

In 'Ferry', Louis Zukofsky could begin:

'Gleams, a green lamp
In the fog:
Murmur, in almost
A dialogue

Siren and signal
Siren to signal.'

And in longer poems a strange haunting and exacting simplicity could break through as though it were a hidden shape found inside stone. Robert Creeley, for example, could begin his poem 'The Rain':

'All night the sound had
come back again,
and again falls
this quiet, persistent rain.'

In the background, haunting these chiselled images as a conflagration might haunt a candle, entering its dreams as a vast warning, were a number of long poems which attempted to capture culture in all its complexity, taking phrases and cadences from the history of poetry in order to make a poem new. These poems included T.S. Eliot's 'The Waste Land' and Ezra Pound's 'The Cantos'. And there were other poems such as Hart Crane's 'The Bridge' or Lorca's 'Poet in New York' which sought to re-create urban experience and the fierce gleam of the self using fragmentary tones, and jagged, difficult music.

In American poetry after Pound and Eliot, a number of figures continued to work towards creating a poem or a book of poems as something organic, elemental, dynamic. They sought to establish their own authority, as a planner will look at a part of a city ready for renewal, and call first for a bulldozer. These poems built their own autonomous structure out of a voice and a tone which were deeply personal and uncompromising; these poems cleared the ground, but are filled too with strange echoes from the history of poetry. Also, in the work of poets such as Robert Duncan there was a fearless sense of the beauty of phrases and textures in poetry, a sort of restrained wildness, a willingness to see and hear both ordered pattern and chaotic yearning for possibility and transcendence.

In poems also by poets such as Charles Olson and A.R. Ammons, there was the idea of playing with the line and the page itself. They made the poem both patterned and open; patterned by the repetition of sounds or words, and open by the refusal to operate within the rules of the iambic beat or the pentameter line. But open also by the sense of the poem as a sort of gesture, a way of releasing energy and allowing energy to work as both order and disorder, as both pattern and struggle. The poem depends on the intensity and beauty of the image against the immediacy and high-voltage sound of the voice.

***

Philip Taaffe's studio in New York unfolds in a building which seems very drab and ordinary if observed from the street. It is as though the outskirts of the dream-city had faceless roundabouts and streets created in an anonymous, international style. It is only when you come inside the door into a warren of high rooms, some large and bright and others dark and hidden, that you realise that the dream-city has actually been recreated as an artist's studio, or set of studios, complete with reference library.

Philip Taaffe moves around, explaining the work in progress – the techniques he is using and the source material he has available. He talks about culling images from many sources and discovering connections between these sources that attract him, releasing a hidden power within images that will become an aspect of the narrative of what he is working on.

He is working with dream shapes from history, from natural history as much as art history. He works with many different techniques to fuse the images and create an idea of the picture as a place rather than, say, an object. His job is to activate a space, test the boundaries to see how much a picture can take. He moves between the austerity of making decisions to bringing a sense of fullness to the work. Many things fascinate him, delight his eye, and he goes through some of them now as he weaves through the rooms of this place where he works. He talks about the wooden churches of Northern Russia; the history of marbling; early Buddhist sculpture; a convent and church in Portugal from the second half the sixteenth century; he talks about masks; the shape of fish, sea urchins and bats; Italian painting; the work of film-makers such as Pier Paolo Pasolini, Ingmar Bergman and Yasujirō Ozu; years he has spent in the city of Naples and the amount of layering in that city; the work of Barnett Newman and Bridget Riley whose work he has riffed on.

Some of the rooms we move in have a strange order within the untidiness. It is as though the work waiting to be finished is seeking to pull in some of the images that are piled up uneasily in books on tables and on shelves, or images that live restlessly in the dream-places in his mind. His dream-city has a bank of images and hieroglyphics; they come to him now in New York in the way images in dreams come, or life under water seems to us – floating, without the ties and limits of history, or precise time. It is as though these images came to him distorted, without context, gorgeously jumbled together. His job is to separate them, take what he needs, create pattern, fusion, allow certain images to dominate in a context he has created for them.

In a room at the back is a library which the old book-seller would have been proud of. It is as though the essence of the dream-city has been captured and brought here – the strange old churches, the modern art museum, the natural history museum, the layers of archaeology, the objects that ships carried here from Africa and the Orient, the colours and textures of fruit and seafood in the market, the history of medicine. He has made in his work a new history of the world from the images the world has left to him, using the energy and the sense of the autonomy of the imagination which the American poets, and some of the painters, of the past century have used. He allows his work to be 'born very young in a world already very old', in a phrase from Louis Zukofsky which Robert Creeley once quoted to him in an interview. In the same interview, Philip Taaffe offered a quote from Robert Duncan which fits the work which is resting against the wall, waiting for completion: 'The work is shaped by its own energies.' His dream-palace in New York gathers in these energies, the energies that have come from all over the world, the energies which Robert Creeley distils and releases in his short poem 'Here':

'What
has happened
makes

the world.
Live
on the edge,

looking.'

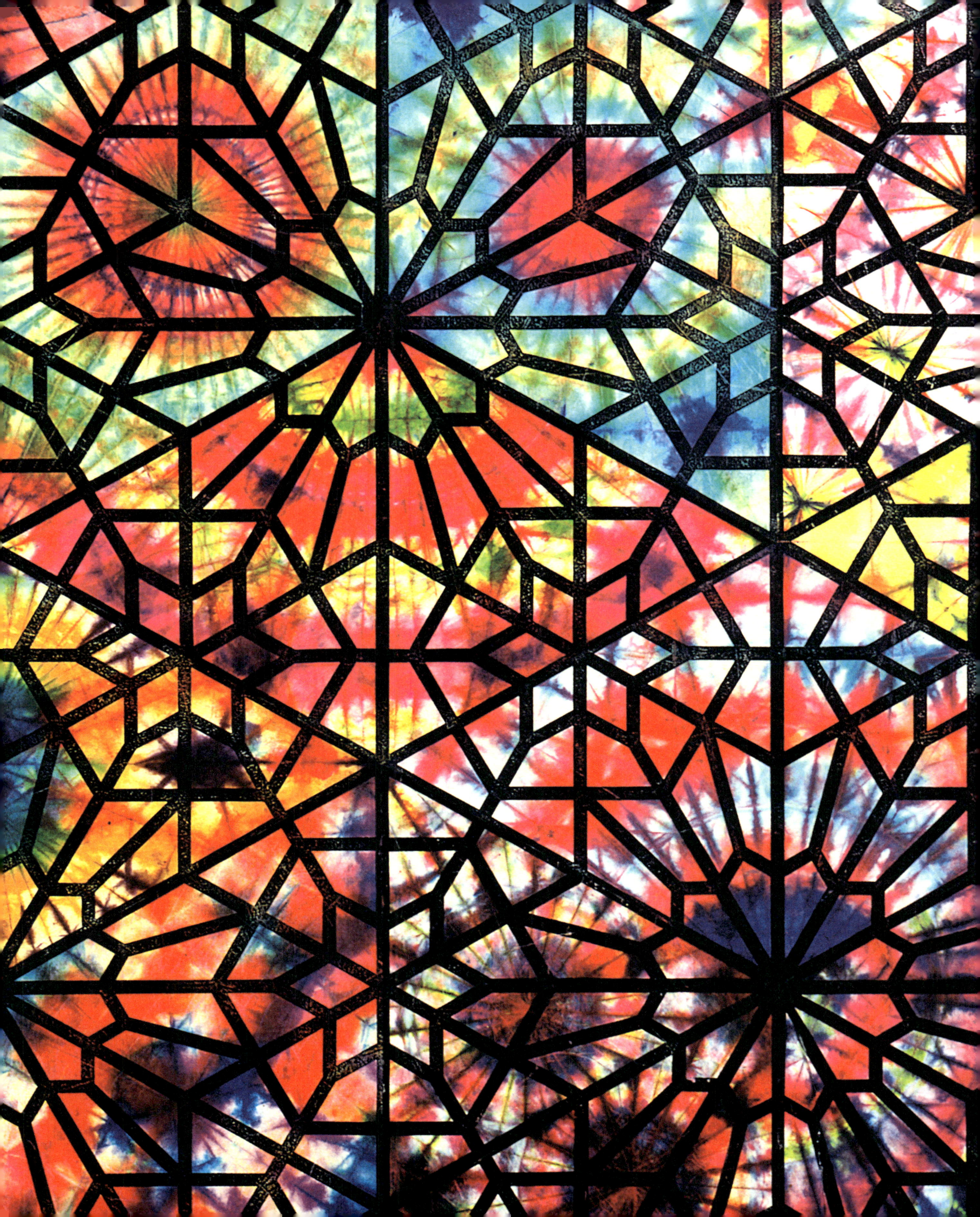

Interview

David Brody and Philip Taaffe

Brody Let me ask you specifically about painters whom you took a very analytical view of, in terms of how you began to use their formal ideas: Bridget Riley, Paul Feeley, Barnett Newman, Ellsworth Kelly, and others, all of whom are somewhat situated within post-painterly abstraction – Barnett Newman at the very beginning of it all. Were you making a statement about what a painting should be by choosing those particular painters for whom an analytical, formal position seems to be primary?

Taaffe Yes, probably I was, because those were the painters for whom I felt the closest affinity. As a young artist, that analysis was a way of bringing myself into a closer state of artistic intimacy with the material evidence that I had to come to terms with in order to find my way. We're all lost, in a sense. We're all voyagers; we're all navigating a certain cultural terrain of our own choosing. At that phase of my artistic life I felt I had to understand myself through coming to terms most intimately with the work I loved, in order to find a way forward. But I don't want to get bogged down in any kind of autobiographical dimension to this.

Brody So let me be your analyst: why don't you want to talk about Barnett Newman?

Taaffe I *do* want to talk about Barnett Newman.

BRODY Okay, great. In Barnett Newman's writing, he rails against formalism in art, which he calls, the "Pagan Void." Instead he wants abstraction to regain its primitive, religious function. Mel Bochner writes (in 2002) that "one can only conclude that metaphysical and theological issues have been avoided or repressed in recent writing about Newman because they fall outside the conceptual prejudices of late 20th century criticism."

TAAFFE I'm in complete agreement with that. The primitivist aspect of Newman was crucial to me when I was starting out. To my mind, what I was doing was releasing the spirit of Newman's intentions. I've said this before: I was bringing in the dimension of liturgy, religious stagecraft, almost treating this arena as sacred theatre, or the painting as a sacred object that I sought to internalise. Newman is insisting upon a weighted subject matter for an abstract work. I always considered that extremely important. I felt very close to that position. I was including myself in a tribal situation that was loaded with subject matter. That's where I wanted to be at the time. I wanted to declare my affinity with this position. I didn't make the work as a parody of Newman. It was a very genuine wish to be part of the tradition. Newman uses the title "Onement," to be "at one" with something. I responded to that religiosity and the sense of wanting a deeper connection to a reality outside of any formalist considerations.

BRODY Crucially, his "zips" were gestural – textured along their sides. Your remaking them as ready-made patterns, things that looked like they could have come from a sewing trimming shop, it seems to me, cannot be read as other than critique.

TAAFFE Yes, I was imposing a more illusionistic element, but I had seen Newman's paintings as having an illusionistic dimension, especially the one at the Metropolitan Museum with the masking tape left on, *Concord* (1949). That's what enabled me to say that I could collage something there and make it illusionistic, to do something with that space. I know there's a deeper psychological component to these gestures. It's not necessarily a very friendly environment when you are starting out as an artist. So one has to find a way to proceed.

BRODY Does your idea of religion involve play, involve pleasure?

TAAFFE Yes, of course. It's not sanctimonious. It's about liberating the spirit.

BRODY What about Newman, do you think he was sanctimonious?

TAAFFE No, I don't think he was sanctimonious. I think he was trying to take a serious position. He was trying to instill content, to demonstrate that an abstract work had content, that it was not a formalistic product. I came from a very anti-formalist background in my schooling. I was a student of Hans Haacke and formalism was anathema, so I never wanted to make a formalist work of art. I wanted to make an investigation. First of all, I consider painting to be a field of visual research – that's what it is for me. I was conducting research. I wanted to find my way, to move into a certain area where I would be able to make discoveries. I was always interested in finding out what it is that we are confronted with? As painters we are confronted with a certain history, and we have to respond to this somehow.

BRODY If there was iconoclasm in your investigation, there was also love, that seems clear. W. J. T. Mitchell wrote a book called *What Do Pictures Want?,* and in it he writes that to destroy an image, for example, the World Trade Center or the golden calf, is to make a new image.

TAAFFE An act of destruction is merely a temporary displacement. You're just making another image, yes.

BRODY So aniconism actually empowers images. False idols are so dangerous that they have to be destroyed. But instead of seeking to destroy images, Mitchell says the critic, or by implication the artist, should sound them out like Nietzsche's Zarathustra, wielding his hammer as a tuning fork. In Mitchell's words, "it would be a delicate critical practice to strike images with just enough force to make them resonate but not so much as to smash them." That seems like an apt description of your re-enactments of Newman, Still, Riley, Kelly etc. – aniconists all. They tried to destroy the image, to make an art beyond pictures, but in doing so just made more pictures. Your painterly re-enactments sound these new idols, they don't smash them.

TAAFFE As I've said before, I felt modern art was a collective situation, which is why I decided that I would just do a version of an optical work by Bridget Riley, because it didn't matter that it existed before. It was determined tribally. I like to travel in time and make connections, culturally, to figure out what came from where and to decipher the direction of things. It's a way of navigating my way through the world. You're choosing what you want to inhabit, visually. I do it still, only now I am going further back in time, culling things and telling stories that didn't previously have a connection. I'm trying to find ways of bringing things together that have never been brought together before. And ritual is still an important part of my method. It's not just what I do, but how I do things, that is important to me in my work.

BRODY When you cull images, you don't use much in the way of photography, and as far as I can see, no contemporary photography. If you use computers it's incidental, I imagine. This is a very significant kind of rejection. Rather than sample directly from the digitised ocean of images you cut stencils, you re-draw source images for silkscreening. And when you work with images from natural history, they usually come through the filter of nineteenth century drawings rather than photographs, and never contemporary scientific imaging. So these are very deliberate decisions that you make, and it seems to connect with your interest in making work that is not about being reproduced, but is singular, individual, and has an "aura" – that quality which can only be experienced in person.

TAAFFE What you describe is an essential crisis in art today, a paradox. What we love about art, why we think about it and make it and discuss it has to do with a shared physical environment. We are a part of the same physical space, and we experience art directly, with a sense of immediacy. To me it matters that art exists in a physical place. I defend the aura and the presence of a work of art. Maybe this is why I am dubious about digital media and cyberspace; I have no problem using those things if they can be of help, but I worry that they are being used as a substitute for interpersonal practices. As I mentioned, I was a student of Hans Haacke, so I still see things in the context of social critique: I think to a large extent it's corporate capitalism that is pushing this technology down our throats in order to make a ton of money and to control people's lives and their spending habits and to gather information in order to market consumer goods. Perhaps there needs to be a little more resistance to things like this.

BRODY I've been looking at your works in reproduction, but it wasn't until I walked into the studio and was reminded of how one's experience of texture changes depending on distance, with the very particular way the paintings take light, with the irreproducible character of their colour saturation – it's a physical engagement, an optical trip. Your work is clearly meant to overwhelm.

TAAFFE Overwhelm is too strong a word. I want to present a complete experience. I want to believe that we can sustain a high level of intimacy and involvement with painting and imagery, one that has a certain visual complexity that people are interested in coming to terms with, that it's somehow pointing a way, in a creative direction.

BRODY Is it an obligation as an artist with a position like yours to seduce the viewer?

TAAFFE I think it's less a question of seduction than of creating a dialogue, enabling an exchange to take place. For example when you go to a poetry reading, you're sitting there listening to the poet read their poems, and that is a very different experience than reading a book of poetry. I think such an exchange is culturally essential, and I think there is a lot of passion out there for this type of experience. Art is about an exchange between one person and another – that's the beauty of it, that one person has shaped this poem or this painting, and another person comes to that situation and is transported by it. Art is ultimately about desire, and when you see a painting you love, you feel the desire that went into the making of it. It's a very personal, one-on-one thing; it's not about systematic or technical questions. It's about feeling the story behind what's there, and how the artist has filtered the information to make it personal, how the artist has assimilated those ideas and images and worked with them and made them their own, to reveal something about the world. But there is an almost Manichean schism between, on the one hand, what we are talking about, what we want, what we're engaged with, and all the rest – these kind of media-driven, larger, more anonymous constructions. That's just a recapitulation of the alienation that most people experience in their lives, imitating the worst aspects of Hollywood or fashion or a kind of technological overload. I don't think that's useful. It's not what I think people want. I don't think that people know what they want, but I don't think that's it.

BRODY I don't want to belabour this point, but I'm really interested to know why you don't use photography?

TAAFFE I do use photography. This piece of bark you see in the studio was taken from a Douglas-fir tree and sent to me by a friend in Seattle. I wanted to use it in a painting (*Dryadic Figures,* 2004). In order to generate the imagery, I photographed these pieces of bark with a Polaroid camera, and I lit them with a certain kind of raking light. I do studio photography.

BRODY Have you done that all along?

TAAFFE From time to time I've photographed seashells, razor ribbon wire, just very specific objects I want to include in my paintings.

BRODY And if you do use photography by other people, it tends to be photography of an earlier era. Is it because of the textures of older techniques?

TAAFFE Yes, I prefer gravure, the continuous tone.

BRODY So I'm wrong. You do use photography. You're not religiously opposed to it.

TAAFFE No, not at all. I want it both ways. Categorical ambivalence is in the nature of what I do. It has to do with a kind of mediation – it's about being inside the work and outside the work at the same time. I'm finding ways to construct a picture that is very much me, but I also fade away, and I no longer exist at the end of the process. I'm absorbed into the imagery; I enter the work in that way. It also has a psychological dimension because of the emotional struggle that takes place. The decisions involved in making a painting are clearly not objective ones, although they have their own logic that is geared toward allowing the painting to move forward in its own right.

BRODY In the 1990s you moved away from the analytical approach that characterised much of your work from the 1980s. You were analytical in the forms that you chose, but you began to get very complicated and permutational and combinatorial.

TAAFFE I think I had no other choice at the time. All of these different tropes and strategies that we have been talking about were tools in my development. They were ways of developing the vocabulary and means whereby I could move in a more emotional direction. I was always interested in shaping a situation that would have a kind of emotive signification. You used the word 'seduction,' but I would say, rather, 'presenting a set of emotions.' Seduction is a very problematical way of describing what goes on. It's *almost* seductive. I think what the viewer finds seductive are the traces of emotion and the decisions that are physically evident that created these emotions. How are these images constructed? The constructive aspect to what you're looking at carries emotional content and power.

BRODY The New York School work that you focused on was at the relatively un-gestural end of the spectrum. What do you think of European expressionist painting of the same period – Tachisme, Art Informel, COBRA? Painters like Pierre Soulages, Antoni Tàpies and Jean Fautrier have never made much headway in New York, being seen as neither wild enough nor calculating enough. Their international reputation is much higher though, and there have been attempts to look at this work afresh here.

TAAFFE As interesting as the European counterparts in the 1950s were, compared to what was going on in New York they always seemed rather aestheticised, even though there were some good things that came out of that. Soulages, Fautrier, Tàpies. I like all of these artists, but in my view they don't remotely stand up to Rothko and Still and Newman. The context of the United States and New York provided a rawness. Here artists recognised they were faced with an artistic frontier. Even the European painters who came to New York in the forties and fifties were compelled to seek a less cultured or less refined version of abstraction, in keeping with the American standard. On the other hand, I am not seduced by the heroic myth of Abstract Expressionism: I actually prefer the psychic claustrophobia of early Pollock to the drip paintings.

BRODY You use words like "trance" and "ritual" to talk about your practice, which suggests, if not drug use per se, an orientation toward shamanic disruption of ordinary reality. Sigmar Polke never made it a secret that he was sometimes taking LSD when he was painting, as I understand it, and there's plenty of other examples. Pollock's great surrealist meltdowns, pre-drip, might well have been fueled by alcohol. Utterly sober art practice, of course, can produce parallel insights. Do you see any fundamental distinction between these two ways of knowledge?

TAAFFE Psychedelic is a word that only was invented in the late forties, but I think it applies to a lot of earlier work. The sixteenth century Sienese painter Domenico Beccafumi is a prime example. He was the most psychedelic Renaissance painter, to my mind. I don't think the question of drugs matters. I've experimented with these things, but I've never used drugs ritualistically in the work. When I talk about the trance-like state that results from the work, a good example is the *Floating Pigment* paintings that I started to make in 2002. In making those works I constructed two enormous pools of liquid in the middle of this room. I mixed gigantic quantities of carrageen moss, which is a liquid, viscous porridge, and then I had another swimming-pool-like vat of water. I was pouring and throwing and manipulating liquids and pigments, for days and weeks on end. The entire studio was dedicated to this process, and it is was an incredibly hallucinatory experience – ectoplasmic, bordering on delirium, like watching the origin of the cosmos every time. I was not taking any drugs, but a process like that does something to your brain. It's extremely chimerical. In this case the pigment is like a drug.

BRODY Are you comfortable with your paintings being seen in the context of a new psychedelic vanguard?

TAAFFE Certainly. I think psychedelics are informational. It's like going to church. It's a way of achieving a certain moment of internal focus. The same thing can be achieved in meditation, in prayer, in reading good poetry or listening to a great piece of music. It's all part of that fabric of existence that we need to reiterate to be able to understand who we are and what we're here for. Psychedelics can put one in touch with the archaic nature of one's own being, digging deeper into our DNA and the genetic code. It's about our humanity, not just the pulsating vibratory visual experience. It takes one very far back – frightening, but essential to getting at a certain knowledge of who we are and where we come from. Psychedelics are a form of wisdom.

BRODY I see a real relationship between the kind of profusion you seek in your work, the dense clarity, and those early Miró paintings, beginning with *The Farm*, (1921–22), and well into the pure abstractions of the thirties. And also a sense of color as a substance whose texture can go all the way into the weave of the canvas. There's something hallucinatory in almost every mark that Miró makes. Of the School of Paris masters, he seems to be the one that influenced you the most.

TAAFFE Miró is pure mind. Those early paintings you mention, especially *Harlequin's Carnival*, (1924–25), in the Albright-Knox, are absolutely essential images for me. They are intimist, yet incredibly expansive. The implications for abstraction are so far-reaching, yet there is such an economy of means. There is a richness and luxury to them that emerges from the poverty of pure invention.

BRODY Matisse's near abstraction of hovering planes also seems important in your work, notably in your use of Moorish ornament to similarly spacious ends. The sovereignty of geometry, and the light, has always been part of Orientalism, beginning with Delacroix and Ingres, going through Gérôme and the "*grandes* machines" salon paintings, and climaxing in Matisse's *The Moroccans*, (1915).

TAAFFE There's nothing preventing me from moving in any direction at any given moment now. I'm poised, I'm open. I've constructed my pictorial world in such a way that I can move between these things in an instant. I was examining recently the Portuguese Renaissance architect Diogo de Arruda who was active during the early years of the sixteenth century. The Portuguese went to India and established trade colonies, and the ships returned festooned with all types of exotic specimens and crustaceans and other exotica. The ships were just dripping with all this stuff they found. It was mind-blowing to this architect, so he incorporated marine ropes and strange coral formations and other items. There are also sculpted arms and other parts of human anatomy in his architecture. It's an absolutely amazing conflation of symbolic, exotic imagery, all commingled. It's figurative as well.

BRODY So in a work like *Old Cairo*, (1989), were you consciously commingling French Orientalism, and all its baggage, with those architectural motifs?

TAAFFE No, it was really a diaristic concern. For me the paintings are always experiential. It was made after a trip to Cairo – the only city in the world I've ever gotten lost in. I was just wandering aimlessly, ten hours a day. I was breathing it in, taking notes and doing drawings as a way of possessing all the things I was seeing. I had a desire to see a painting that did not yet exist. When I returned to my studio in Naples, I made *Old Cairo* by reconstructing these notations and visual materials, to try to shape an extravagant, rapturous experience. I wanted to create a synthesis, using all these diverse materials. It was a constructivist effort. The point is to have a world that is open to all these things, to have a decision making process that allows for openness – or rather, how to build openness into the decision making process.

BRODY There are a few paintings where you use balustrade shapes, if that's the right word – staircases that intersect and cross over in the middle. In those paintings there is flatly applied ornament, as ornament would be applied in Arabic architecture, generally.

TAAFFE You are absolutely right. It's flatly applied.

BRODY But then you make this very interesting space that is quite different from the other paintings you had been making up to that time. You almost imply that they're three-dimensional. You're making an atmospheric fold in space, not quite illusionistic.

TAAFFE I want my paintings to separate from the three-dimensional. I want them to exist on a flat surface. I don't like a lot of built-up things on the surface. The paintings have a lot of layers but are also very thin. I don't like them to be too physical. I try to put them in a more cerebral frame, so you read them as you would poetry. I don't want the viewer to be hit over the head by the physical experience. I'm seeking more of a synesthetic encounter. All of this extends from that very limited, focused, flat surface. I want them to be talismans, in a sense.

BRODY In the kind of painting space that you're interested in, which is related to colour field painting, the colours are absorbed into the surface. It's like Rothko space.

TAAFFE Colour field painting for me is always very limited. The problem for me is that I see a lot of abstract work as being fragmentary, when it settles into systematic niceties, or is somehow self-congratulatory, or accepts a certain mannered inevitability of outcome. I'm seeking more of an orchestrated whole, I'm not satisfied with just a colour field. I want more *stuff* in the painting.

BRODY Are you a skeptic of the kind of sacred veneration with which many people regard Rothko?

TAAFFE No, I venerate Rothko – I actually have a small painting of his from 1943.

BRODY From his surrealist period?

TAAFFE Yes, I love the Surrealist Rothko. *Slow Swirl at the Edge of the Sea* (1944) is one of my favorite paintings in the world, and the polyform paintings are fantastic, too.

BRODY Rothko was very similar to Newman in that he was explicit about the sacred aims of his work. There's tremendous analysis in their work, but they're seeking to go into the poetic beyond, and they're explicit about that. Whereas the artists who took Rothko and Newman as founding fathers were radical in disavowing the poetry: what you see is what you see. So in a sense, your Newman paintings were misunderstood in the same way the originals were.

TAAFFE Yes, perhaps. The psychic gravity of Rothko's work and the emotional space that he was trying to create in the paintings is what appeals to me.

BRODY The kind of ornament that you brought into your work, from Celtic carving and tribal art and Hindu art, some Gothic and Romanesque art, Islamic art of course, all these traditions of ornament equate visual intricacy with a sacred dimension. They are sacred texts, in some cases literally. Your work seems to be in sympathy with the luxuriant, hallucinatory richness of invention of these anonymous artists. Is a Persian carpet equal to a Mondrian?

TAAFFE No. A Mondrian is a Mondrian and a Persian carpet is a Persian carpet – something entirely different. I have a great Persian carpet, but it's an entirely different species from a Mondrian. You could learn how to organize every aspect of your life from looking at a Mondrian; it's a very stimulating thing that can inform many aspects of existence. A Mondrian painting is the ultimate paradigm for life, in a sense. There's also a profound metaphysical dimension to his work. It's like watching a mystic be a mystic. It's the spiritual dimension of the work that sets it apart. And the intensity of the involvement, the material physical involvement, the artistic transformation of this prescribed space, the decisions that were made to make this thing, the way he brought his intellect and his mystical concerns to this situation is what gives it this power.

BRODY It seems that your work is evolving from the Mondrian end of the spectrum to the super-profuse end with the recent folded, marbled works on paper, which are positively phantasmagoric in their density.

TAAFFE My work goes through phases of being more or less dense or complex. It reaches a point of saturation and then it becomes possible to empty it out. What I've always tried to do in my work is allow myself complete freedom to change directions and to move in different areas of research and exploration, and to change the weight and velocity of certain kinds of things in the work. I think it's good to periodically change course and work on something that has a very different quality, although I will say that a certain amount of density is important to me. I like a rich visual field, however the way I arrive at that changes. Even though I take certain minimalist approaches to things, in terms of the organisational austerity of a work, I like a certain fullness. That comes in the editing process, too.

BRODY Let me ask you about *Martyr Group* (1984). The target practice figures have something that look like halos. They're overlapped in a way that relates to Byzantine art, but they also seem to point to Andy Warhol's repeating silkscreen appropriations, especially because of the dark subject matter of gunshots, assassinations.

TAAFFE You're the first person who ever made that comparison, I never thought about Warhol in relation to that.

BRODY You didn't think about Warhol when you began using silkscreen?

TAAFFE Not particularly. I have a much more hands-on gestural approach to silkscreen. I use silkscreen as a gestural tool, like a paintbrush.

BRODY Can I psychoanalyse a little more? I wonder if your aversion to using contemporary photographs might be related to making a distinction between your work and Warhol's.

TAAFFE Maybe. There's something inevitable about Warhol, almost like a cultural fact.

BRODY I'm curious about the mindset of the young Philip Taaffe who had an enormous poetic ambition about art, and was willing to take the kinds of risks, social risks, to form friendships with older outlaw artists such as William Burroughs, Harry Smith, and others.

TAAFFE Thanks to Diego Cortez, early in 1985, I first collaborated with William Burroughs. It seems he was interested in getting involved once again with painting, and he was looking for new ways to be inspired, and to refamiliarize himself with this type of work. I had been deeply involved with William's books since I was in high school. He was very much a hero of mine. I also knew of his involvement with the visual arts through Brion Gysin, also an important figure for me. We made a lot of work together. That was a very rewarding collaboration; we exhibited the results at Pat Hearn's gallery in 1987. Harry Smith I never met. I moved into the Chelsea Hotel in 1991, the same year he died there. I was living in Italy for three and a half years, and then I moved into the Chelsea. I knew he was there, and I donated a drawing to help pay his rent at one point. I was very familiar with Harry Smith's work, but unfortunately I never met him.

BRODY I've been looking at his films and there's one where he uses Hindu hand gestures, mudras, and they're just cut one to the next, with other imagery on top. His montage and use of nineteenth century engravings, his layering of images, the way he physically imprints and saturates colour onto the film stock, strike me as being influential, directly or indirectly, with how you work.

TAAFFE Oh, he's my relative. I'm related to Harry Smith, there's no doubt about it.

BRODY You had a friendship with Stan Brakhage. He has a similar approach to space, which has to do with endless saturations of layers.

Taaffe He was also a hero of mine when I was a student. I went to see him at Millennium Film Workshop a couple of times, where he would always present his new films. I loved his work. I also saw it at Anthology Film Archives.

Brody He was really a poet, it seems to me. His talking about his films is part of what they are.

Taaffe He was a Bard. He was hand painting on film when I met him, and he liked to work in public. He would sit in the cafes in Boulder, an incredibly expansive individual, totally accessible, but he was doing this visionary work, very precise, like a watchmaker. Painting and scratching away, hour after hour, shaping these masterpieces. It was almost like he was manufacturing a bomb or something, making this thing that would explode and alter your sense of reality.

Brody Obviously today we have non-linear editing techniques, and image processing, and all this ubiquitous digital fantasy. But with Brakhage, all the layering is essentially manual. They're not strictly unique objects – Brakhage could distribute prints, and you use reproductive techniques – but the experience of viewing his films and your paintings is not reproducible.

Taaffe That's true. One thing that always impressed me about his filmmaking is the rhythmic aspect, the fact that you have lyrical passages combined with frenetic moments, hypnagogic pulsations. There's a controlled velocity. He was always experimenting with pauses and lengths of sustained visual incident and changes in the velocity and changes in the colour and quality of the gesture. I think there's a direct parallel there to my work. I'm very interested in different speeds of gesture in a work. What you noticed about the painterly backdrop in my paintings could consist of three or four different applications. There are different speeds and physical forces. Those are locational clues, and they become an important part of the time-based gestural narrative that underlies the work as it develops. There's a lot of editing in my work, piecing together gestural sequences or visual passages. That definitely parallels many of the things Brakhage was doing in film.

Brody In reading *What Do Pictures Want?*, Mitchell talks about how it was only in the 1790s that western European imperial societies became in contact with tribal art, and it was at exactly the same time they came to understand the meaning of fossils. You've used tribal art and fossils, as well as nineteenth century scientific drawings of discovered species, plants, microbotany. It seems like a lot of your imagery does converge on the nineteenth century imperial worldview. It's tempting to read some kind of critique into that.

TAAFFE I'm more of an explorer, although of course I have a dim view of empire. I'm more interested in exploration and the slow gathering of knowledge.

BRODY Is there nostalgia for a time when knowledge and aesthetics seemed unified?

TAAFFE In a sense, though I wouldn't say it's particularly nostalgic. The material has to fit a certain psychological profile. I perform a type of detective work to find material that has potency. It's true that scientists today are extremely atomized in hyper-specialisations, that's just how it is. But it's not like I have great nostalgia for the nineteenth century, I simply feel it's more available to me, in terms of its aesthetic use-value. Getting back to exploration, I will say that a lot of what I find is not readily available. I deliberately try to find things that are fairly obscure, because I'm interested in unique material. For me, these nineteenth century scientific memoirs are fossils in and of themselves.

BRODY You spoke earlier about the sense of the immediate presence of the work, something like the return of the 'aura,' and the sense of a community of viewers created by their common experience of that presence.

TAAFFE I try to instill sensitivity to the surface through the sense of touch. There are certain things that cannot be achieved without that direct relation to a work. It also has to do with the organisation of the space and the scale of a work and the quality of the line and how weak or strong it is. There are lots of little things that go on that are barely noticeable at first, and yet the cumulative effect of these subtle marks constitute a painting's presence or being in the world. Art is caressing, it's erotic. Isn't that why we like looking at art? I think that's what we like most about art, whether we realise it or not. It's about the intimacy of one person shaping something in a very delicate, personal way, that another person can experience, and that's what we need more of in the world today. We're losing that sense of the tactile.

BRODY Painting was once high technology, it was once virtual reality. But now, vivid technological microcosms are available on one's phone. Yet your work eloquently proves that painting can still do things that technological fantasy and spectacle can't. Does painting matter less and less or more and more?

TAAFFE I think that painting informs the visual culture *essentially*: that painting is a paradigmatic synthesis and that it can inform other kinds of cultural activities such as design and architecture. I see art as intrinsically at the center of our culture, whether it is realized at the time or not.

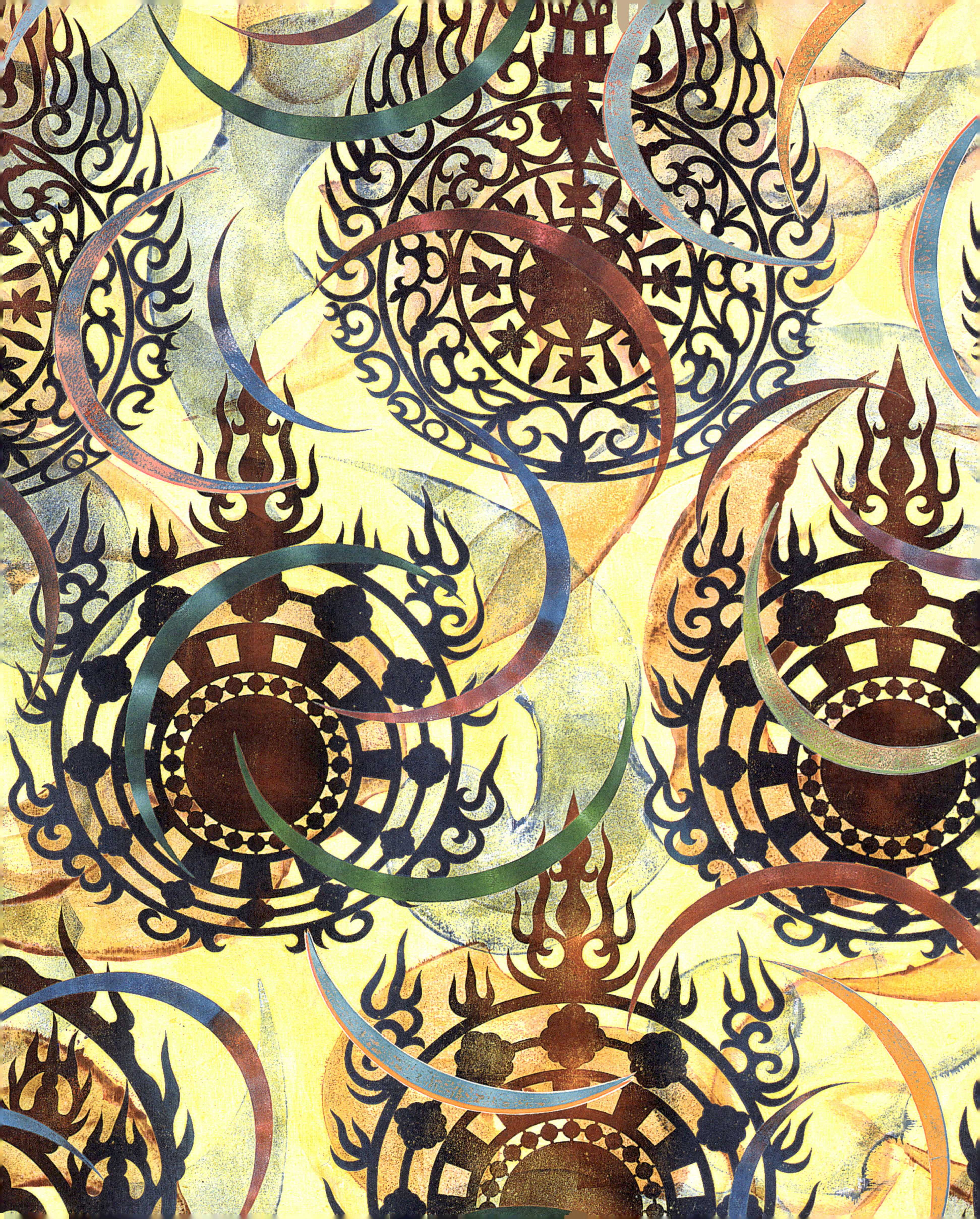

Plates

Porte Amur, 2001
Mixed media on canvas, 270 × 228 cm

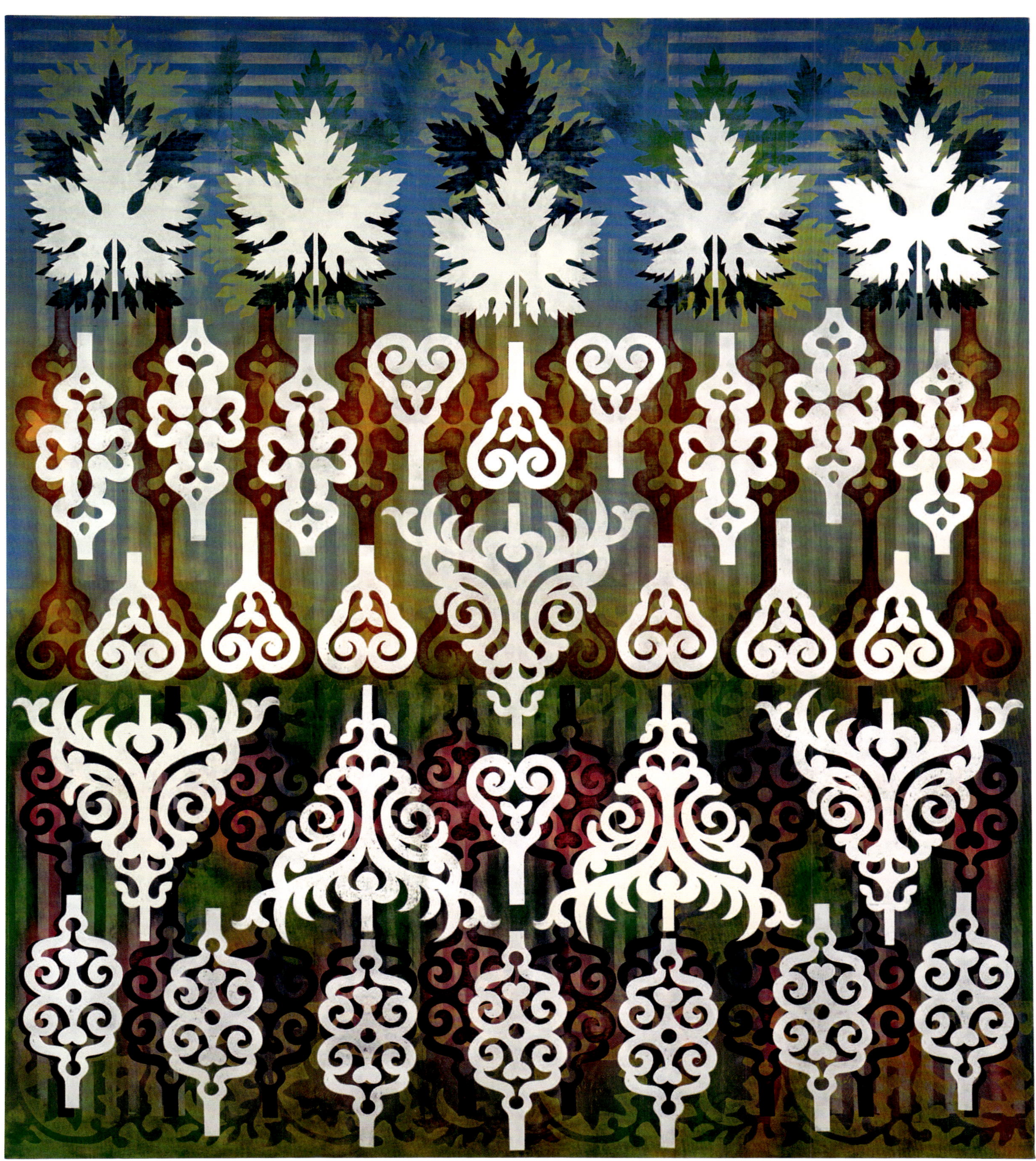

Rose Nocturne, 2002
Mixed media on canvas, 221 × 97 cm

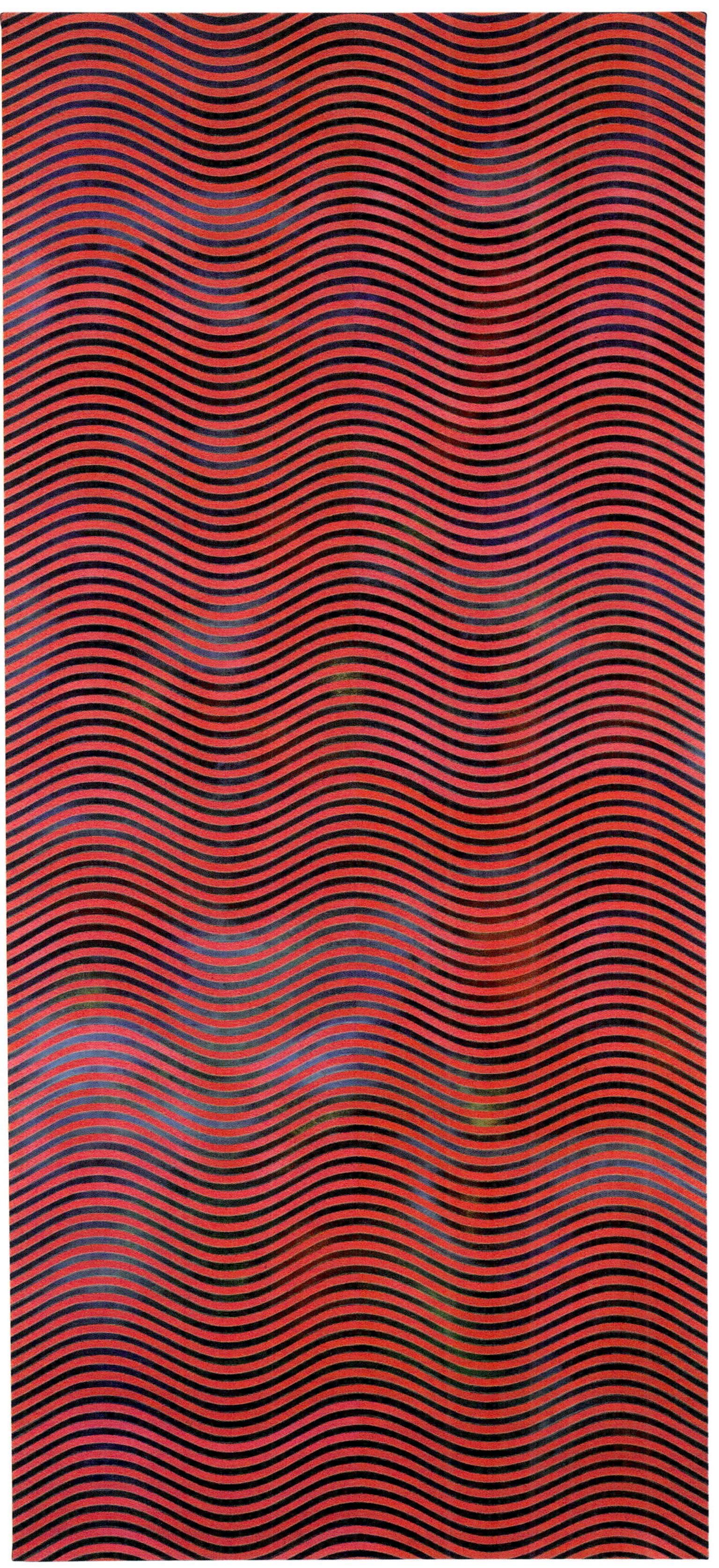

Composition with Gemstones II, 2001–02
Mixed media on canvas, 158 × 217 cm

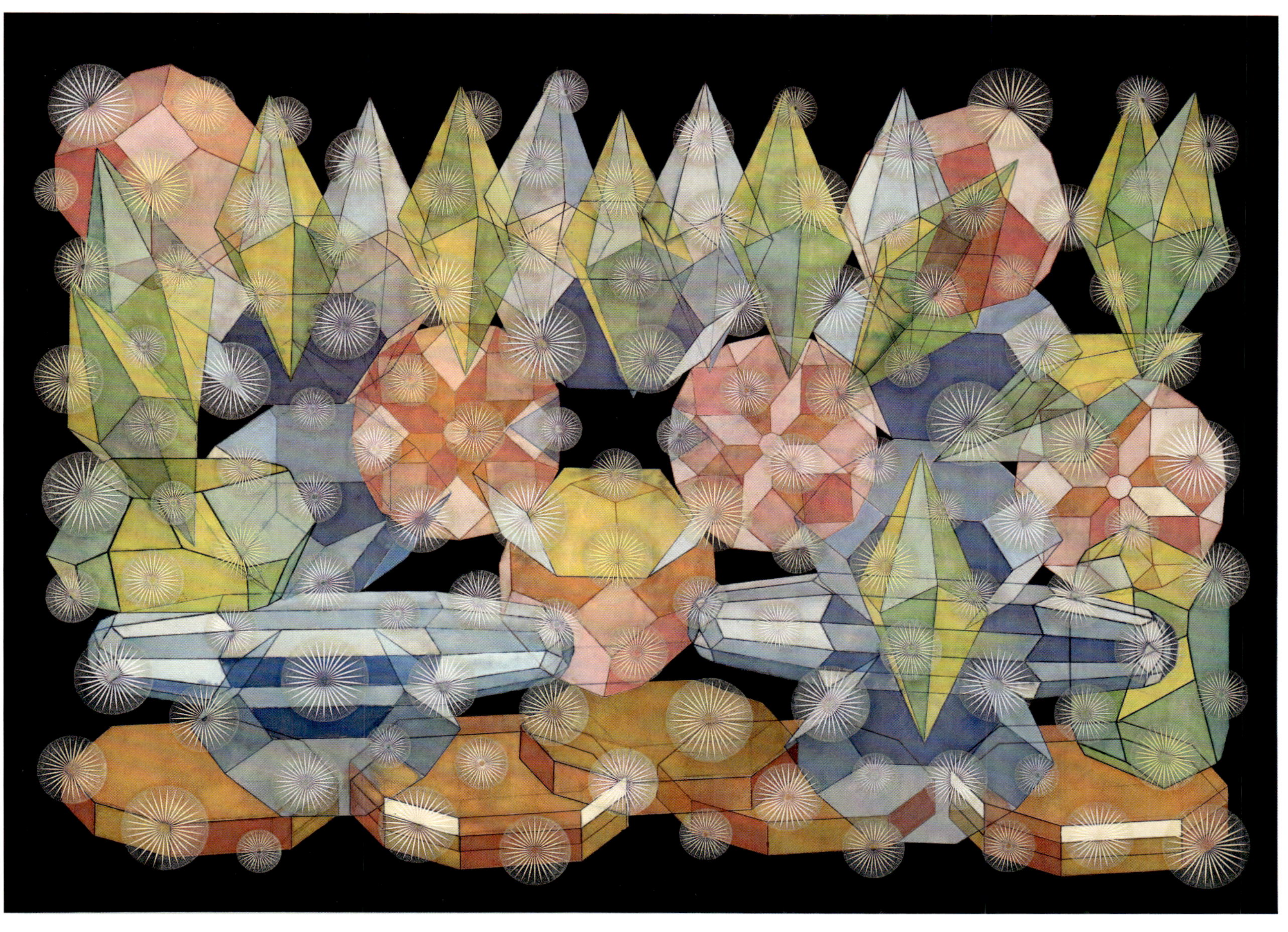

Phasmidae, 2002
Mixed media on canvas, 142 × 177 cm

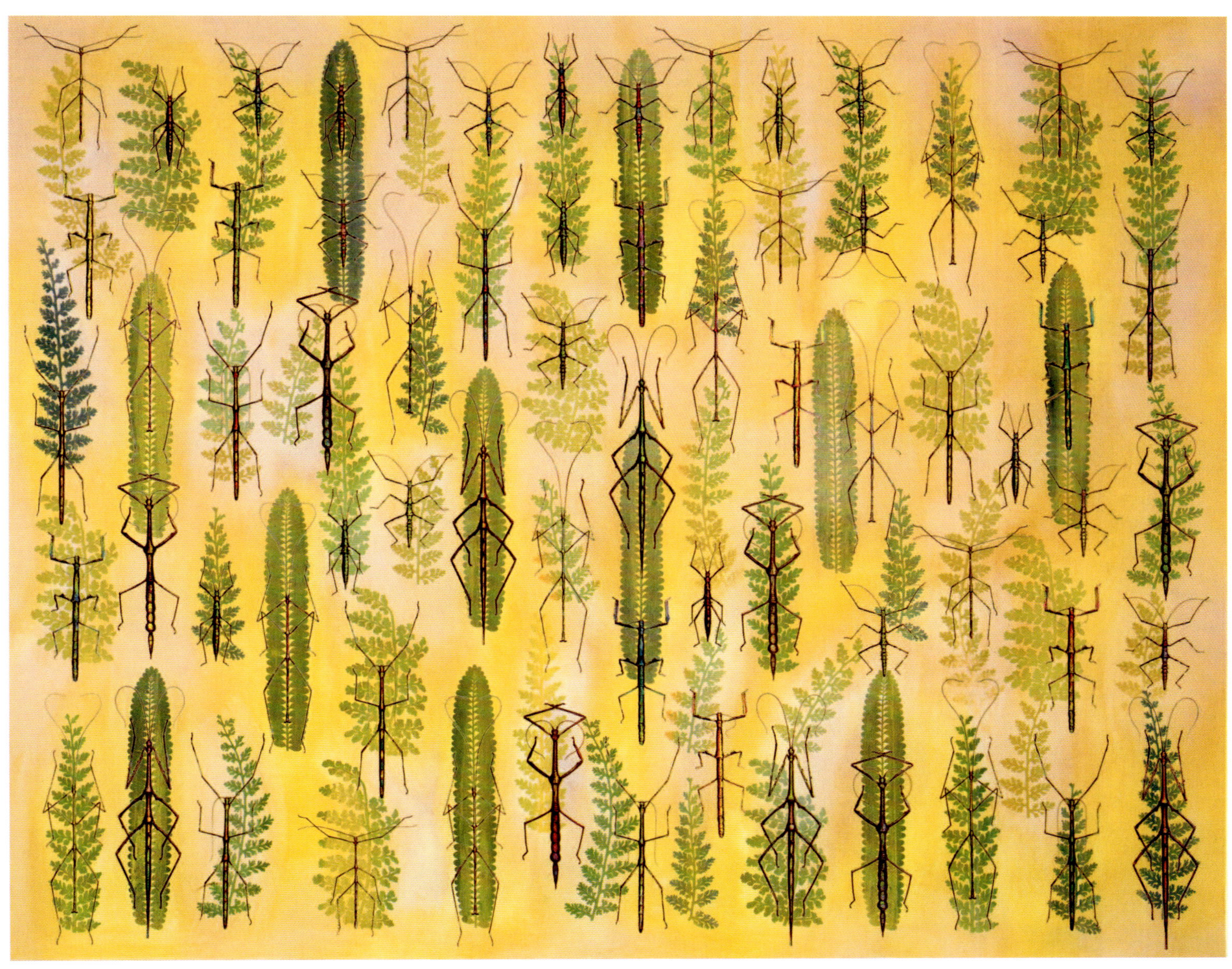

Abstract Painting (Vipera Russelli), 2002
Mixed media on canvas, 141 × 100 cm

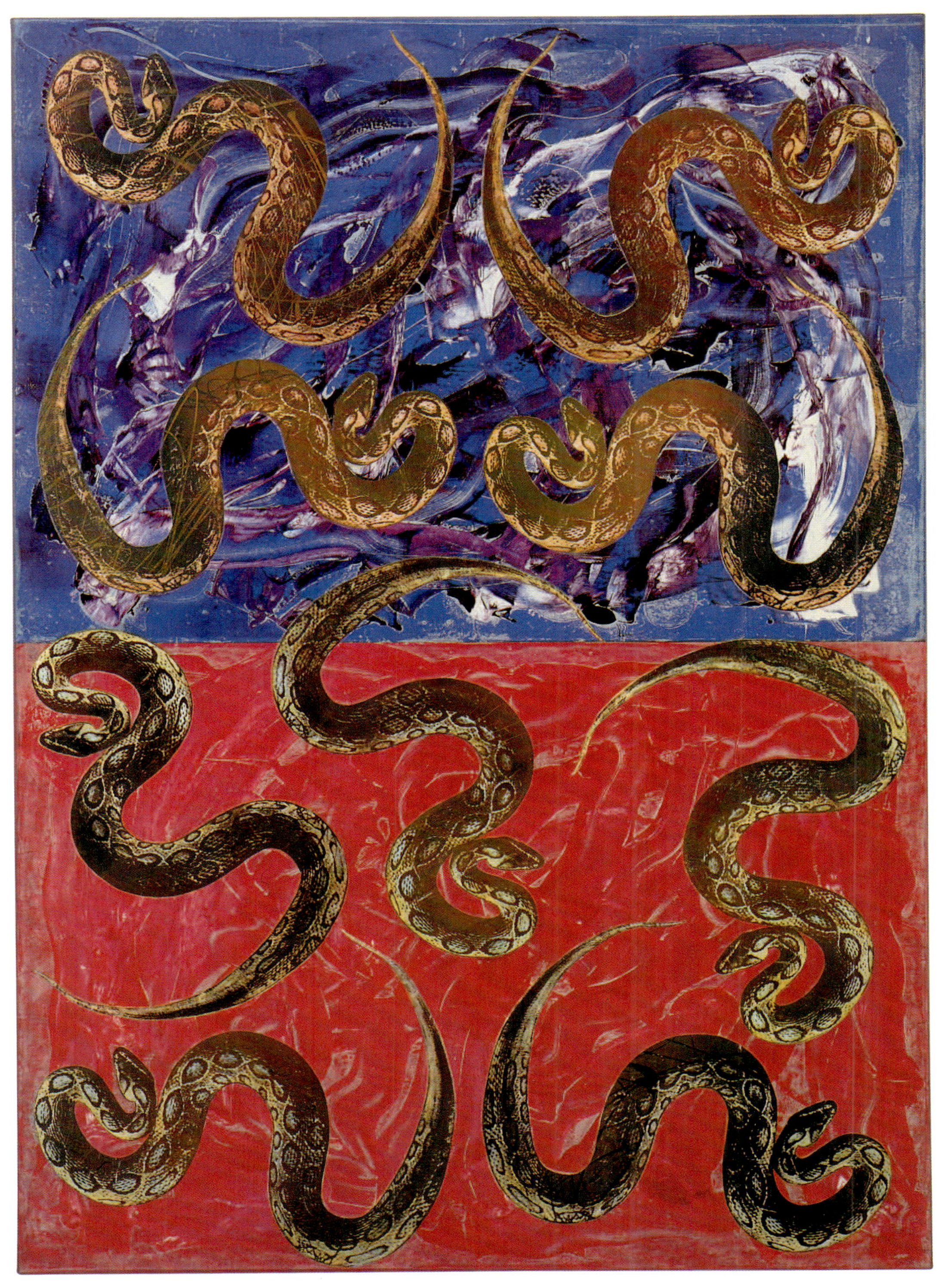

Painting with Teeth, 2002
Mixed media on canvas, 113 × 138 cm

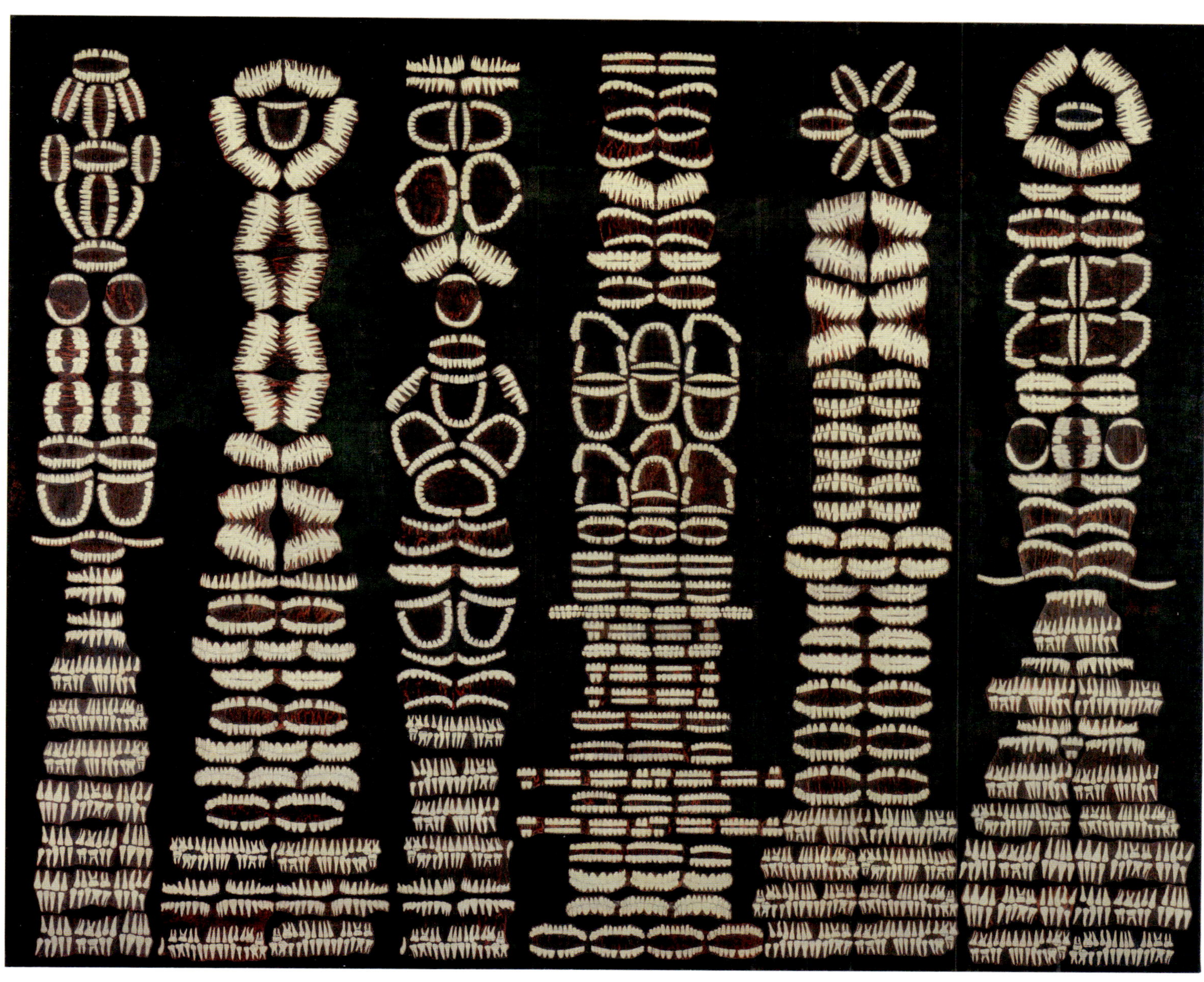

Sanctuary, 2002
Mixed media on canvas, 201 × 302 cm

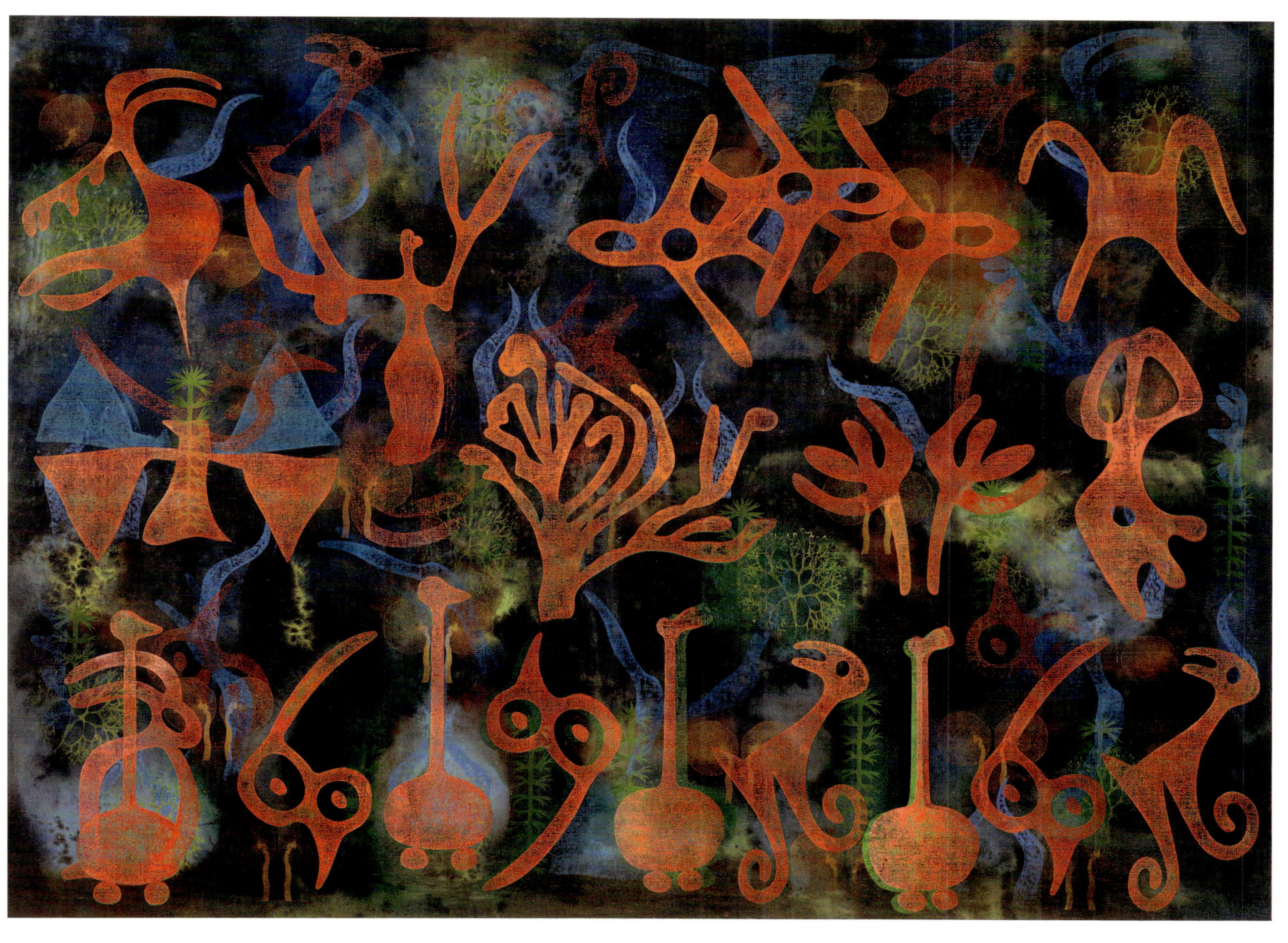

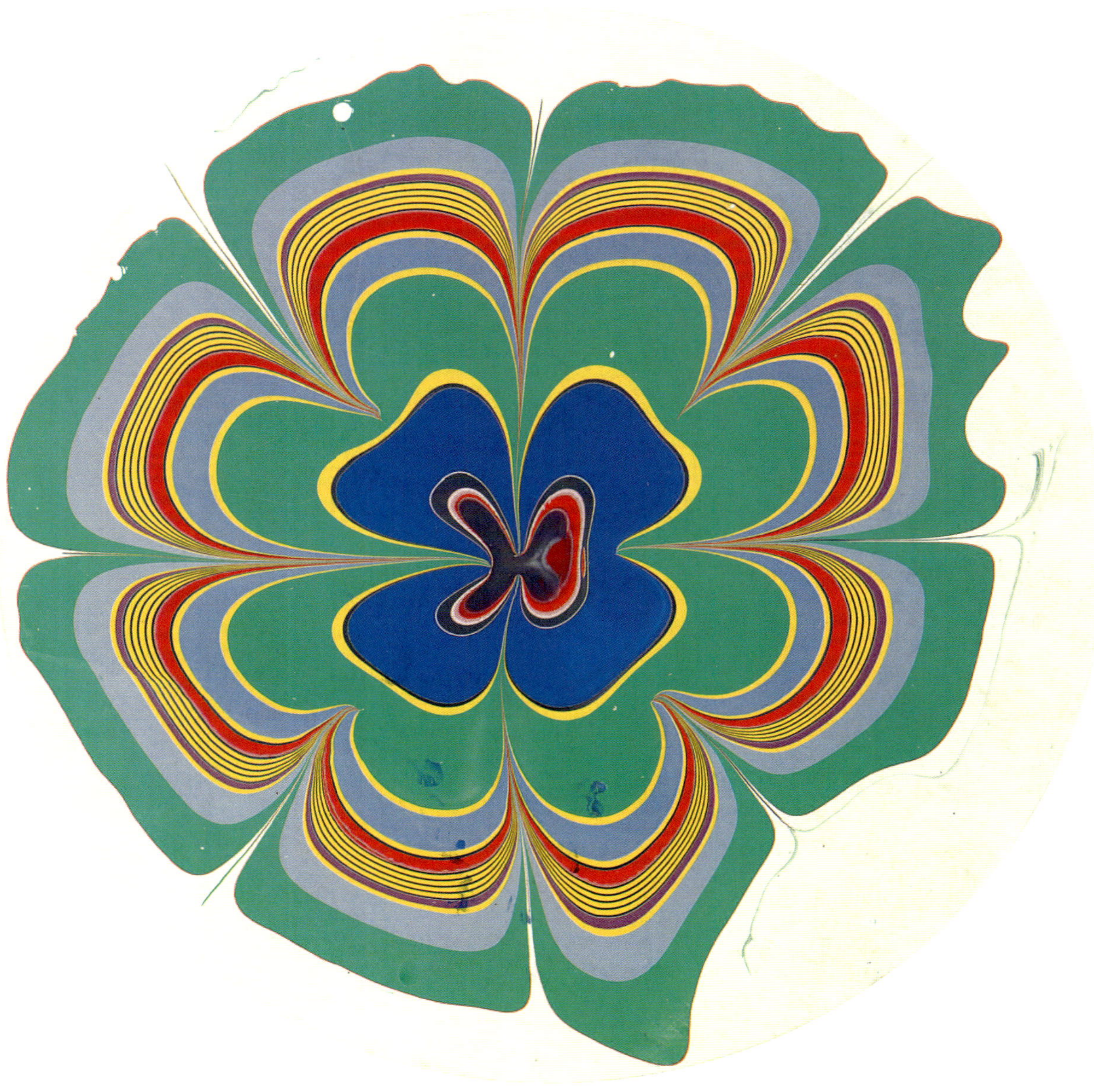

Otranto, 2002
Mixed media on canvas, 36.5 cm

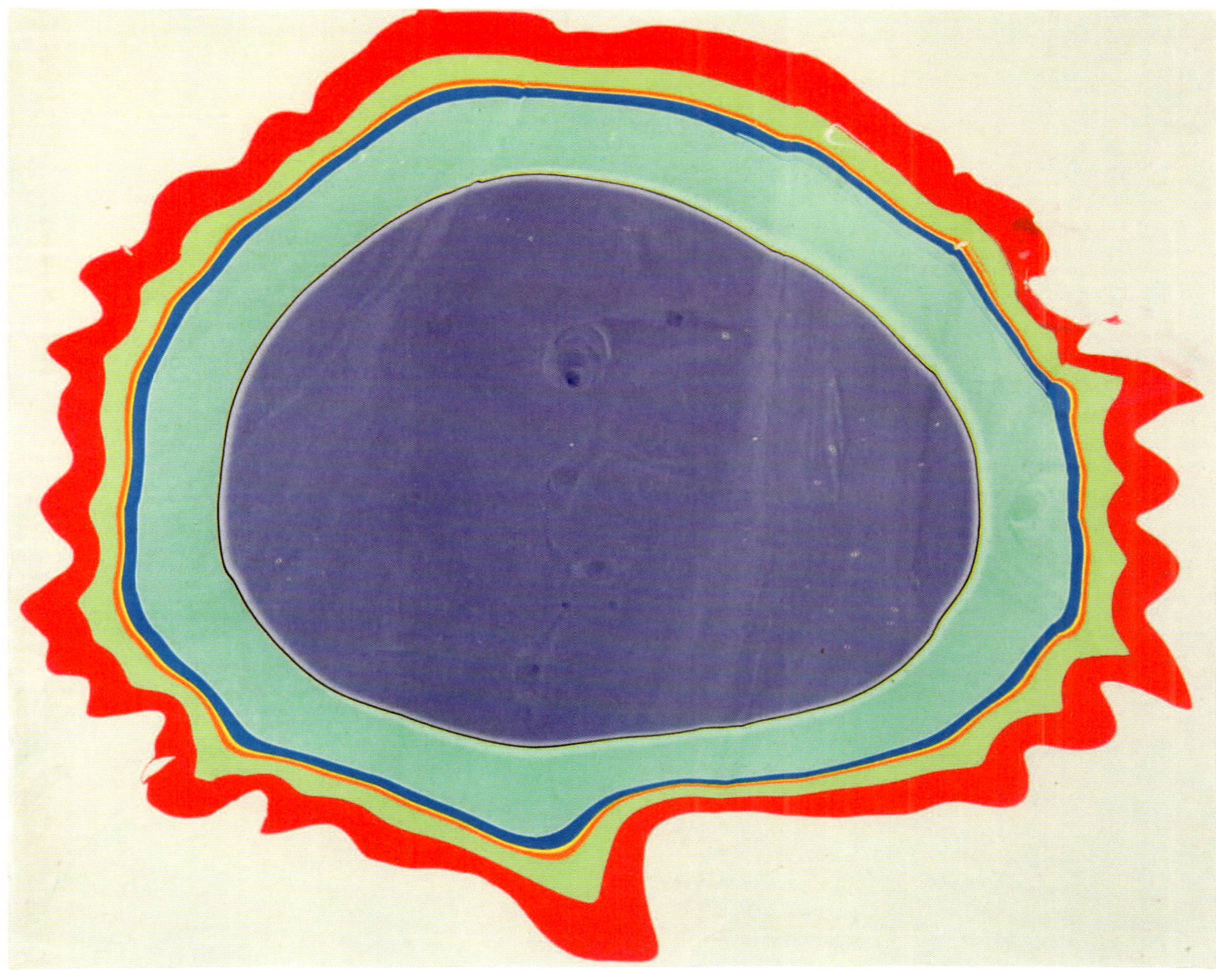

Specchio, 2002
Mixed media on canvas, 26 × 31.7 cm

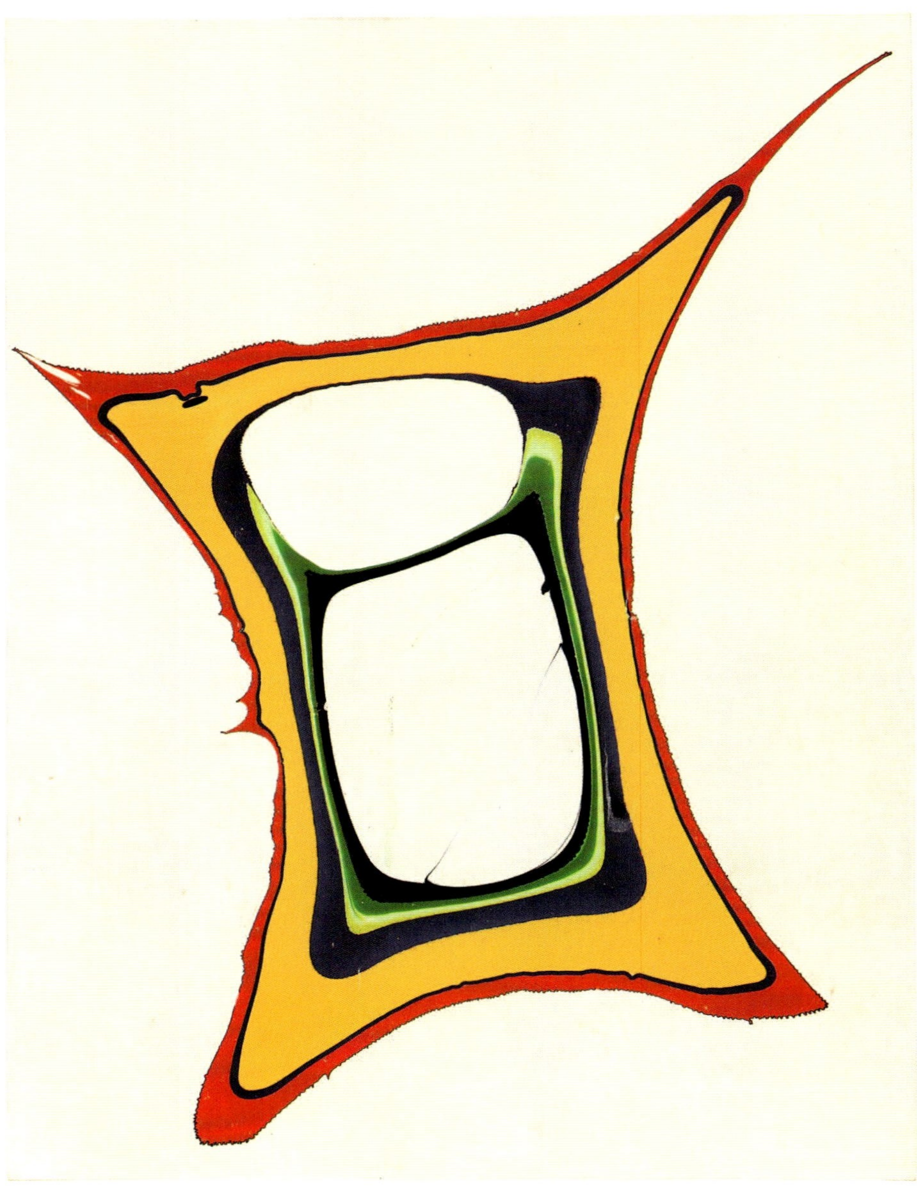

Helm, 2002
Mixed media on canvas, 43.8 × 33 cm

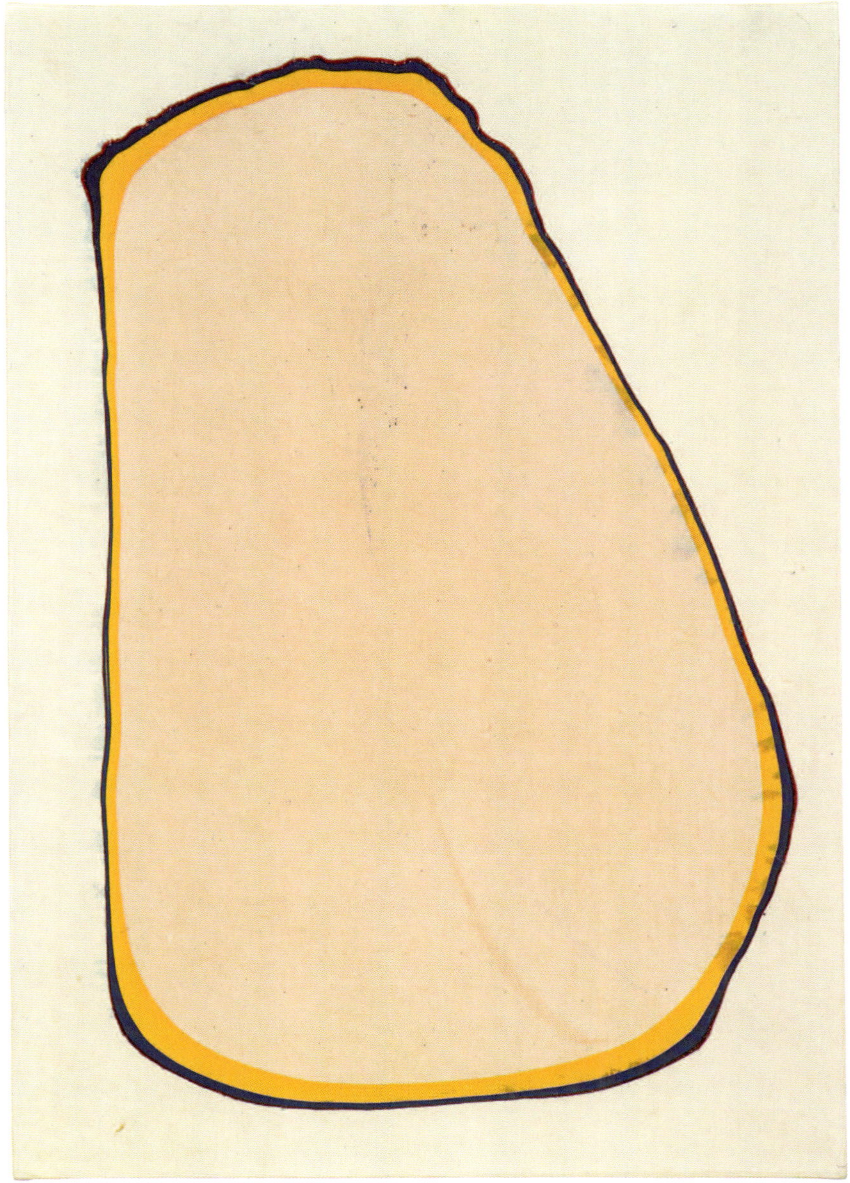

Cairn, 2002
Mixed media on canvas, 30.4 × 20.9 cm

Field Station, 2003
Mixed media on canvas, 105 × 145 cm

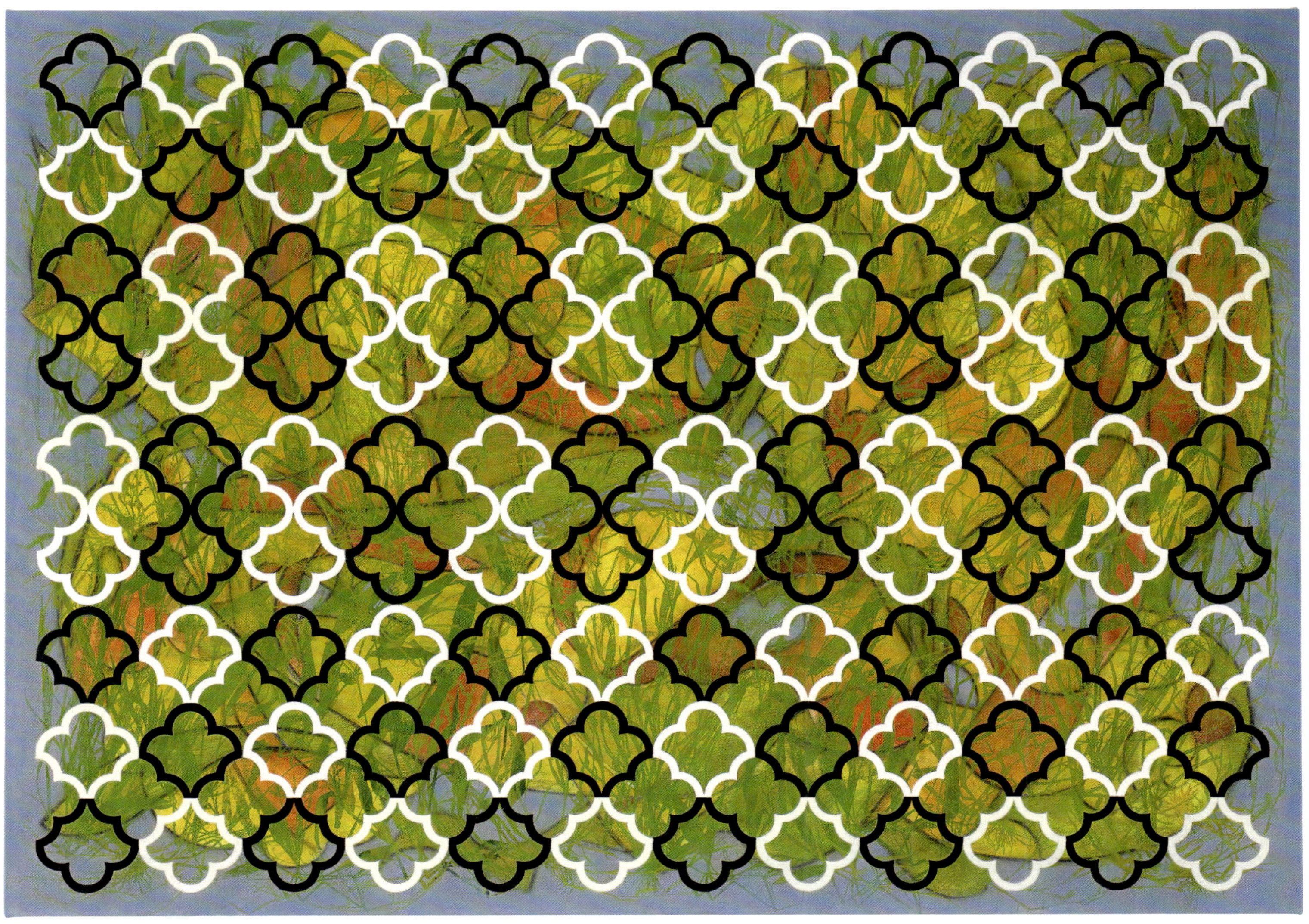

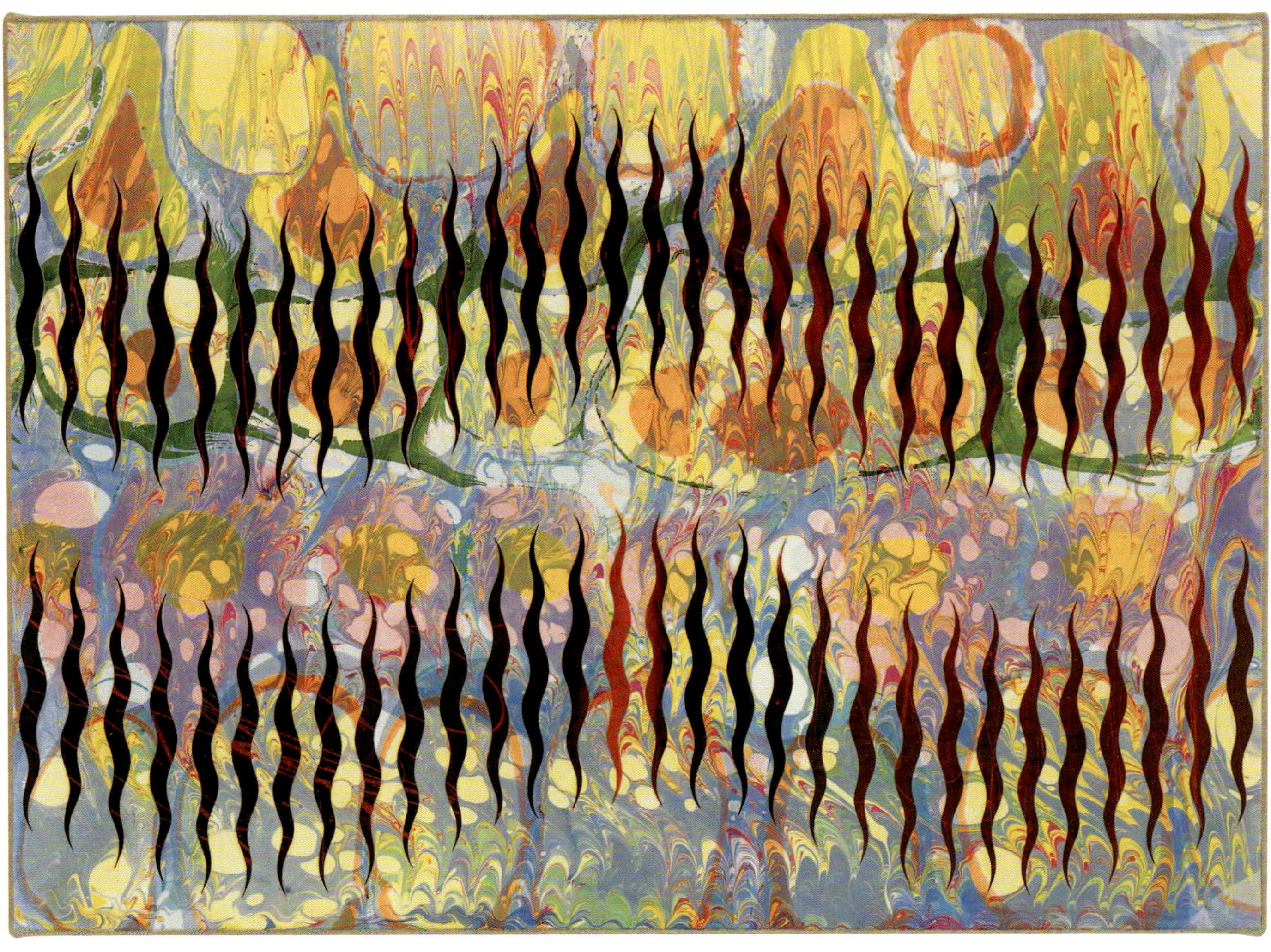

Split, 2004
Mixed media on canvas, 58 × 77 cm

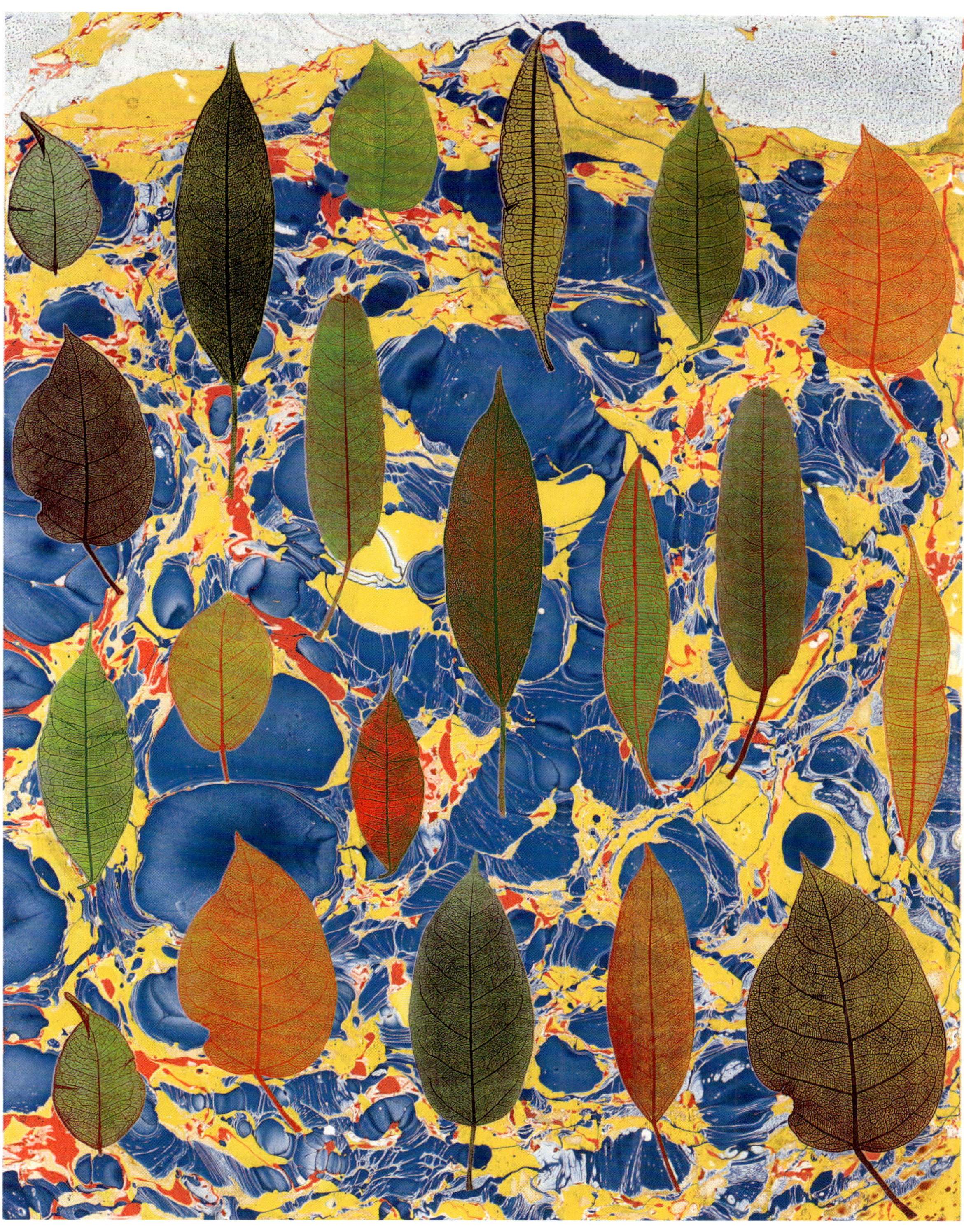

Devonian Leaves, 2004
Mixed media on canvas, 127 × 99 cm

Composition with Shells and Algae, 2005
Mixed media on canvas, 226 × 300 cm

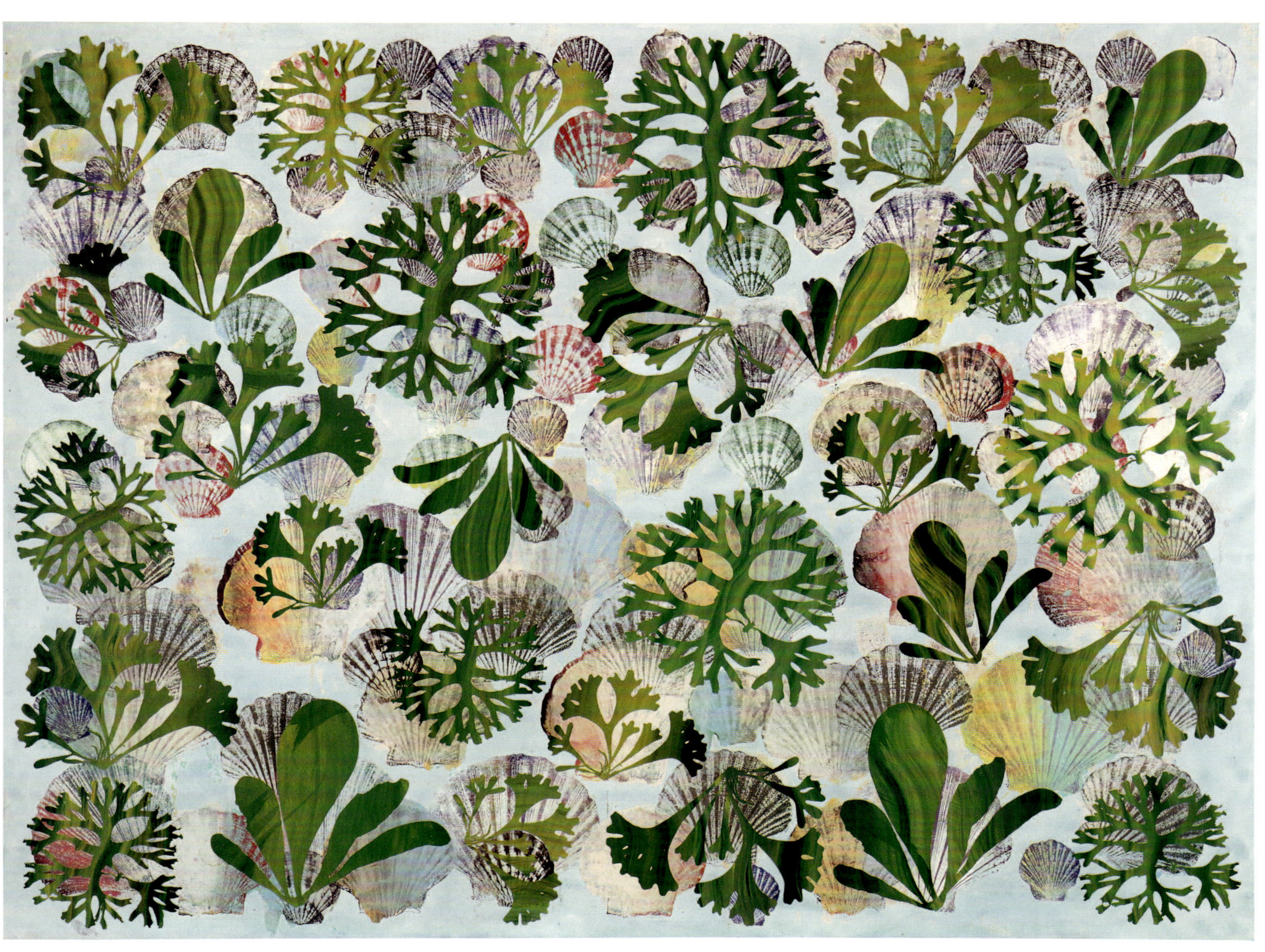

Plinth, 2006
Mixed media on canvas, 294 × 127 cm

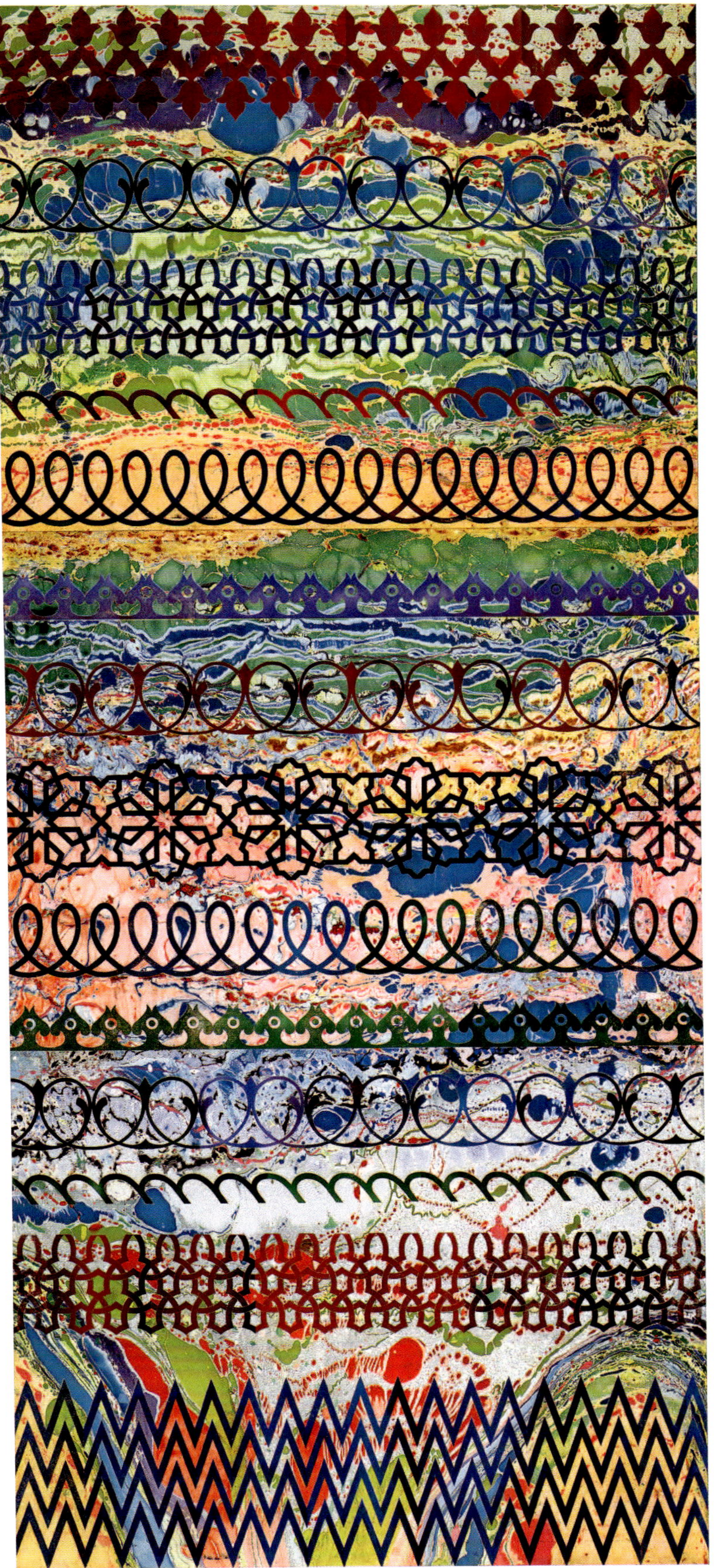

Asuka Passage, 2006
Mixed media on canvas, 296 × 255 cm

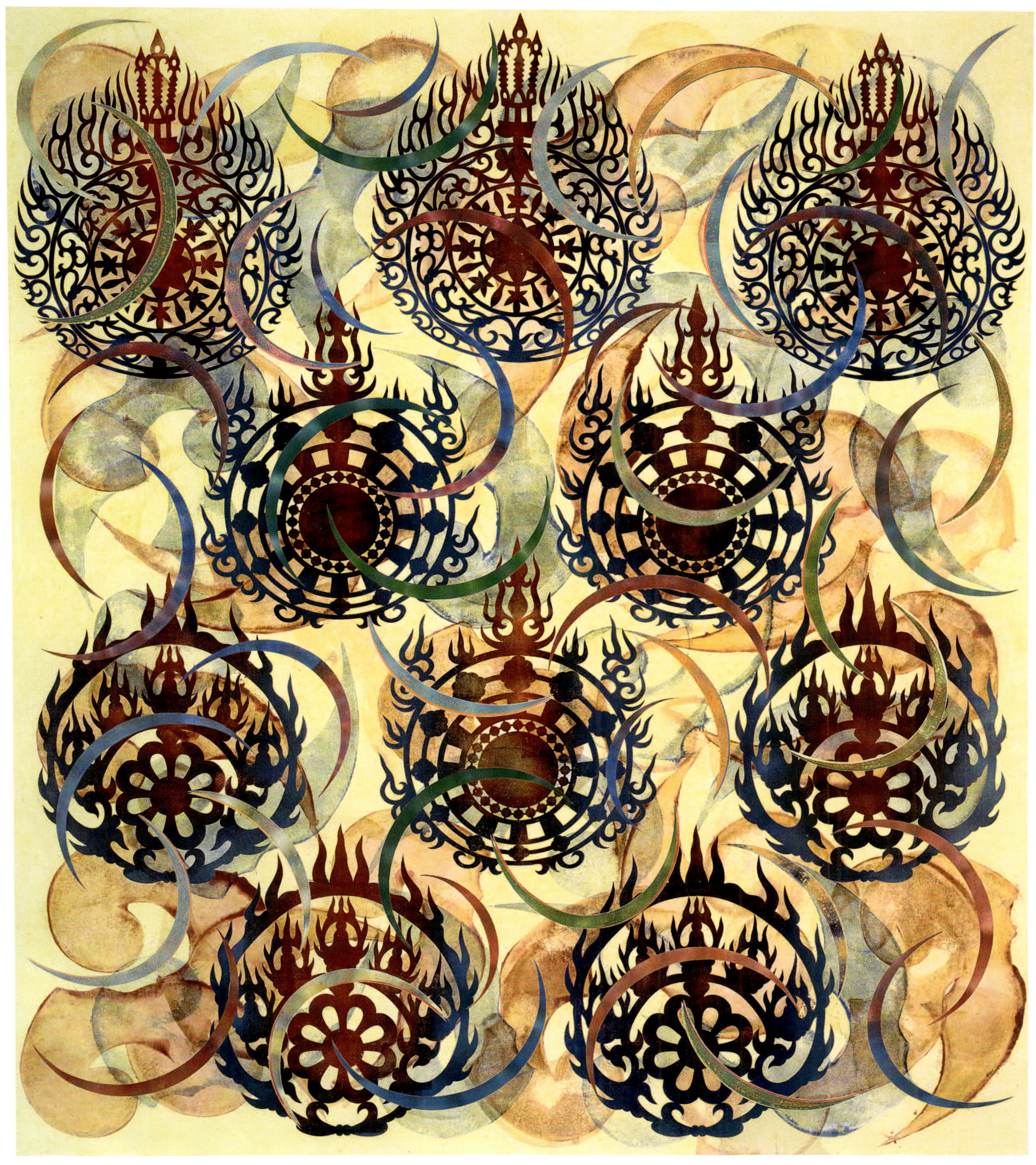

Dryadic Figures, 2006
Mixed media on canvas, 215 × 258 cm

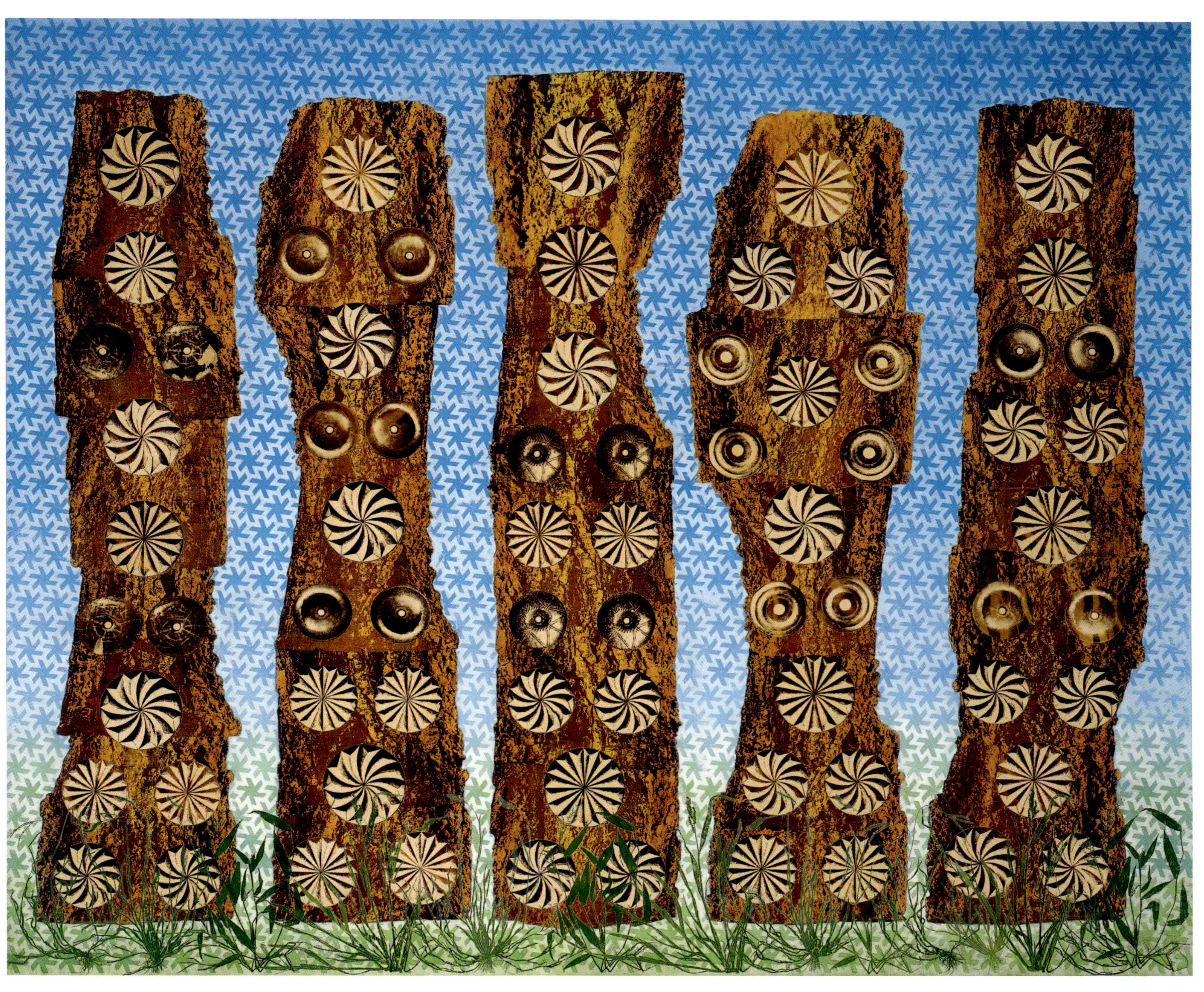

Cape Siren, 2008
Mixed media on canvas, 296 × 243 cm

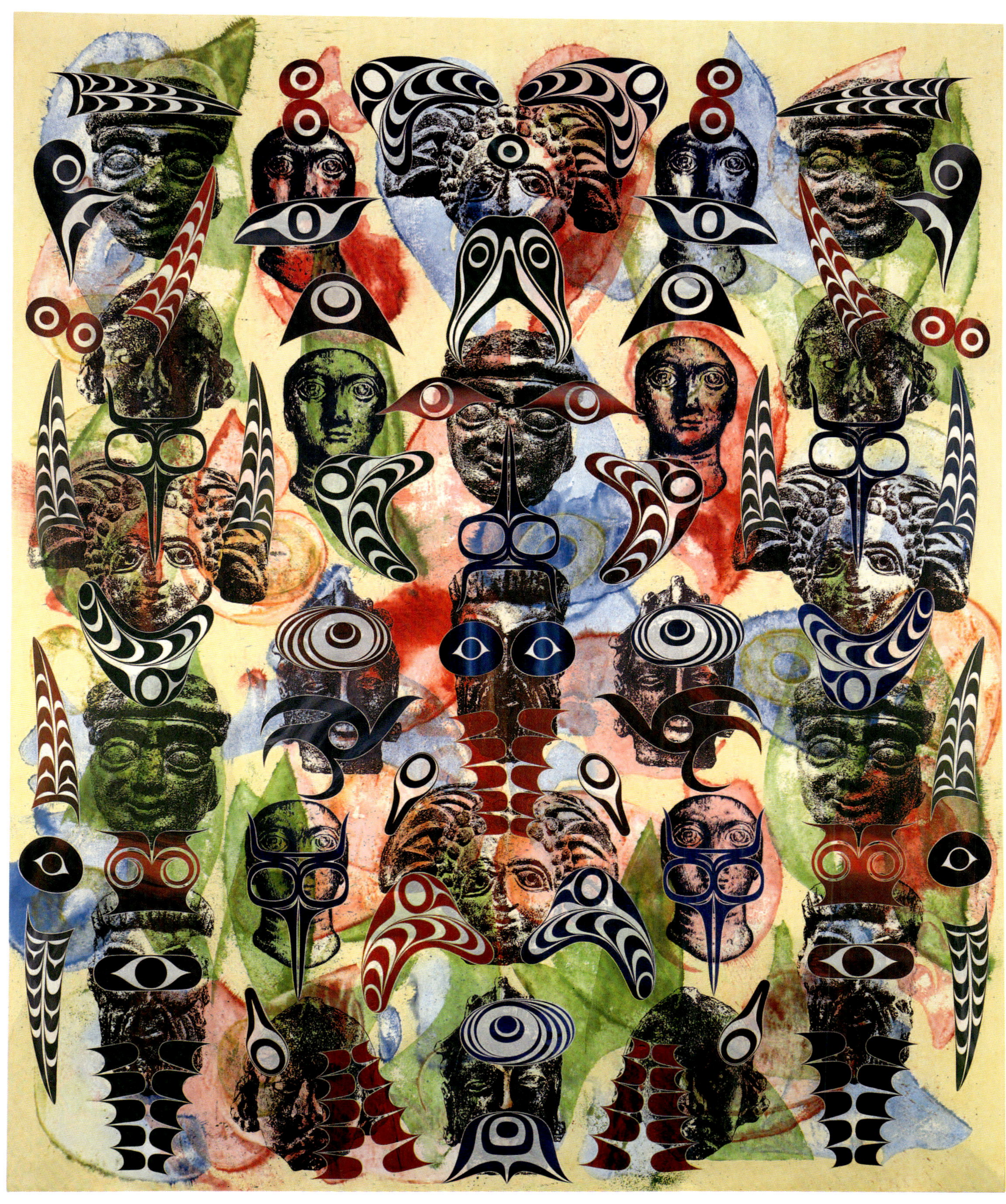

Dance of the Phasmidae, 2007
Mixed media on canvas, 7 × 81 cm

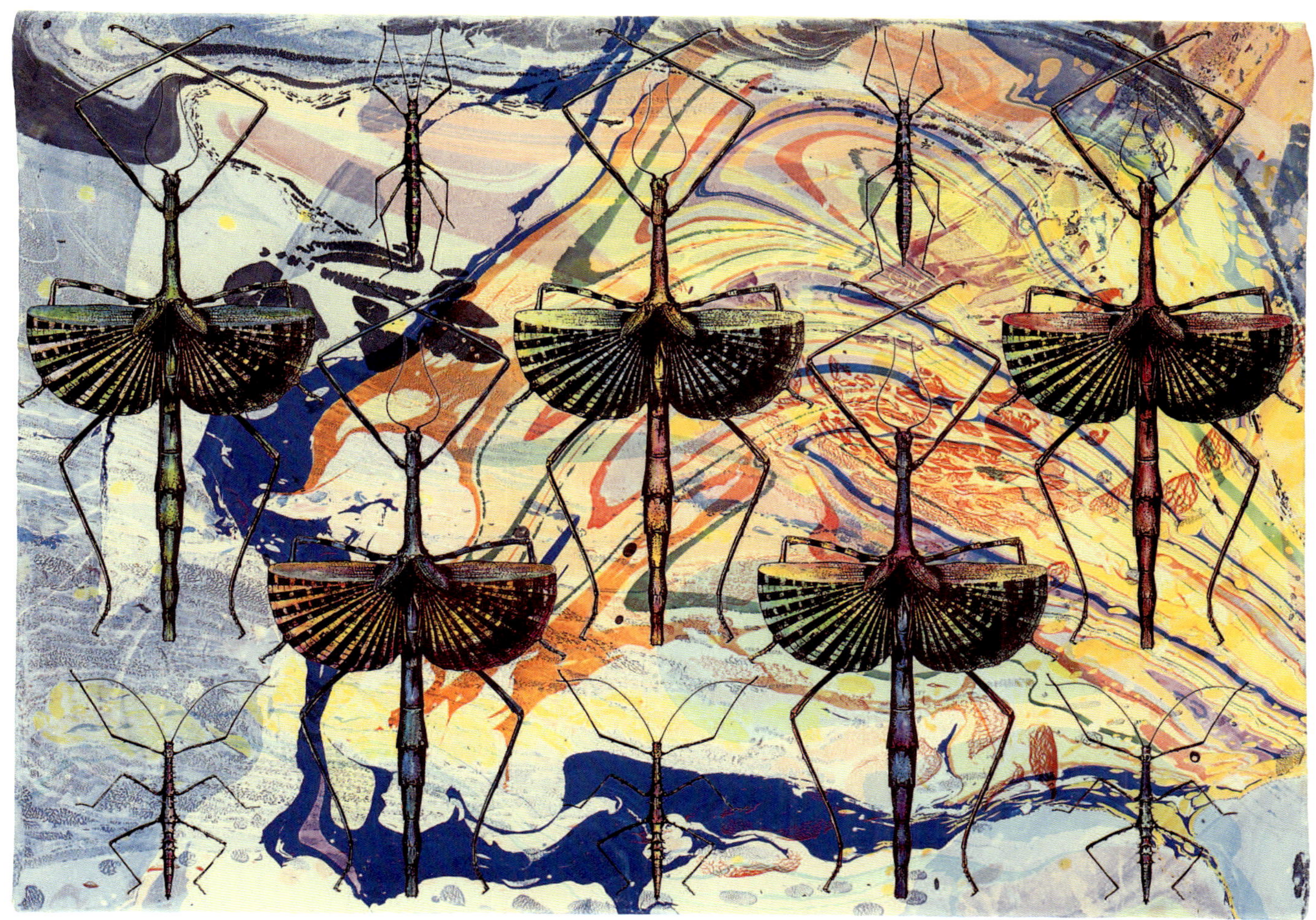

Cosmati, 2007
Mixed media on canvas, 196 × 127 cm

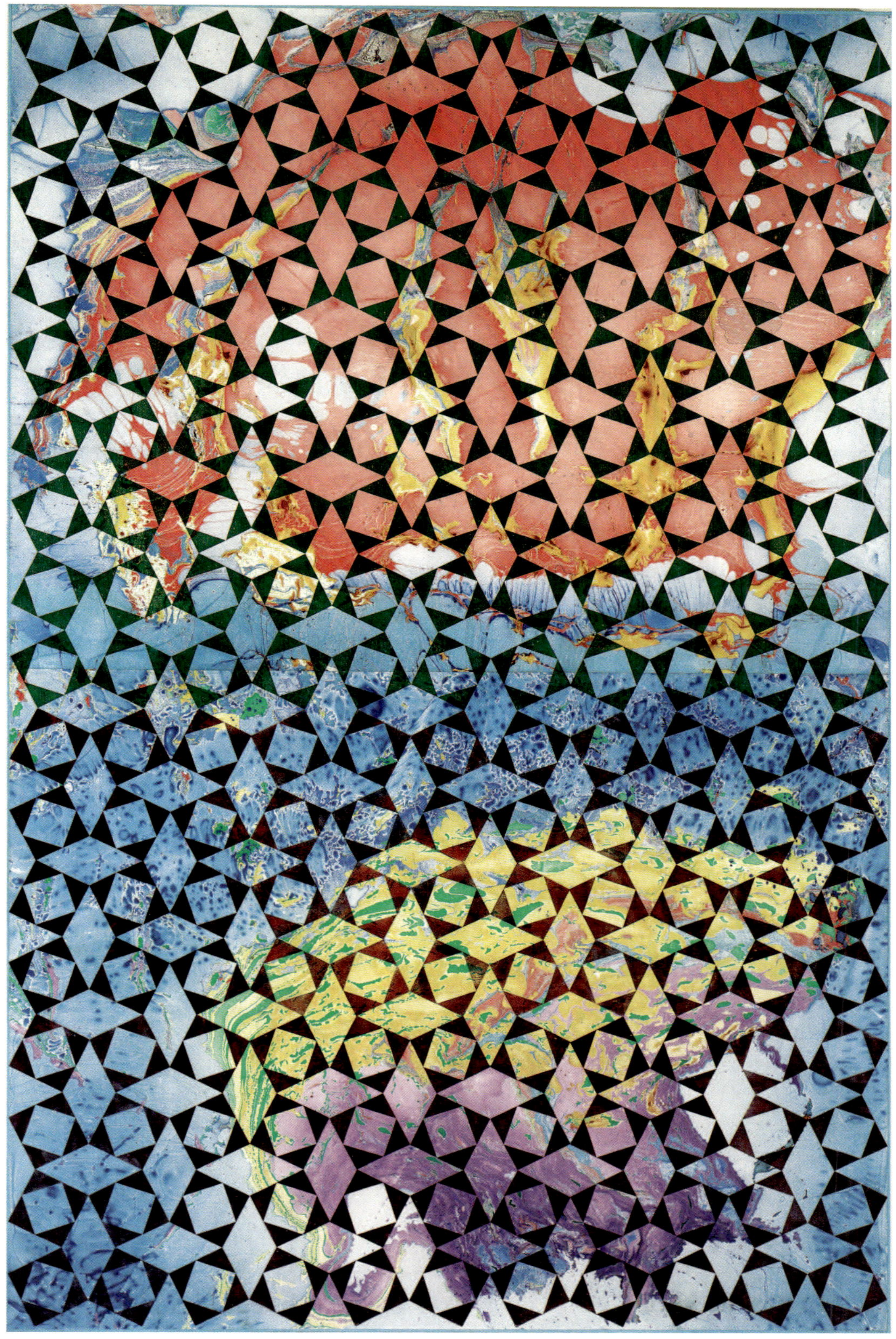

Port of Saints, 2007
Mixed media on canvas, 307 × 245 cm

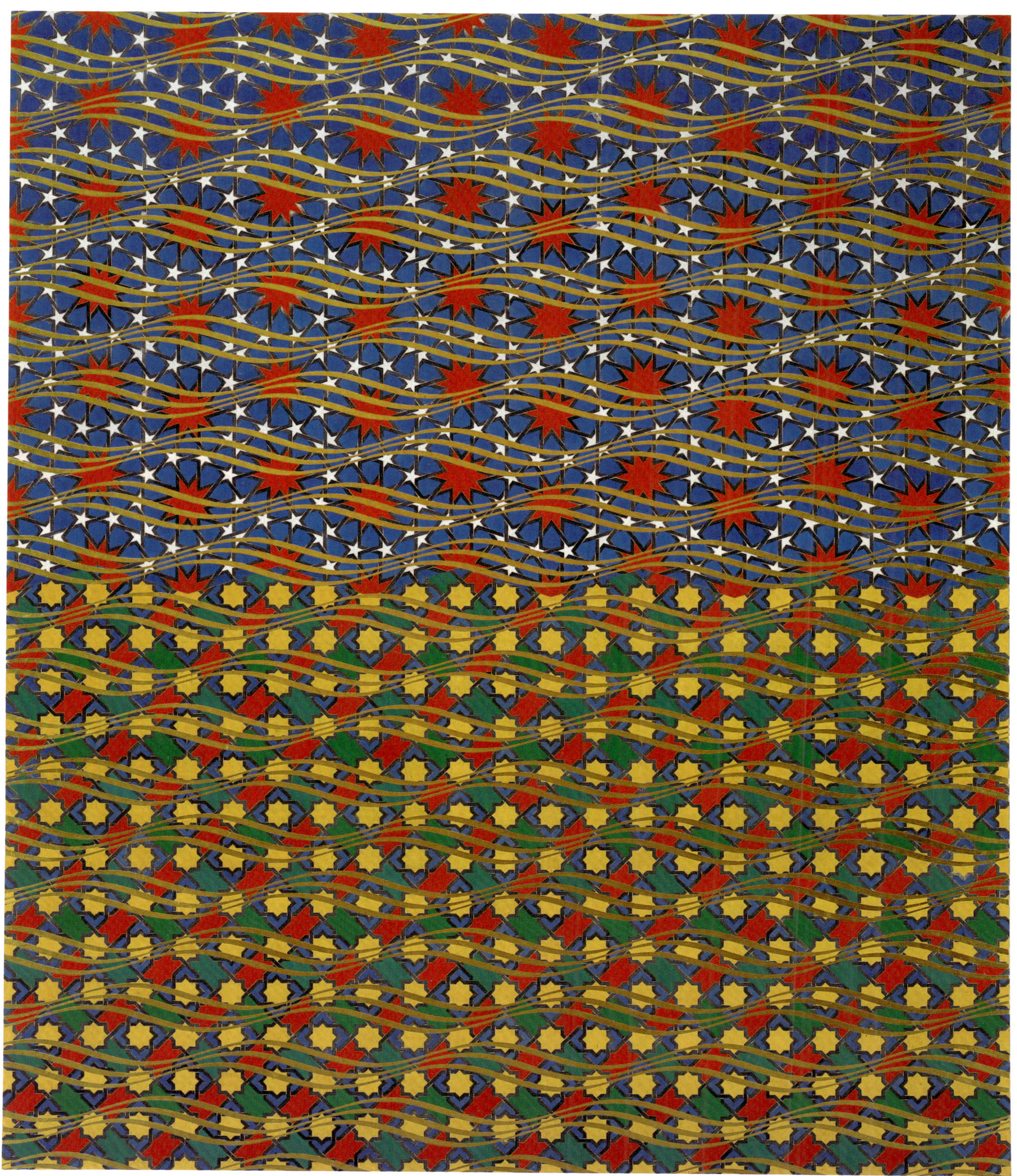

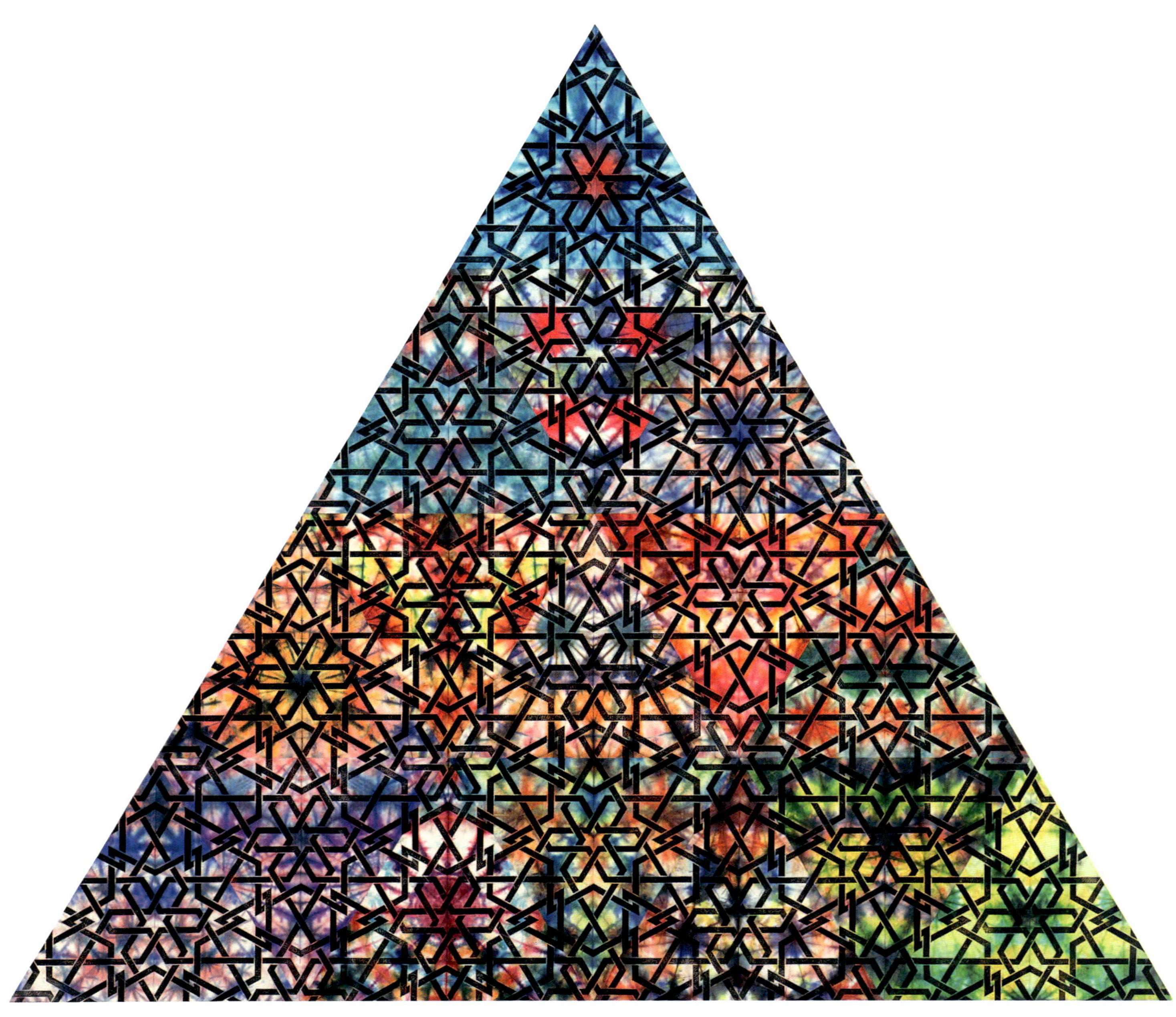

Damascene Triangle I, 2008
Mixed media on canvas, 179 × 179 cm

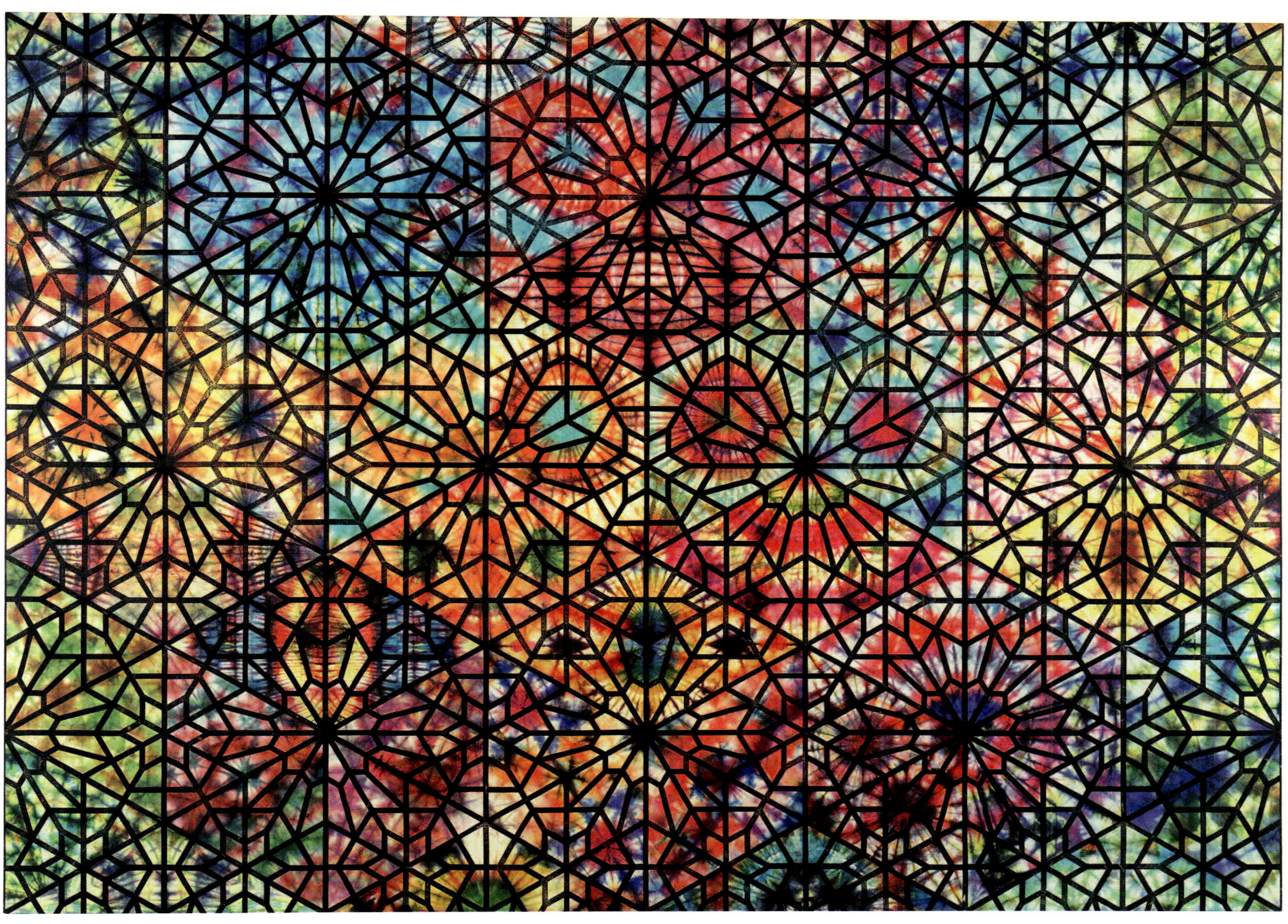

Cairene Window II, 2008
Mixed media on canvas, 50 × 213 cm

Artificial Paradise (Loculus), 2008
Mixed media on canvas, 350 × 381 cm

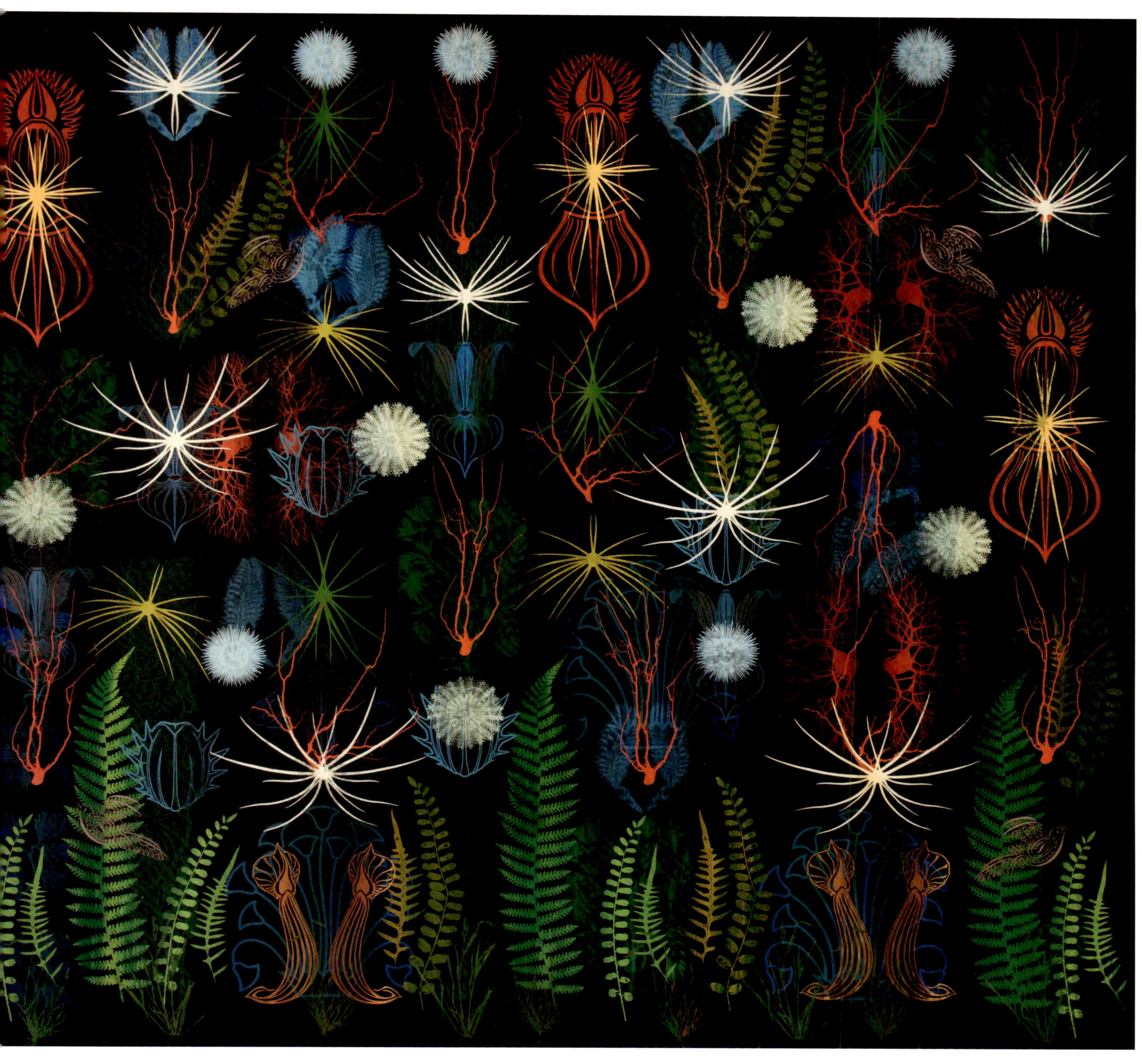

Large Viking Filigree Painting, 2008
Mixed media on canvas, 327 × 277 cm

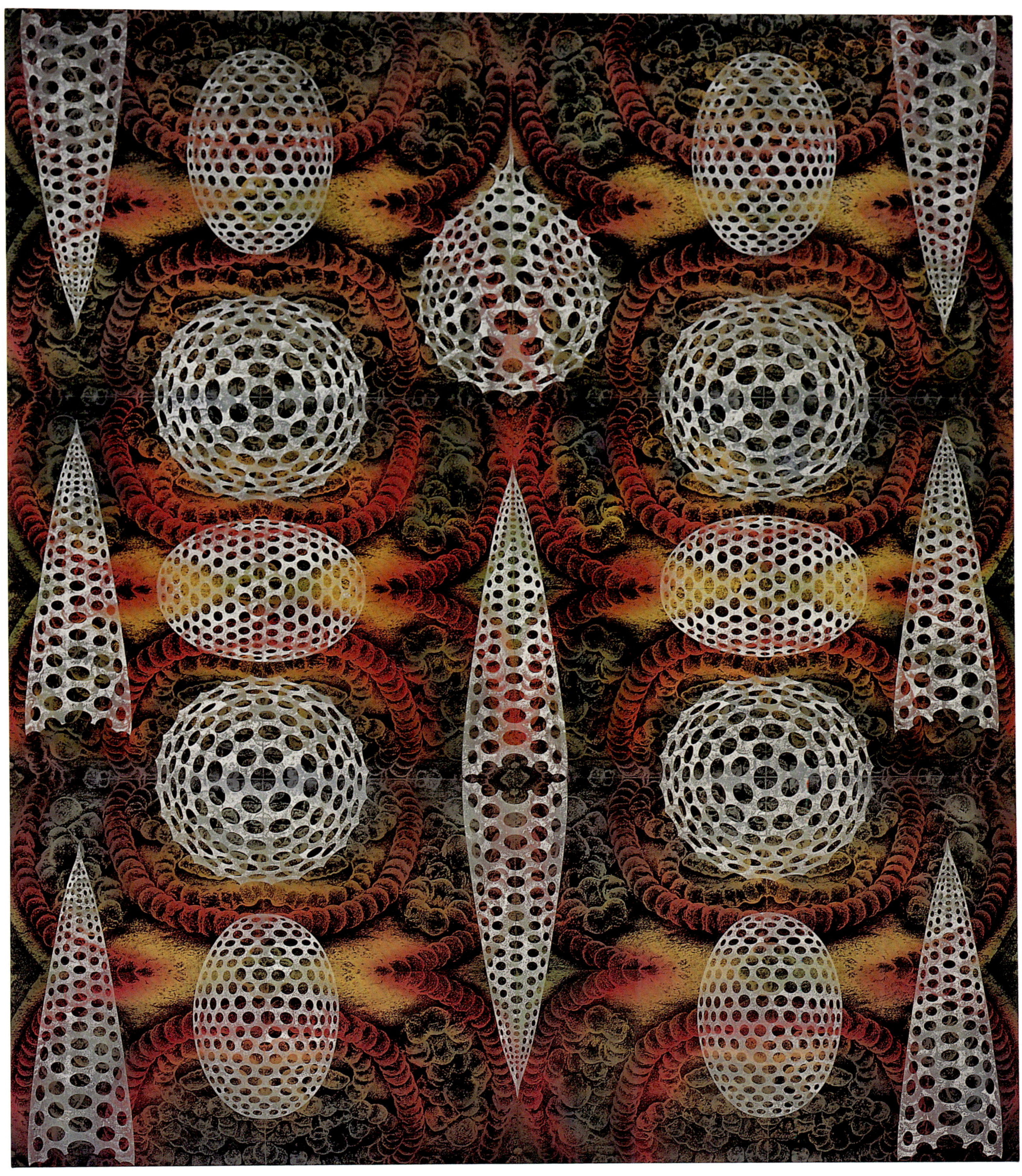

Painting with Byzantine Fragments, 2008
Mixed media on canvas, 288 × 288 cm

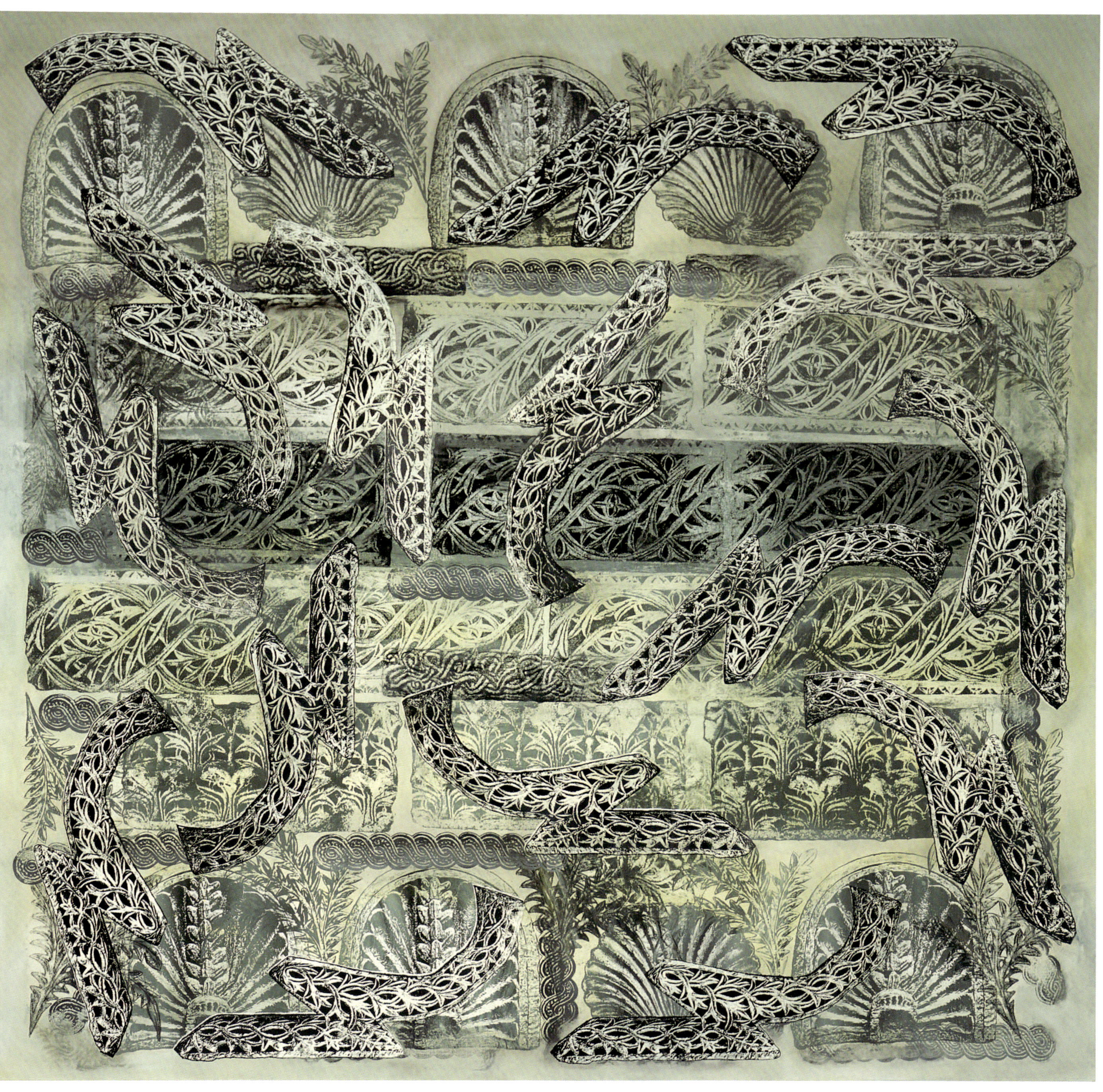

Peregrine Falcon over King Snake, 2008
Mixed media on canvas, 77 × 77 cm

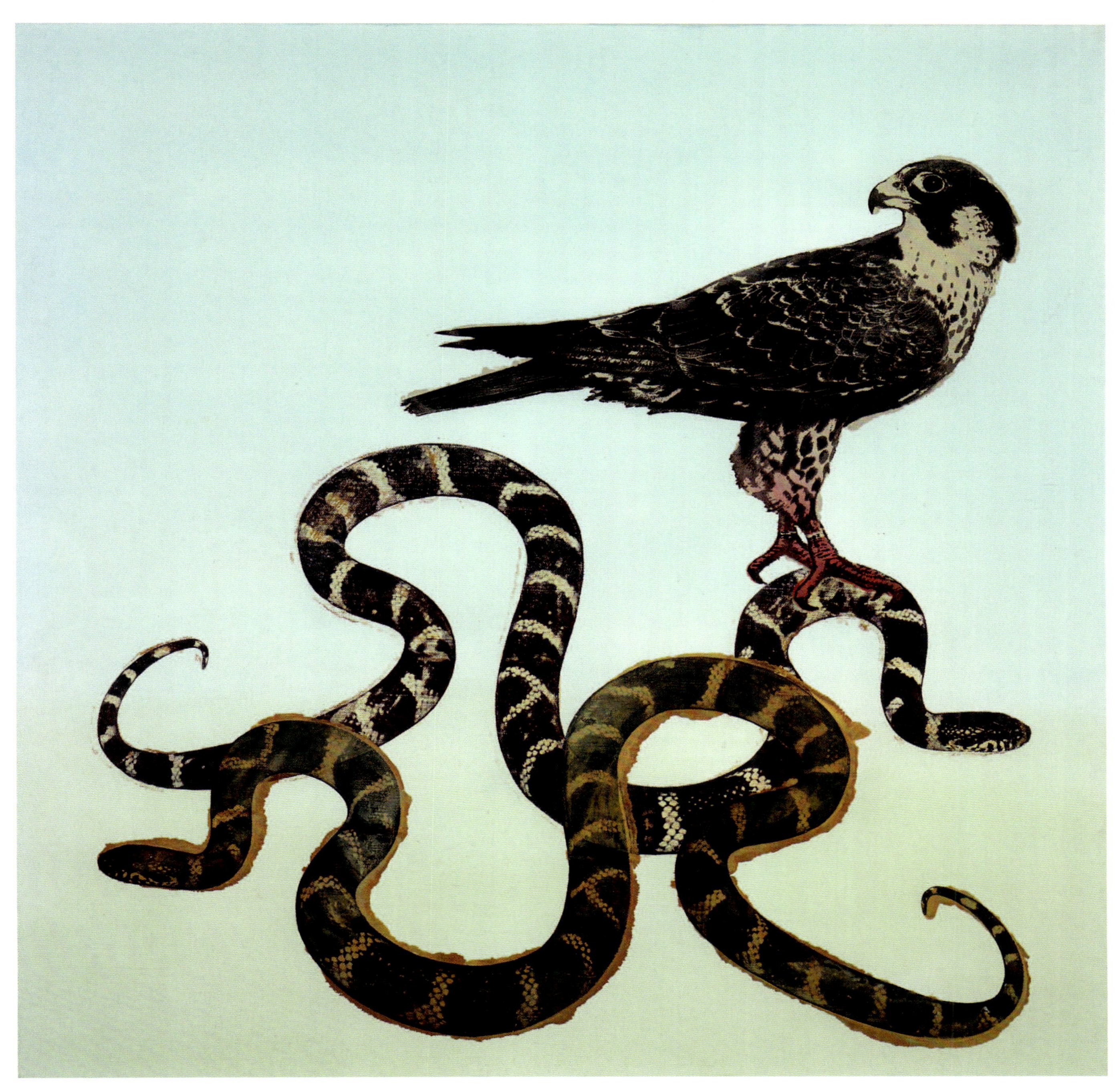

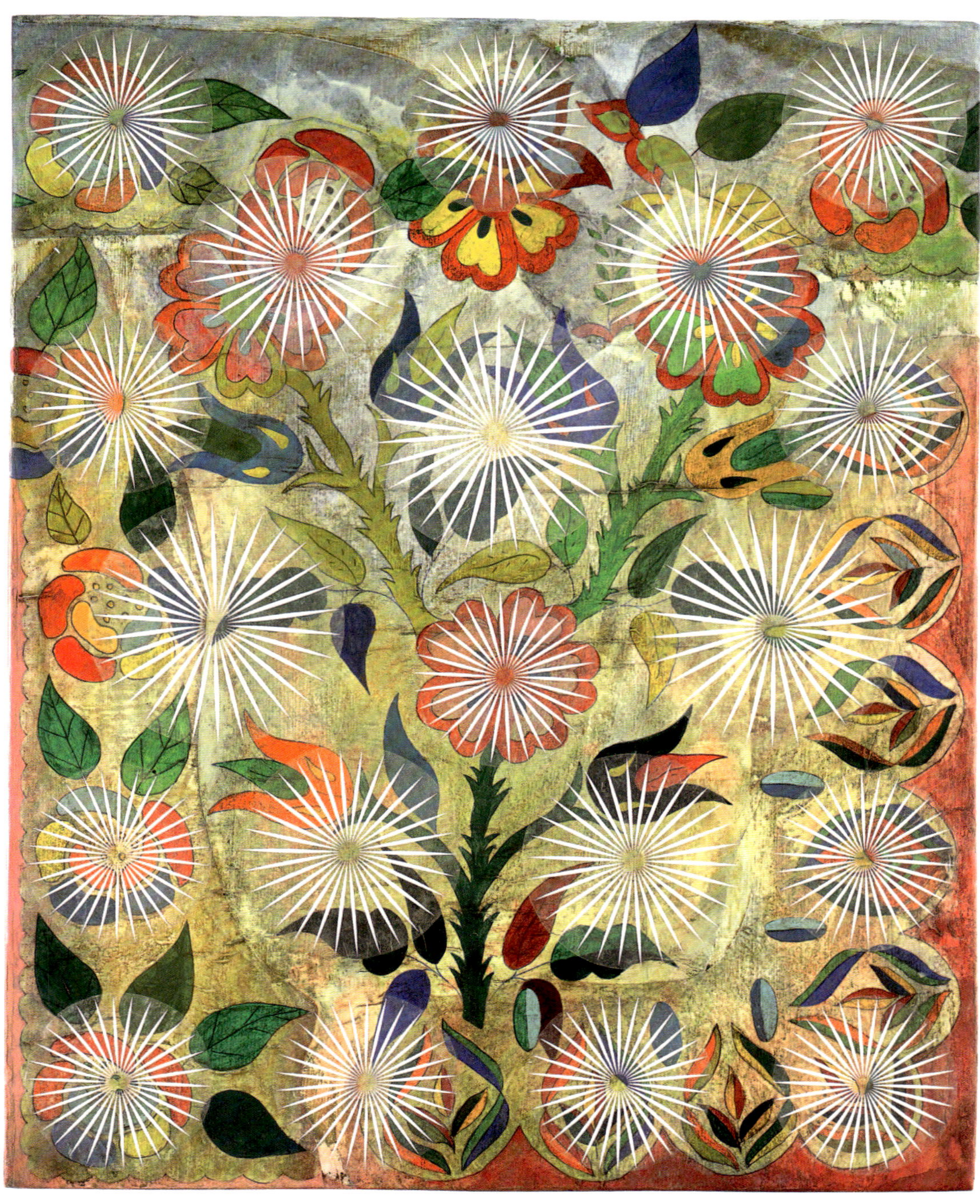

Composition with Ornamental Fragments 1, 2009
Mixed media on canvas, 51 × 41 cm

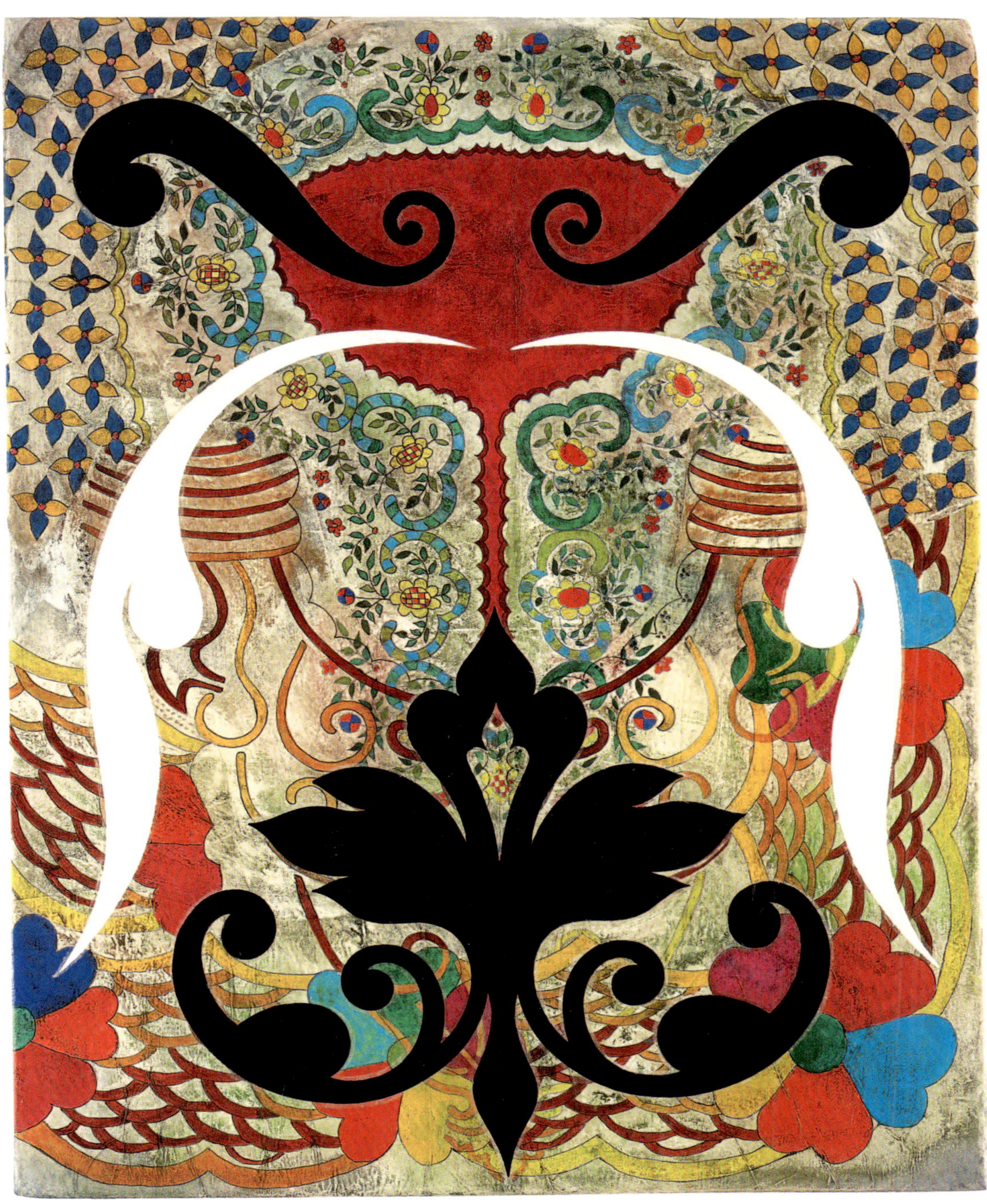

Composition with Ornamental Fragments 2, 2009
Mixed media on canvas, 51 × 41 cm

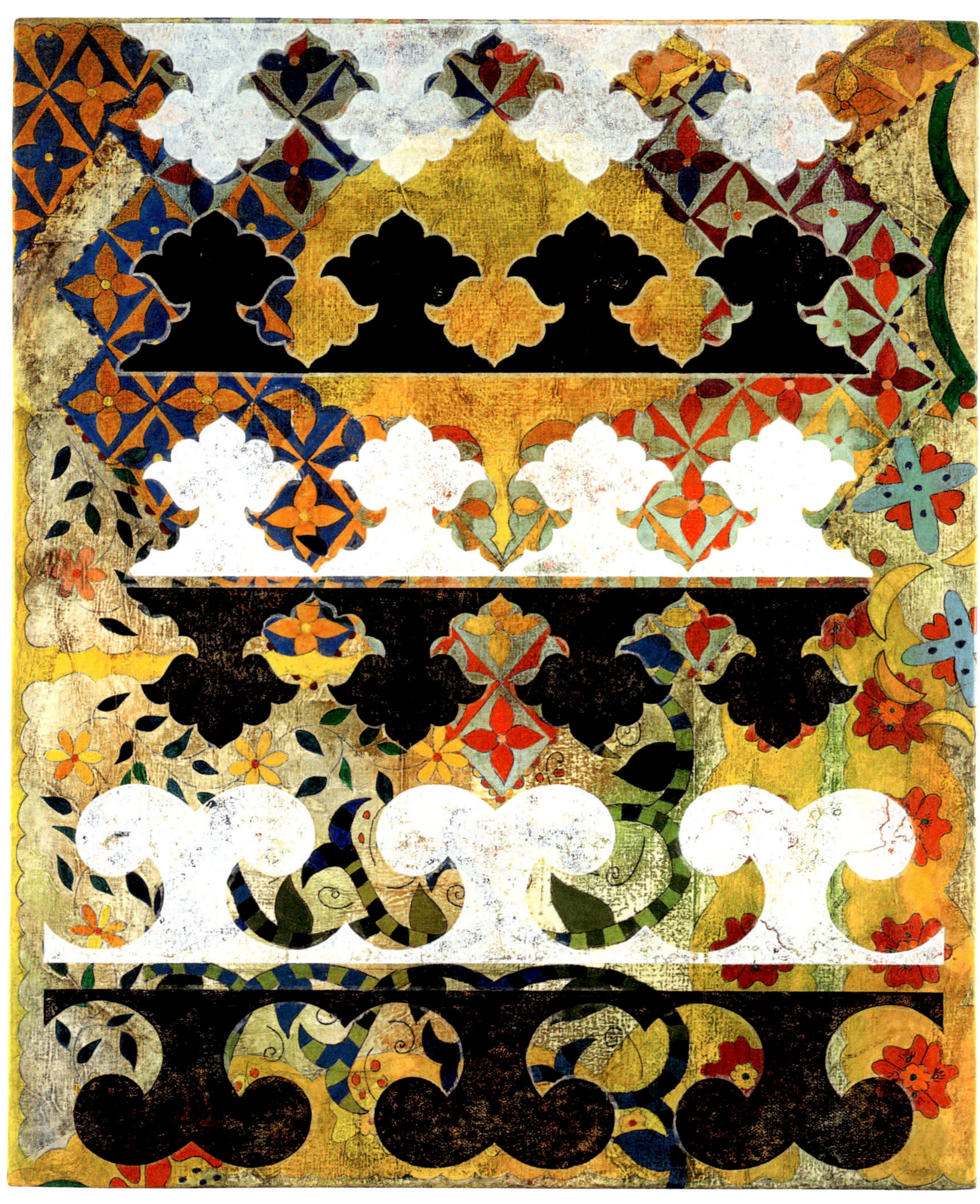

Composition with Ornamental Fragments 3, 2009
Mixed media on canvas, 51 × 41 cm

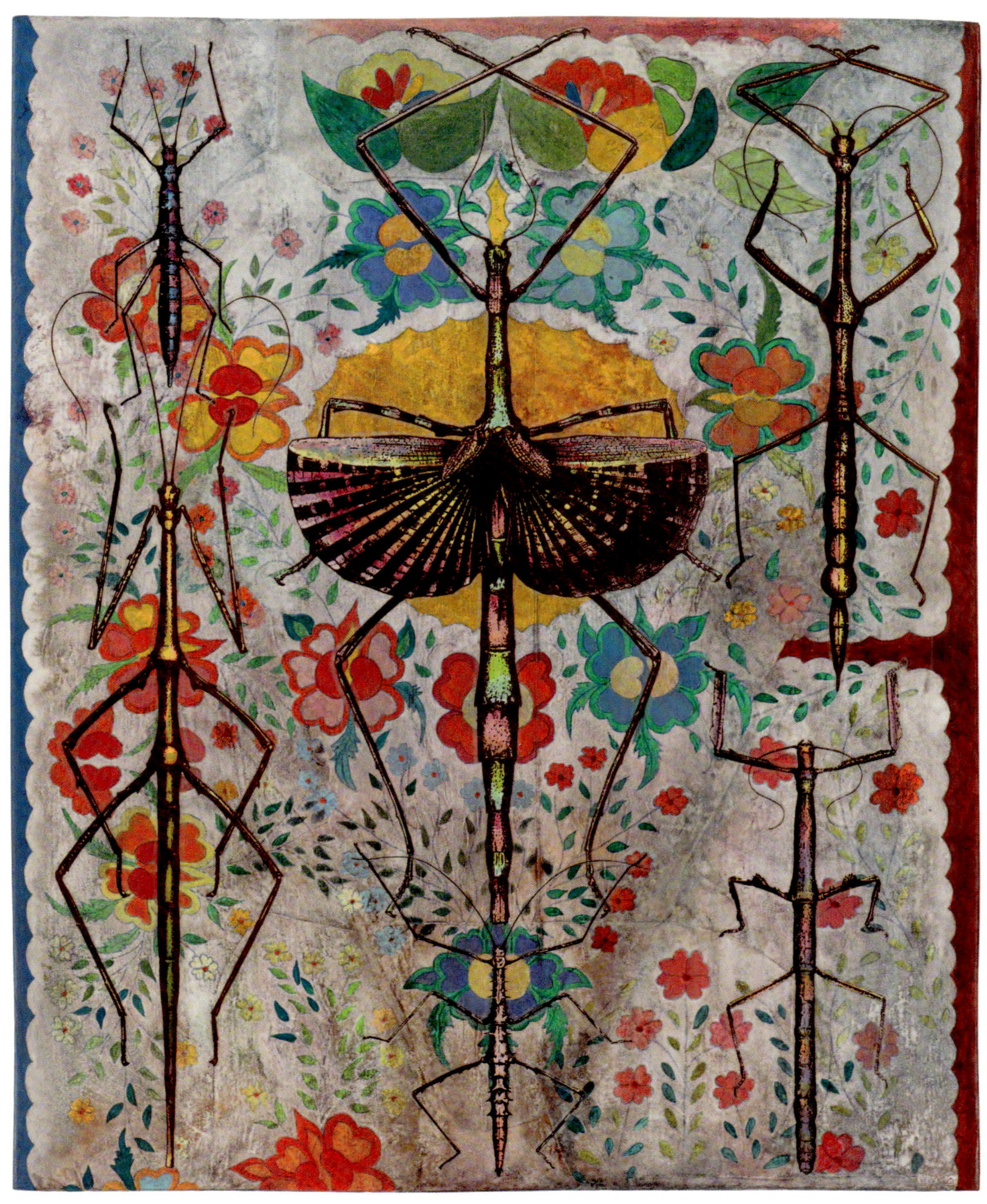

Composition with Ornamental Fragments 6, 2009
Mixed media on canvas, 51 × 41 cm

Composition with Ornamental Fragments II, 2009
Mixed media on canvas, 82 × 61 cm

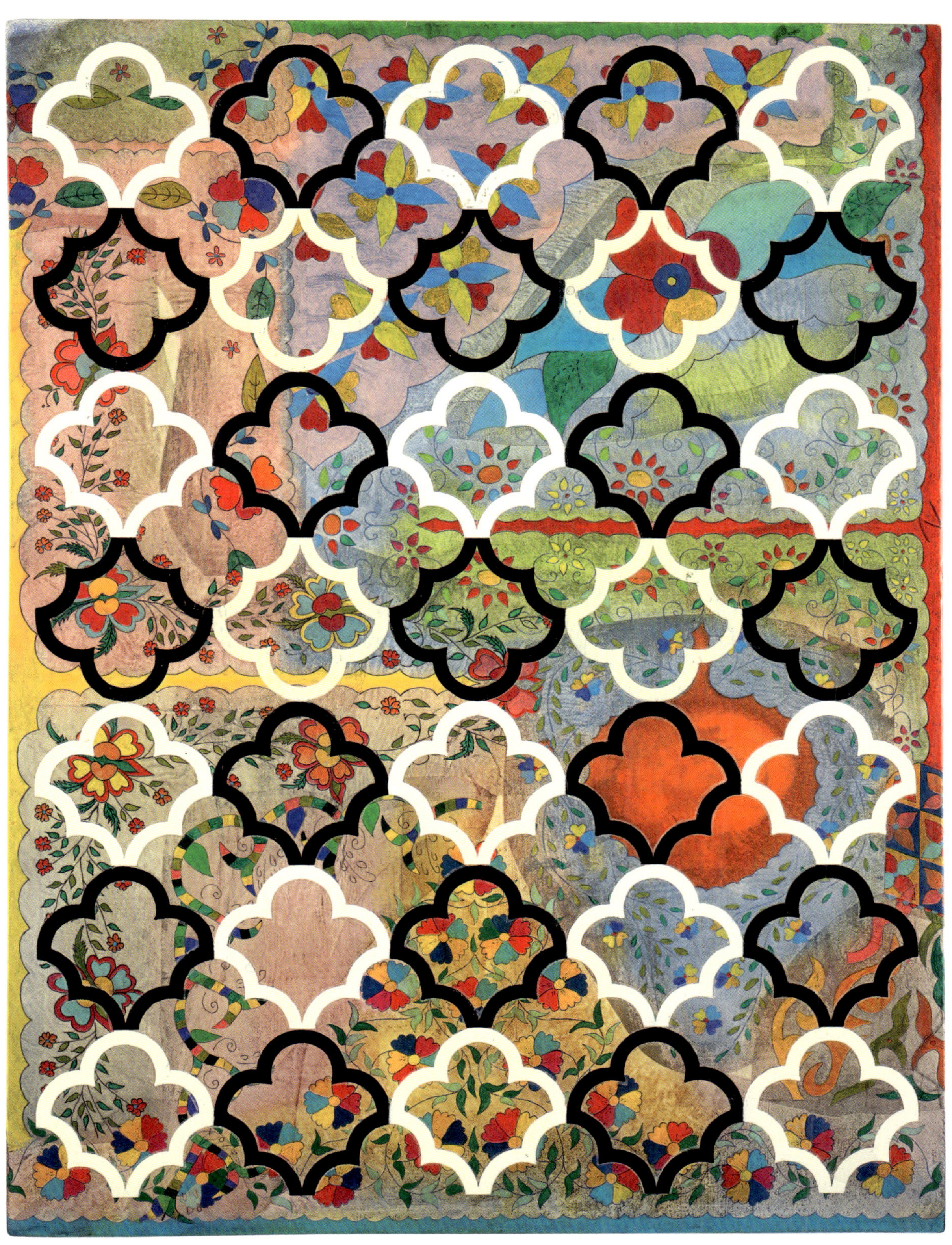

Bal Asterie, 2009
Mixed media on canvas, 152 × 200 cm

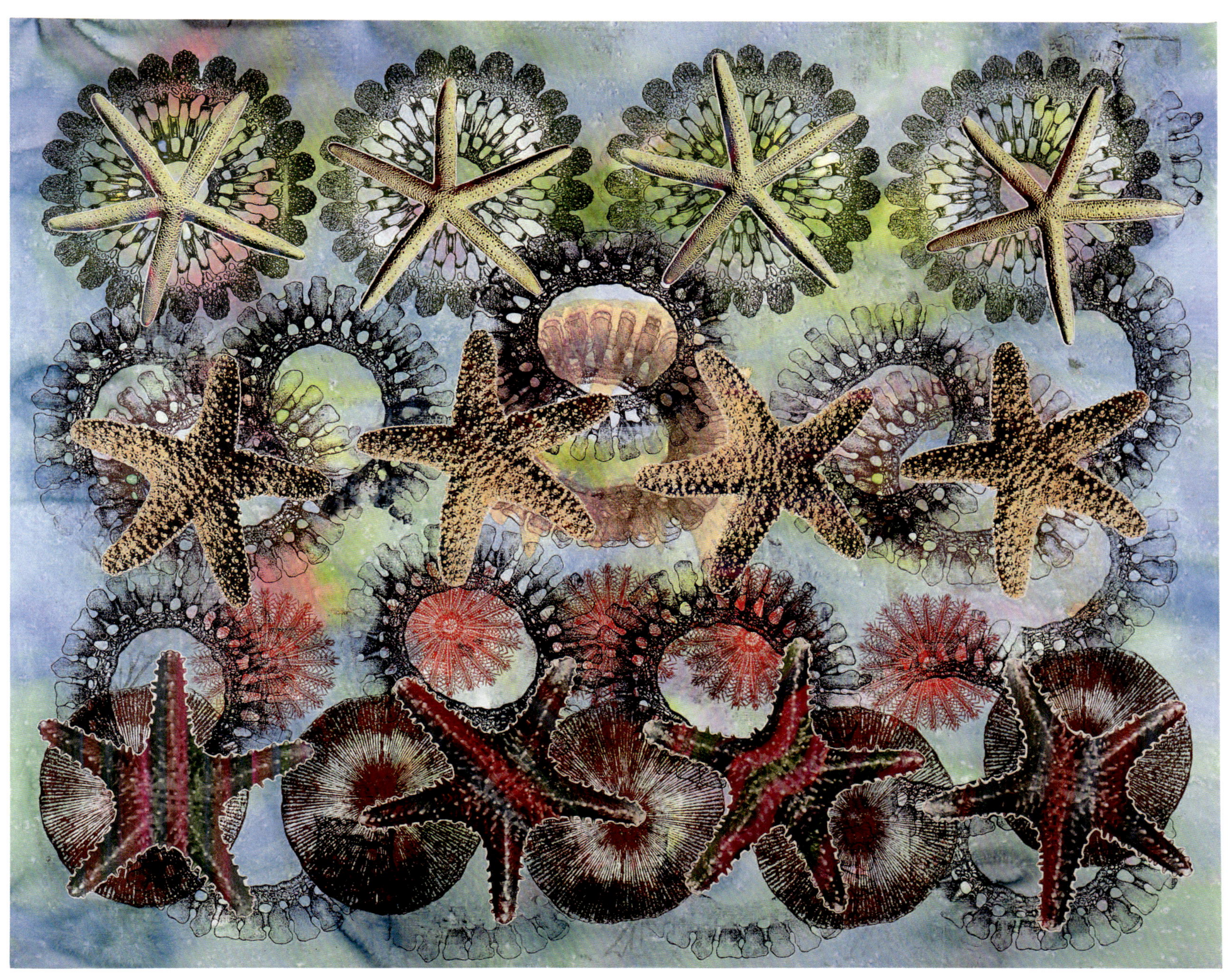

Flag, 2009
Mixed media on canvas, 78 × 103 cm

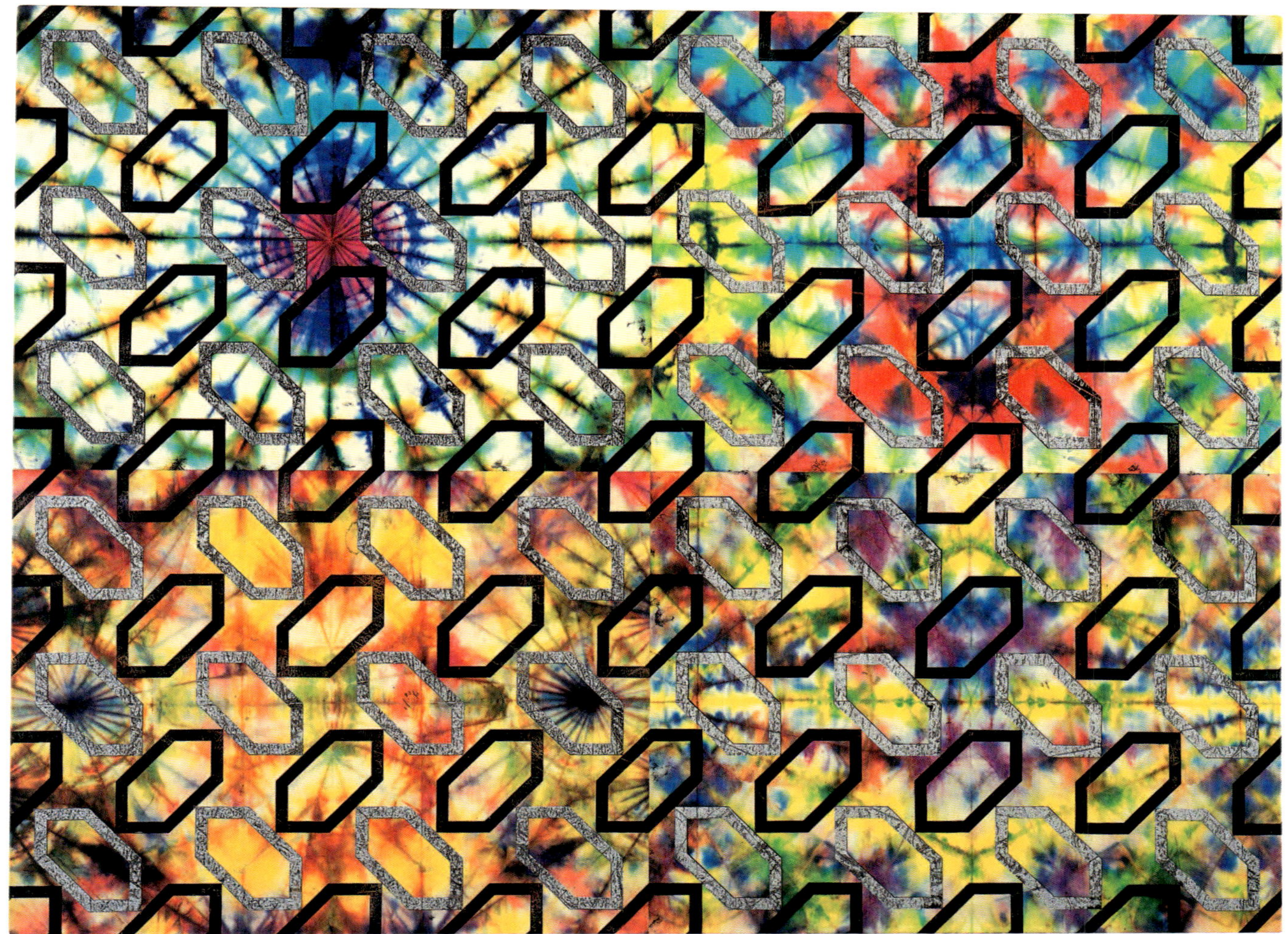

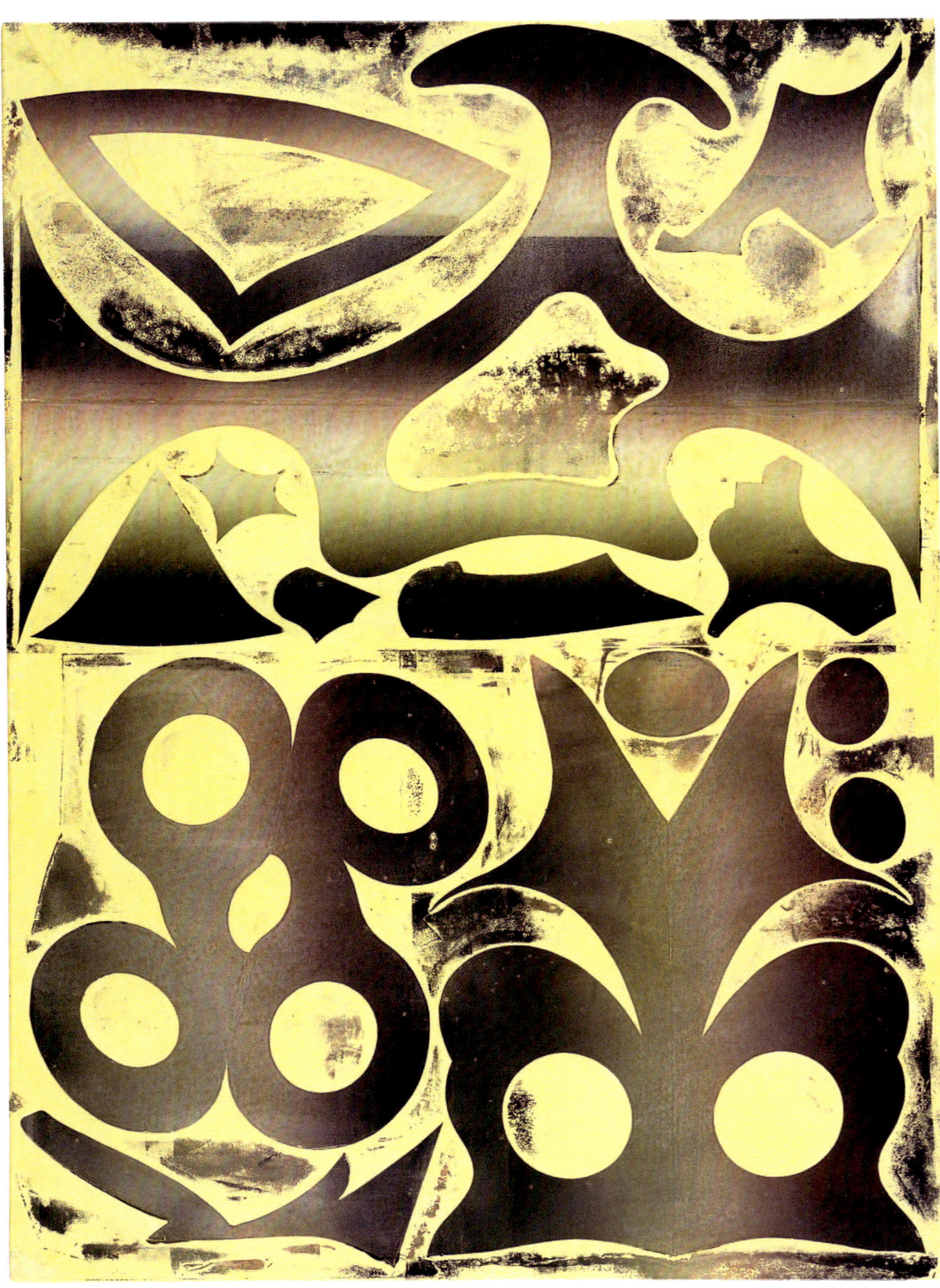

Anthology (Yellow), 2009
Mixed media on canvas, 99 × 71 cm

Anthology (Red), 2009
Mixed media on canvas, 71 × 99 cm

Anthology (Green), 2009
Mixed media on canvas, 71 × 99 cm

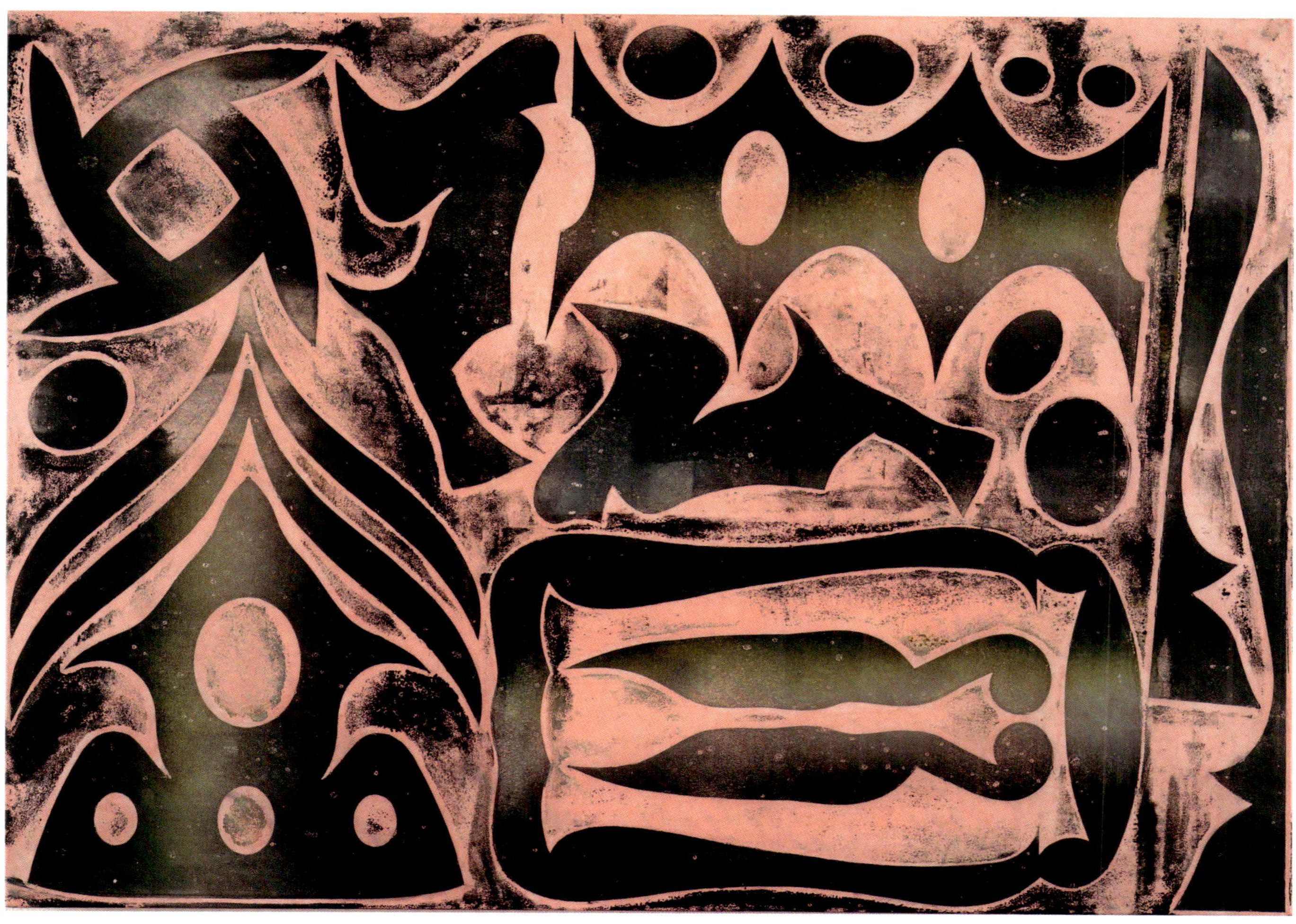

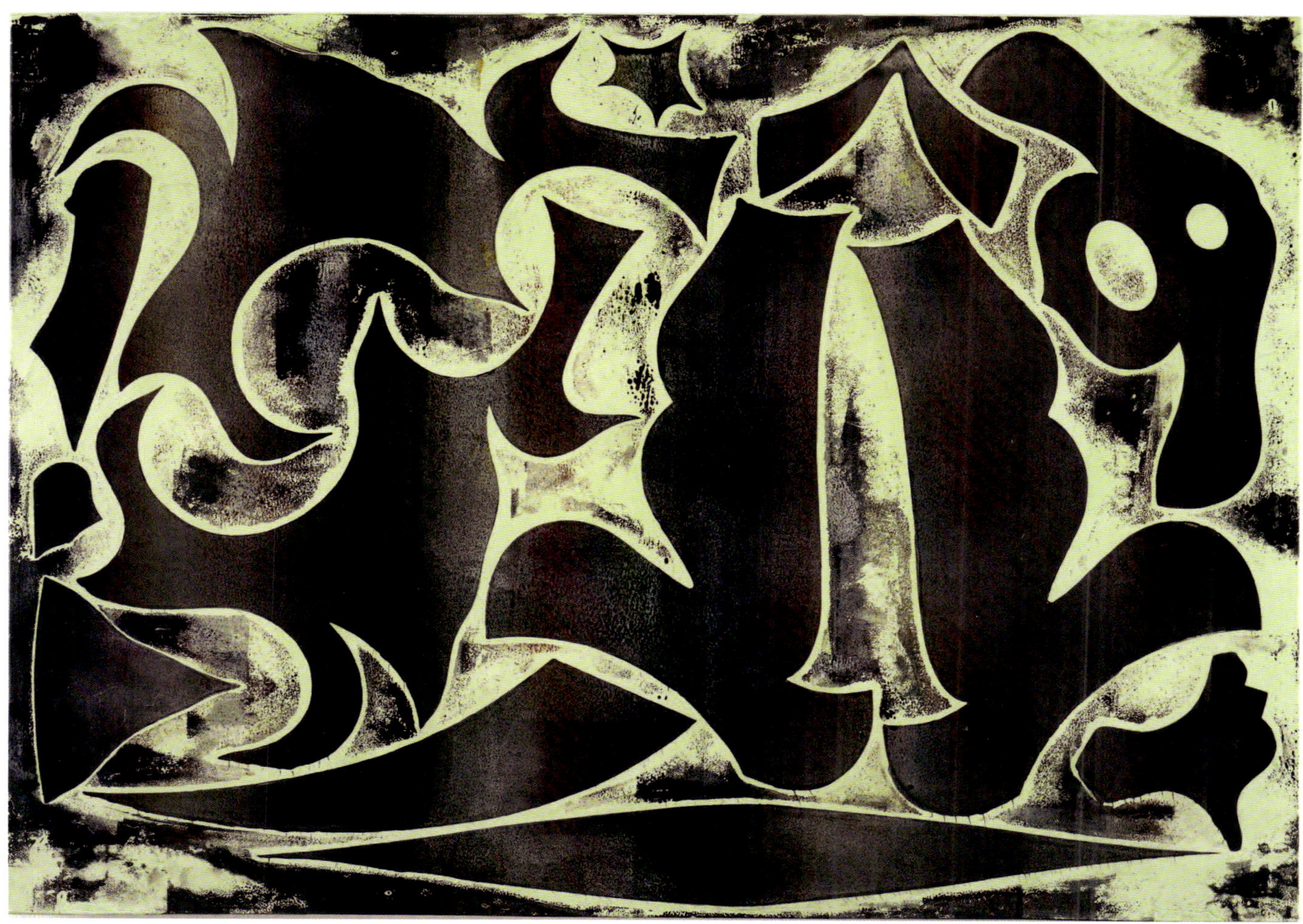

Epiphany, 2009
Mixed media on canvas, 152 × 200 cm

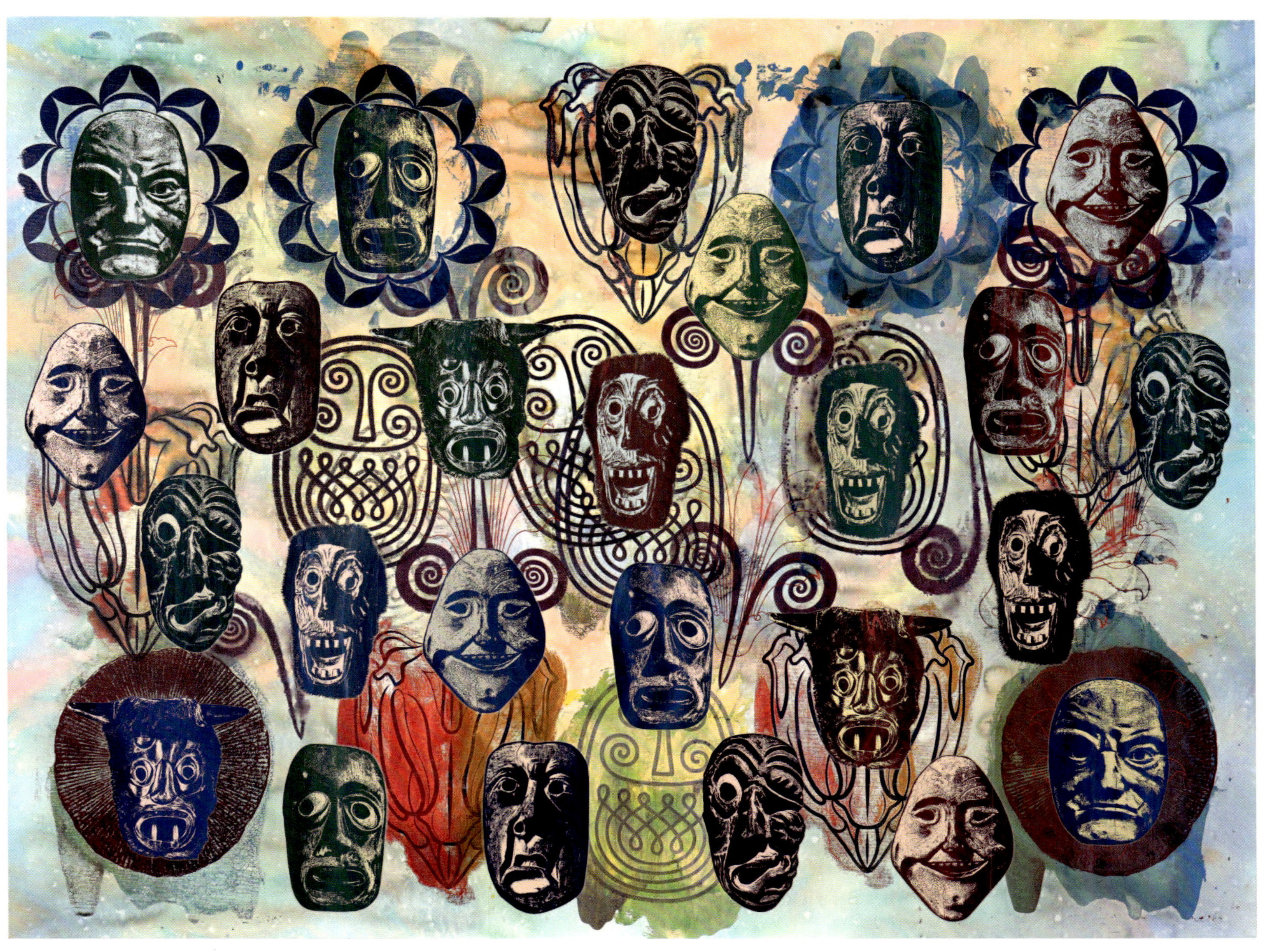

List of Works

Porte Amur
2001
Mixed media on canvas
270 × 228 cm
Courtesy Gagosian Gallery
p. 51

Rose Nocturne
2002
Mixed media on canvas
221 × 97 cm
Courtesy Stellan Holm Gallery
p. 53

Composition with Gemstones II
2001–02
Mixed media on canvas
158 × 217 cm
Collection of Katia and Howard Read
p. 55

Phasmidae
2002
Mixed media on canvas
142 × 177 cm
Private Collection
p. 57

Abstract Painting (Vipera Russelli)
2002
Mixed media on canvas
141 × 100 cm
Collection Diego Cagol, Trento
Courtesy Studio d'Arte Raffaelli
p. 59

Painting with Teeth
2002
Mixed media on canvas
113 × 138 cm
Courtesy Philip Taaffe
p. 61

Sanctuary
2002
Mixed media on canvas
201 × 302 cm
Private Collection
p. 63

Otranto
2002
Mixed media on canvas
36.5 cm
Courtesy Philip Taaffe
p. 64

Specchio
2002
Mixed media on canvas
26 × 31.7 cm
Courtesy Philip Taaffe
p. 65

Helm
2002
Mixed media on canvas
43.8 × 33 cm
Courtesy Philip Taaffe
p. 66

Cairn
2002
Mixed media on canvas
30.4 × 20.9 cm
Courtesy Philip Taaffe
p. 67

Field Station
2003
Mixed media on canvas
105 × 145 cm
Courtesy Philip Taaffe
p. 69

Split
2004
Mixed media on canvas
58 × 77 cm
Private Collection
Courtesy Studio d'Arte Raffaelli
p. 70

Devonian Leaves
2004
Mixed media on canvas
127 × 99 cm
Private Collection, Bologna
Courtesy Studio d'Arte Raffaelli
p. 71

Composition with Shells and Algae
2005
Mixed media on canvas
226 × 300 cm
Private Collection
Courtesy Thomas Ammann Fine Art AG
Zurich
p. 73

Plinth
2006
Mixed media on canvas
294 × 127 cm
Courtesy of Jeff and Ashley McDermott
p. 75

Asuka Passage
2006
Mixed media on canvas
296 × 255 cm
Courtesy Gagosian Gallery
p. 77

Dryadic Figures
2006
Mixed media on canvas
215 × 258 cm
Private Collection
Courtesy Thomas Ammann Fine Art AG
Zurich
p. 79

Cape Siren
2008
Mixed media on canvas
296 × 243 cm
Collection Irish Museum of Modern Art
Heritage Gift by Lochlann and Brenda Quinn
p. 81

Dance of the Phasmidae
2007
Mixed media on canvas
57 × 81 cm
Private Collection, Trento
Courtesy Studio d'Arte Raffaelli
p. 83

Cosmati
2007
Mixed media on canvas
196 × 127 cm
Private Collection, Modena
Courtesy Studio d'Arte Raffaelli
p. 85

Port of Saints
2007
Mixed media on canvas
307 × 245 cm
Essl Museum Klosterneuburg, Vienna
p. 87

Damascene Triangle I
2008
Mixed media on canvas
179 × 179 cm
Act Art Collection, S. Lock, Berlin
Courtesy Jablonka Gallery, Cologne
p. 88

Cairene Window II
2008
Mixed media on canvas
150 × 213 cm
Courtesy Jablonka Galerie, Cologne
p. 89

Artificial Paradise (Loculus)
2008
Mixed media on canvas
350 × 381 cm
Private Collection
p. 91

Large Viking Filigree Painting
2008
Mixed media on canvas
327 × 277 cm
Courtesy Jablonka Galerie, Cologne
p. 93

Painting with Byzantine Fragments
2008
Mixed media on canvas
288 × 288 cm
Private Collection
p. 95

Peregrine Falcon over King Snake
2008
Mixed media on canvas
77 × 77 cm
Jablonka Galerie, Cologne
p. 97

Composition with Ornamental Fragments 1
2009
Mixed media on canvas
51 × 41 cm
Private Collection, Trento
Courtesy Studio d'Arte Raffaelli
p. 98

Composition with Ornamental Fragments 2
2009
Mixed media on canvas
51 × 41 cm
Private Collection, Trento
Courtesy Studio d'Arte Raffaelli
p. 99

Composition with Ornamental Fragments 3
2009
Mixed media on canvas
51 × 41 cm
Private Collection, Trento
Courtesy Studio d'Arte Raffaelli
p. 100

Composition with Ornamental Fragments 6
2009
Mixed media on canvas
51 × 41 cm
Collection Gretchen Carlson, New York
p. 101

Composition with Ornamental Fragments II
2009
Mixed media on canvas
82 × 61 cm
Private Collection, Trento
Courtesy Studio d'Arte Raffaelli
p. 103

Bal Asterie
2009
Mixed media on canvas
152 × 200 cm
Private Collection Milano
Courtesy Studio d'Arte Raffaelli
p. 105

Flag
2009
Mixed media on canvas
78 × 103 cm
Courtesy Studio d'Arte Raffaelli
p. 107

Anthology (Yellow)
2009
Mixed media on canvas
99 × 71 cm
Private Collection, Munich
Courtesy Studio d'Arte Raffaelli
p. 108

Anthology (Red)
2009
Mixed media on canvas
71 × 99 cm
Courtesy Studio d'Arte Raffaelli
p. 109

Anthology (Green)
2009
Mixed media on canvas
71 × 99 cm
Private Collection, Napoli
Courtesy Studio d'Arte Raffaelli
p. 109

Epiphany
2009
Mixed media on canvas
152 × 200 cm
Private Collection
p. 111

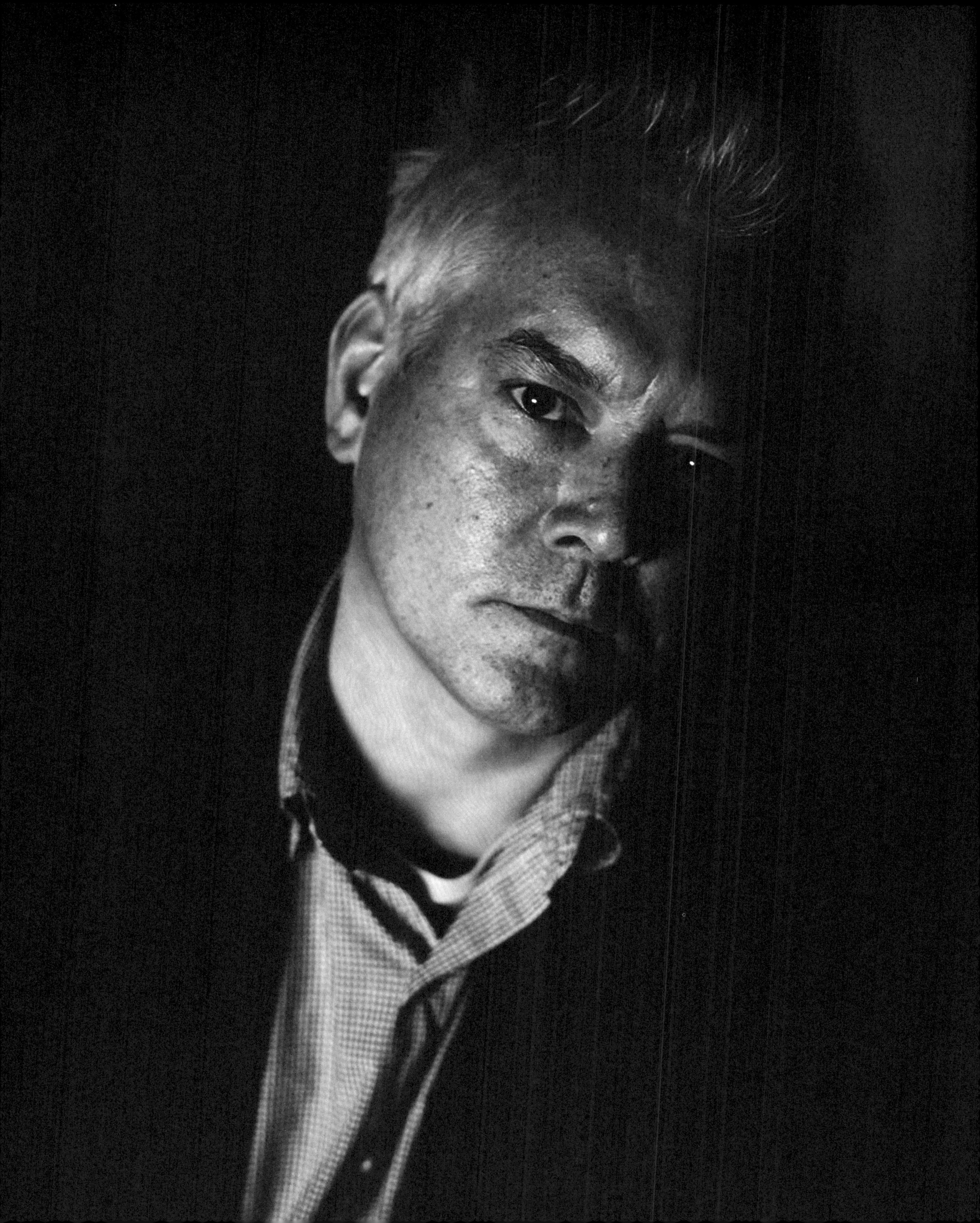

Biography

Born in 1955, Elizabeth, NJ
Lives and works in New York

Education

1974–77
The Cooper Union for the Advancement of Science and Art, New York

Solo Exhibitions

2011
Philip Taaffe, Gagosian Gallery, London
Anima Mundi, Irish Museum of Modern Art, Dublin, Ireland

2010
Disvelamenti/Unveilings, MAGI'900 – Museo delle eccellenze artistiche e storiche, Bologna, Italy
Works On Paper, Gagosian Gallery, New York
Ekstasis, Gagosian Gallery, Athens, Greece

2009
Philip Taaffe: New Works, Jablonka Galerie, Berlin
Recent Work, Studio d'Arte Raffaelli, Trento

2008
Philip Taaffe: Das Leben der Formen. Werke 1980–2008, (*The Life of Forms. Works 1980–2008*) Kunstmuseum Wolfsburg, Germany
Philip Taaffe, Jablonka Galerie, Berlin

2007
Philip Taaffe, Gagosian Gallery, New York (Madison Avenue)
The Portalakis Collection, Athens, Greece

2004
Philip Taaffe: Recent Paintings and Drawings, Jablonka Gallery, Cologne
Galleria d'Arte Moderna e Contemporanea della Repubblica di San Marino

2003
Recent Paintings and Drawings, Thomas Ammann Fine Art, Zurich

2002
Philip Taaffe, Jablonka, Gallery, Cologne, Germany
Studio d'Art Raffaelli, Trento

2001
Thaddaeus Ropac, Paris
Confluence: Selected Works from 1990 to Present, University Art Gallery, University of California, San Diego, CA
Galleria Civica di Arte Contemporanea Trento, Italy

2000
IVAM Centre Carme, Valencia, Spain
New Paintings, Gagosian Gallery, Beverly Hills

1999
Gagosian Gallery, New York (SoHo)
Baldwin Gallery, Aspen, CO

1998
Thomas Ammann Fine Art AG, Zurich
Rebecca Camhi Gallery, Athens

1997
Recent Paintings, Gagosian Gallery, Beverly Hills
Mario Diacono Gallery, Boston, MA
Peter Blum, New York

1996
Galerie Max Hetzler, Berlin
Vienna Secession, Vienna

1994
Gagosian Gallery, New York (SoHo)

1993
Gerald Peters Gallery, Dallas, TX
Center for the Fine Arts, Miami
Galerie Max Hetzler, Berlin

1992
Galerie Max Hetzler, Berlin

1991
Galerie Max Hetzler, Cologne
Gagosian Gallery, New York

1990
Galerie Samia Saouma, Paris

1989
Mary Boone Gallery, New York
Pat Hearn Gallery, New York

1988
Donald Young Gallery, Chicago
Galerie Lucio Amelio, Naples, Italy

1987
Mario Diacono Gallery, Boston, MA
Pat Hearn Gallery, New York

1986
Pat Hearn Gallery, New York

1986
Galerie Ascan Crone, Hamburg
Galerie Paul Maenz, Cologne

1984
Galerie Ascan Crone, Hamburg
Pat Hearn Gallery, New York

1982
Roger Litz Gallery, New York

Group Exhibitions

2011
Alchemy & Inquiry: Philip Taffe, Fred Tomaselli, Terry Winters, Wave Hill Cultural Center, Bronx, New York
Invitation Exhibition of Visual Arts. American Academy of Arts and Letters, New York
Artist's Collect: Prints from the Collections of Kiki Smith, Philip Taaffe, Richard Tuttle and the Estate of Sol LeWitt. International Print Center, New York

2010
Looking Back/The Fifth White Columns Annual, Selected by Bob Nickas. White Columns, New York
Signs of Life: Ancient Knowledge in Contemporary Art, Kunstmuseum Lucern, Swizterland
Philip Taaffe, Christine Streuli, Timo Nasseri, Galerie Sfeir-Semler. Beirut, Lebanon
The 80s Revisited. The Bischofberger Collection
Accrochage, Jablonka Galerie, Cologne
Your History Is Not Our History, New York in the 1980's, New York
Psychedelic: Optical and Visionary Art since the 1960s, San Antonio Museum of Art

2009
Slough (curated by Steve di Benedetto), David Nolan Gallery, New York
Blue, John Graham & Sons, New York

2008
Harry Smith Anthology Remixed, Centre for Contemporary Arts, Glasgow
Fuentes. Non-European Influences on Contemporary Artists, Galerie Thaddaeus Ropac, Salzburg and Paris (exhibition travels)
Die Macht des Ornaments/The Power of Ornament, Belvedere, Vienna
Donald Baechler/Philip Taaffe: Four Masterworks of Contemporary American Painting From a Private European Collection. Galerie Nikolaus Ruzicska, Salzburg
Sensory Overload: Light, Motion, Sound, and the Optical in Art Since 1945, Milwaukee Museum of Art
First Step: Towards a Collection of Western Contemporary Art, National Museum, Krakow
For What You Are about to Receive, Red October Chocolate Factory, Gagosian Gallery, Moscow
Reverb, Jablonka Galerie, Cologne
How To Cook A Wolf: Part One, Dinter Fine Art, New York
Invisible Rays: The Surrealism Legacy, The Rose Art Museum, Waltham, MA
Harry Smith Anthology Remixed, Center for Contemporary Art, Glasgow
Social Diagrams. Planning Reconsidered, Künstlerhaus Stuttgart, Germany

2007
Harry Smith Anthology Remixed, alt Gallery, Newcastle upon Tyne

The Naked Ape, Museo Tridentino di Scienze Naturali, Trento
Optic Nerve: Perceptual Art of the 1960's, Columbus Museum of Art, Ohio
Camouflage. Portland Museum of Art, Oregon
Painting as Fact – Fact as Fiction, de Pury & Luxemnbourg, Zurich
Passion for Art, 35 Jehre Essl Museum, Sammlung Essl Kunsthaus, Klosterneuburg, Austria

2006
The Painted World, P.S.1 Contemporary Art Center, Long Island, New York

2005
Experiencing Duration, Lyon Biennial of Contemporary Art, France
Actualités, Musée d'Art Moderne de la Ville de Paris
A Benefit for the Drug Policy Alliance, Cheim & Read, New York
Printemps de Setembre, Toulouse, France
Nach Rokytnik-Die Sammlung der EVN, Museum Moderner Kunst Stiftung Ludwig-MUMOK, Vienna
Lyon Biennial, Experiencing Duration, Lyon Contemporary Arts Museum, Villeurbanne Institute of Contemporary Art
Works on Paper, Gagosian Gallery, Beverly Hills

2004
A Collection's Vision, Museum der Moderne Mönchsberg, Salzburg, Austria
Contemporary American Art from Misumi Collection, Tottori Prefectural Museum, Japan
Drawings, Gagosian Gallery, New York
The Mountains between Art and Science: From Leonardo to Beuys, MartRovereto, Trento, Italy
Greetings from New York: A Painting Show, Galerie Thaddeus Ropac, Salzburg, Austria
The Spirit of White, Galerie Beyeler, Basel, Switzerland
The Invisible Thread: Buddhist Spirit in Contemporary Art (organized by Roger Lipsey), Newhouse Center for Contemporary Art at Snug Harbor Cultural Center, Staten Island
East Village USA (curated by Dan Cameron), New Museum of Contemporary Art, New York (through 2005)
Angelo Filomeno, Simon Periton, Philip Taaffe, and Francesco Vezzoli, Gorney Bravin & Lee Gallery, New York

2003
Art After DNA, The Hecksher Museum of Art, Huntington, New York

2002
Living Room, Jablonka Galerie, Cologne, Germany
The Heavenly Tree Grows Downward: Selected Works by Harry Smith, Philip Taaffe and Fred Tomaselli, James Cohan Gallery, New York
Art Downtown (sponsored by Wall Street Rising), five buildings in the financial district, New York

2001
Ornament and Abstraction, Fondation Beyeler, Basel, Switzerland
Give & Take, Victoria and Albert Museum, London

1999
Drawings 2000. Barbara Gladstone Gallery, New York
Post-hypnotic, University Galleries of Illinois State University, Normal, IL. Traveled to the McKinney Avenue Contemporary, Dallas, TX; the Contemporary Arts
Center, Cincinnati, OH; the Atlanta College of Art Gallery, GA; the Chicago
Cultural Center; the Tweed Museum, University of Minnesota, Duluth, MN
Itinere.2, Palazzo Delle Papesse, Siena, Italy
Real Stories II, Marianne Boesky Gallery, Friedrich Petzel Gallery, New York

1998
New York Launch of Evergreen Review Silent Auction and Exhibition, New York
WallPaper, Nicholas Davies Gallery, New York
Now and Forever: Part I, Pat Hearn Gallery, Matthew Marks Gallery, New York
Ensemble Moderne: à Propos de la Nature Morte, Galerie Thaddaeus Ropac, Paris

1997
Theories of the Decorative: Abstraction and Ornament in Contemporary Painting, Edinburgh International Festival 1997, Scotland. Traveled to Edwin A. Ulrich Museum of Art, Wichita, KS
Celebration for the Opening of the Getty Center, Eli Broad Family Foundation, Santa Monica, CA
Animal Tales, The Whitney Museum of American Art at Champion, New York

1996
Screen, Friedrich Petzel Gallery, New York
On Paper, Marlborough Gallery, New York
Nuevas Absracciones, Museo Nacional Centro de Arte Reina Sofia, Madrid. Traveled to: Kunsthalle Bielfeld, Germany; Museu d'art Contemporani de Barcelona
Biennial of Sydney: International Exhibition of Contemporary Art, Australia
Wiener Secession, Friedrichstrasse, Vienna

1995
A New York Time: Selected Drawings of the Eighties, The Bruce Museum, Greenwich, CT
ARS 95 Helsinki, Museum of Contemporary Art/Finnish National Gallery Helsinki, Finland
Pat Hearn Gallery, A Selected Survey, Pat Hearn Gallery, New York
1995 Biennial Exhibition, The Whitney Museum of American Art, New York
25 Americans: Painting in the 90's, Milwaukee Art Museum, Milwaukee, WI

1994
The Magic Magic Book, The Whitney Museum of American Art, New York

1993
Doubletake: Collective Memory & Current Art, Kunsthalle Wien, Vienna
The Brushstroke: Painting in the 90's, Ruth Bloom Gallery, Santa Monica, CA
Skowhegan '93, The Colby College Museum of Art, Waterville, ME
An American Homage to Matisse, Sidney Janis Gallery, New York

New York on Paper, Galerie Beyeler, Basel. Traveled to Galerie Thaddaeus Ropac, Paris
New York Painters, Sammlung Goetz, Munich

1992
Theoretically Yours (curated by Collins & Millazo) Chiesa di S. Lorenzo, Aosta, Italy
Lineart Internationale Kunstbeurs. Nov 5-9
Dark Décor (curated by Janine Cirincione and Tina Potter), Independent Curators Incorporated, New York
There Is A Light That Never Goes Out, Amy Lipton Gallery, New York
Doubletake: Collective Memory & Current Art, Haywood Gallery, London
Works on Paper, Schmidt Contemporary Art, St. Louis, MO
Quotations, The Aldrich Museum of Contemporary Art, Ridgefield, CT. Traveled to the Dayton Museum of Contemporary Art, OH
Group Show (in cooperation with Thomas Borgmann Galerie Max Hetzler, Berlin
Ellen Berkenblit, Albert Oehlen, Alexis Rockman, Philip Taaffe, Christopher Wool, Luhring Augustine Gallery, New York

1991
Who Framed Modern Art or the Quantitative Life of Roger Rabbit, Sidney Janis Gallery, New York
1991 Biennial Exhibition, Whitney Museum of American Art, New York
Glen Baxter, Philip Taaffe, James Welling, Galerie Samia Saouma, Paris
Strange Abstraction, Touko Museum of Contemporary Art, Tokyo
Vertigo 'The Remake, Galerie Thaddaeus Ropac, Salzburg, Austria
Carnegie International 1991, The Carnegie Museum of Art, Pittsburgh, PA
Conceptual Abstraction, Sidney Janis Gallery, New York
Parades, and exhibition of artist's work for the stage, ORCOFI, 48 Avenue Montaigne (Barcelo, Bleckner, Garouste, Serra, Taaffe), Paris
Stubborn Painting: Now and Then, Max Protetch Gallery, New York

1990
The International Art Fair, Lucio Amelio, Ascan Crone, and Studio Trisorio booths, Basel, Switzerland
Pharmakon '90, Nippon Convention Center, Tokyo
The Last Decade: American Artists of the 80's, Tony Shafrazi Gallery, New York
All Quiet on the Western Front? (75 Americans in Paris), Espace Dieu 17, Paris
Ross Bleckner, Philip Taaffe, Richmond Burton, Perry Rubenstein Gallery, New York

1989
Abstraction in Question, John and Mable Ringling of Art, Sarasota, FL
The International Art Fair, Lucio Amelio, Ascan Crone, and Studio Trisorio booths, Basel, Switzerland

1988
Who's Afraid of Red, Yellow, and Blue, Museum Fredericianum, Kassel, Germany
Art at the End of the Social, The Rooseum, Malmö, Sweden

American Art in the 80's: The Binational, The Institute of Contemporary Art, Museum of Fine Arts, Boston, MA. Traveled to Stadtische Kunsthalle, Dusseldorf, Germany
Drawings, Luhring, Augine & Hodes, New York
Hybrid Neutral: Modes of Abstraction and the Social, University Art Gallery, The University of North Texas, Denton, TX. Traveled to Galerie Monika Spruth, Cologne, Germany

1987
Whitney Biennial, The Whitney Museum of American Art, New York
Post Abstract Abstraction, Aldrich Museum of Contemporary Art, Ridgefield, CT
Galerie Paul Maenz, Cologne, Germany
Similia/Dissimilia, Kunsthalle, Dusseldorf, Germany
Mary Boone Gallery, New York
Generations of Geometry, The Whitney Museum at Equitable Center, New York
Recent Tendencies in Black and White, Sidney Janis Gallery, New York
New York Art Now, Saatchi Collection, London
Primary Structures, Rhona Hoffman Gallery, Chicago

1986
The Pet Brams Collection. Emerson Gallery, Hamilton College, Clinton, NY
Recent Abstract Painting, John Good Gallery, New York
Terrae Motus, Fondazione Emelio, Ercolano, Italy
Biennale of Sydney, Sydney, Australia
Zurich Art Fair, Zurich
The Science of Painting, Metro Pictures, New York
Donald Young Gallery, Chicago
The Basel Art Fair, Basel, Switzerland
Crescent Gallery, Dallas, TX
Pat Hearn Gallery, New York
The Red Show, Massimo Audiello Gallery, New York
Tableau Abstraits, Centre National d'Art Contemporain, Nice, France
Paravision II, Margo Leavin Gallery, Los Angeles
New City Editions, Venice, CA
What It Is, Tony Shafrazi Gallery, New York
When Attitudes Become Form, Bess Cutler Gallery, New York
Endgame, Institute of Contemporary Art, Boston, MA
Cologne Art Fair, Cologne, Germany
Art & Its Double, Fondacio Caixa de Pensiones, Madrid
Prospekt '86, Frankfurter Kunstverein, Frankfurt, Germany
Geometry Now, Craig Cornelius Gallery, New York
New York: New Strategies, Ursula Kritzinger Gallery, Vienna

1985
Gallery 345, New York
Pat Hearn Gallery, New York
The Chi-Chi Show, Massimo-Audiello Gallery, New York
Paravision, Postmasters Gallery, New York
Galerie Rudolf Zwirner, Cologne, Germany
Pat Hearn Gallery, New York
Visions, Eastman-Wahmendorf Gallery, New York
Post Style, Wolf Gallery, New York
Vernacular Abstraction, Wacoal Art Centre, Tokyo
A Brave New World: A New Generation, Charlottenborg Exhibition Hall, Copenhagen
Geomatrie-Abstraktion Ornament, Galerie Nacht St. Stephan, Vienna
Cult Decorum, Tibor de Nagy Gallery, New York
Primer salon irrealista, Galeria Leyendecker, Santa Cruz de Tenerife, Spain

1984
Basel Art Fair, Basel, Switzerland
Sex, Cable Gallery, New York

1983
Turn it Over, Studio Sandro Chia, New York

MUSEUM COLLECTIONS
Birmingham Museum of Art, Birmingham, AL
The Broad Art Foundation, Santa Monica, CA
Museum of Fine Arts, Boston, MA
The Museum of Modern Art, New York
The Philadelphia Museum of Art, Philadelphia, PA
Museum Moderner Kunst Stiftung Ludwig, Vienna
The Rose Art Museum, Brandeis University, Waltham, MA
The Whitney Museum of American Art, New York
Albright-Knox Art Gallery, Buffalo, NY
Colby College Museum of Art, Waterville, Maine
Des Moines Art Center
Solomon R. Guggenheim Museum of Art, New York
Museum der Moderne Salzburg
Sammlung Essl, Austria
Collection Scharpff, Hamburger Kunsthalle
Museo Nacional Reina Sofia, Madrid
San Francisco Museum of Modern Art
Kunstmuseum Wolfsburg
Irish Museum of Modern Art, Dublin

Bibliography

Books and Catalogues

2010
Nickas, Bob. *Painting Abstraction: New Elements in Painting*. Phaidon
Grabar, Oleg. *Ornement/Ornemental Perspective*
Coen, Vittoria and Giulio Bargellini. *Philip Taaffe*. Magi 900. Bologna
Giulio Bargellini. *Philip Taaffe*. Magi 900. Bologna

2008
Grabar, Oleg. *The Tensions of Visual Creativity, in Philip Taaffe*. Jablonka Galerie, Abu Dhabi International Fine Arts and Antiques Fair
Adams, Brooks; Broeker, Holger; Brüderlin, Markus; Heymer, Kay. *Philip Taaffe:Das Leben der Formen. Werke* 1980–2008, (The Life of Forms. Works 1980–2008) Kunstmuseum Wolfsburg, Germany/Hatje Cantz

2007
White, Edmund, David Moos & Marina Warner *Philip Taaffe*. New York: Gagosian Gallery
Rimanelli, David. *Philip Taaffe: Works from the Portalakis Collection*. Athens: The Portalakis Collection

2004
Wilson, Peter Lamborn. *Philip Taaffe: Carte annuvolate*. San Marino: Galleria d'Arte Moderna e Contemporanea/kira, Milan

2003
Katz, Vincent. *Philip Taaffe: Recent Paintings & Drawings*. Zurich: Thomas Ammann Fine Art

2002
Philip Taaffe: Illuminations. Poem by Wallace Stevens. Trento: Studio d'Arte Raffaelli
Lipsey, Roger. *Philip Taaffe: Ten Paintings*. Galerie Jablonka, Cologne

2001
Fong, Pamela; Troupe, Quincy. *Philip Taaffe: Confluence*. San Diego: University of California, San Diego
Bulteau, Michel. *Philip Taaffe: Ouevres Récentes*. Paris: Galerie Thaddaeus Ropac
Coen, Vittoria; Pellizzi, Francesco. *Philip Taaffe*. Trento: Galleria Civica

2000
Creeley, Robert; Juncosa, Enrique; Rosenblum, Robert. *Philip Taaffe*. Valencia: IVAM Institut Valencià d'Art Modern
Wehrenberg, Charles. *Philip Taaffe*, New York: Gagosian Gallery

1999
Ricard, Rene. *Philip Taaffe*. New York: Gagosian Gallery
Philip Taaffe: *Recent Paintings*. [Notes by the artist.] Aspen: Baldwin Gallery

1998
Liebmann, Lisa. *Philip Taaffe*. Zurich: Thomas Ammann Fine Art
Diacono, Mario. *Philip Taaffe*. Boston: Mario Diancono Gallery
Brakhage, Stan; Taaffe, Philip. Composite Nature. New York: Peter Blum Edition
Philip Taaffe. Poem by James Merrill. Athens: Rebecca M. Camhi Gallery

1996
Cooke, Lynne. 10th Biennale of Sydney. Sydney: Biennale of Sydney
Adams, Brooks. *Philip Taaffe*. Vienna: Wiener Secession

1994
Crone, Rainer. *The Decorative As a Figure of Abstraction*. Munich: Cantz, Sammlung Goetz, pp. 56-57
Grabar, Oleg. *Philip Taaffe: Recent Paintings*. New York: Gagosian
Jay, Ricky. *The Magic Magic Book*. New York: Library Fellows of The Whitney Museum of American Art
Juncosa, Enrique and Arthur Danto. *Nuevas Abstracciones*. Madrid: Museo Nacional Centro de Arte Reina Sofia

1993
(…). *Philip Taaffe*. Japan: The 3-D Museum of Visual Art, Bijutsu Shuppan-Sha, pp. 70-71
Grachos, Louis. *Philip Taaffe*. Miami: Center for the Fine Arts
Mrabet, Mohammed. *Chocolate Cream & Dollars*. New York: Inanout Press

1992
Kaufmann, Ruth. *Stubborn Painting: Now and Then*. New York: Max Protetch Gallery
Dickoff, Wilfried. *Philip Taaffe*. Köln: Galerie Max Hetzler

1991
Who Framed Modern Art or the Quantitative Life of Roger Rabbit. New York: Sidney Janis Gallery
Sukejiro Itani and Jeffrey Deitch. *Strange Abstraction*. Tokyo: Touku Museum of Contemporary Art, pp. 14-18, 76-79
Murkens, Romie. *Art Now Posterbook, Vol. 1*. Berlin: Benedikt Taschen Verlag Berlin GmbH
Wheeler, Daniel. *Art Since Mid Century: 1945 to the Present*. New York: Vendome Press
Hoffman, Katherine. *Exploration: The Visual Arts Since 1945*. New York: Harper Collins, p. 307
Taaffe, Philip. *Presentation on the Embankment*. New York: Gagosian Gallery
Kultermann, Udo. *Amerikanische* Malerei heute. Pantheon, pp. 167-175
Rosenblum, Robert. *Warhol As Art History*. New York: Rizzoli, pp. 22-27
(…). *Towards a Definition of New Art*. New York: Rizzoli, pp. 43-69

Kaufman, Ruth & Mike Mertz. *Stubborn Painting: Now & Then*. New York: Max Protech Gallery

1990
Moszynska, Anna. *Abstract Art*. London: Thames & Hudson
Diacono, Mario. *The Iconographic Abstraction*. New York: Perry Rubenstein Gallery
(…). *Closed Fires: A Non-Introduction to The Last Decade or A Reprise of Joan Didion's The White Album*. New York: Tony Shafrazi Gallery

1989
Vidal, Gore. *Philip Taaffe*. New York: Mary Boone/Pat Hearn Gallery
Collins, Tricia & Richard Milazzo (Translation by Giovanna Minelli). *Hyperframes: A Post-Appropriation Discourse. ("The Yale Lectures"). Vol. 1*. Paris: Editions Antoine Candau

1988
Fairbrother, Trevor, David Joselit & Elisabeth Sussman. *American Art of the Late 80's: The Binational*. Bonn: VG-Bildkunst, pp. 198, 243
Bonuomo, Michele. *Interview with Philip Taaffe*. Naples: Lucio Amelio Gallery

1987
Burroughs, William.; Taaffe, Philip. Drawing Dialogue. New York: Pat Hearn Gallery
Diacono, Mario. *Philip Taaffe*. Boston: Mario Diacono Gallery
Cameron, Dan. NY Art Now: The Saatchi Collection. London: Collier Searle Matfield, Ltd., pp. 13-56
Armstrong, Richard, Richard Marshall & Lisa Phillips. *Biennial 1987, Whitney Museum of American Art*. New York: W.W. Norton & Company, pp. 11-15
Frank, Peter & Michael McKenzie. "New, Used & Improved: Art for the 80's." New York: Abbeville Press, p. 92
Pincus-Witten, Robert. Postminimalism into Maximalism: American Art 1966–1986. Ann Arbor: UMI research Press

1986
Saltz, Jerry. *Beyond Boundaries: New York's New Art*. New York: Alfred Van der Marck Editions, pp 69-71
Bleckner, Ross. *Philip Taaffe*. New York: Pat Hearn Gallery
Cortez, Diego. *Philip Taaffe*. Hamburg: Galerie Ascan Crone
Cameron, Dan. *Art & Its Double*. Barcelona/Madrid: Fondacio Caixa de Pensiones
Weiermair, Peter. *Prospekt '86*. Frankfurt: Frankfurt Kunstverein

1985
Smith, Roberta. *Vernacular Abstraction*. Tokyo: Wacoal Art Centre
Solomon, Thomas. *A Brave New World: A New Generation*. Copenhagen: Charlottenborg Exhibition Hall

Articles and Reviews

2010
Brody, David, "Philip Taaffe at Gagosian". *ArtCritical.com*, Feb
Naves, Mario, "Philip Taaffe Works On Paper". *Cityarts.info*, Jan
Landi, Ann, "The Ecstatic Esthetic". *ARTnews*, Mar

2009
Cortez, Diego, "Philip Taaffe". *Interview*, Jun-Jul
Green, Tyler. "Brought to Light, Microscopy and Taaffe". *Modern Art Notes*, Feb 27
Rigney, Robert. "Philip Taaffe at Jablonka, Berlin". *ARTnews*, Jun

2008
Coggins, David. "Heirloom Varities". *Art In America*, Oct, pp. 158 – 167
Nickas, Bob. "Review: Philip Taaffe at Kunstmuseum Wolfburg". *Artforum*, May
Koroxendis, Alexandra. "An Artist Looks Into the Past". *Ekathimerini.com*, Jan 23
Karcher, Eva, "Mr Universe". *Vogue Germany*, Mar

2007
Coggins, David. "Review: Philip Taaffe at the Gagosian Gallery (Madison Avenue)". *Modern Painters*, May, p. 95
Adam, Alfred Mac. "Review: Philip Taaffe at the Gagosian Gallery (Madison Avenue)". *ARTnews*, May, p. 156
Princenthal, Nancy. "Review: Philip Taaffe at the Gagosian Gallery (Madison Avenue)". *Art In America*, May, pp. 195-196
Smith, Roberta. "Between the Precise Layers, A cultural Narrative". *The New York Times*, Mar 16, p. B27, B31
Cohen, David. "Ornamental Agility". *The New York Sun*, Mar 1, pp. 11, 16
Bowles, Hamish. "memory artist". *Vogue*, Feb, pp. 238-243, 273

2006
Adams, Brooks. "Time After Time". *Art in America*, Feb, pp. 56-63

2005
Thea, Carolee. "The East Village Voice". *Modern Painters*, Feb, pp. 96-99

2004
Yau, John. "Animilistic Light". Art on Paper, Jul / Aug, cover, pp. 32-35

2002
Liebmann, Lisa. "Best of 2002: A Special Issue" . *Artforum*, Dec
Cotter, Holland. Review: 'The Heavenly Tree Grows Downward' Selected Works by Harry Smith, Philip Taaffe and Fred Tomaselli". *The New York Times*, Sep 20
Glueck, Grace. Review: "For Wall Street's Sake: Art to Lure Visitors Downtown". *The New York Tmes*, Jun 14
Attias, Laurie. Review: Philip Taaffe at Thaddaeus Ropac, Paris. *ARTnews*, Feb, pp. 134-135

2000
Moos, David. "Philip Taaffe: The Bees Know He Will Be Great". *artext*, No. 71, Nov / Jan 2001
Gooch, Brad. First Break: Philip Taaffe. *Artforum*, May
Bonetti, David. "So, where are we now?" *Art New England*, Dec 1999 / Jan
Knight, Christopher. Review: "An Upward Spiral: Philip Taaffe at Gagosian". *Los Angeles Times*, Dec 1

1999
Yood, James. "Post-hypnotic: University Galleries of Illinois State University Normal, Illinois". *Artforum*, Apr
Paparoni, Demetrio. "Matissiana". *tema celeste*, May-Jun
Kimmelman, Michael. Review: Philip Taaffe at Gagosian Gallery (SoHo). *The New York Times*, May 28
Naves, Mario. "Hindered by Impeccable Taste". *The New York Observer*, Jun 14
Saltz, Jerry. "Pattern & Dissipation". *Village Voice*, Jun 22

1998
Kuspit, Donald. Review: Philip Taaffe at Peter Blum, *Artforum*, Apr
Hogrefe, Jeffrey. "Taaffe's Tortured Transition". *The New York Observer*, May 18
Koplos, Janet. Review: Philip Taaffe at Peter Blum. *Art in America*, Jun
Hilty, Greg. "Snakes and Daggers". *Frieze*, Jun-Jul-Aug

1997
Hofleitner, Johanna. "Philip Taaffe: Wiener Secession," *Flash Art*, Mar / Apr

1994
Adams, Brooks. "The Tabernacle of Philip Taaffe". The Print Collector's Newsletter Jan / Feb, pp. 206-210
Liebmann, Lisa. "Taaffe's Temple". *Elle Decor*, Dec/Jan, pp. 24-30
Lewis, Jim. "The Beauty Addict". *Bazaar*, Jan, pp. 100-104; 128; 132
Smith, Roberta. "Philip Taaffe, Beyond mere Painting". *New York Times*, Apr 29, p. 38
Choon, Angela. "Taking Roads Less Traveled". *Art and Antiques*, May
Katz, Vincent. "Traveling Man". *Paper Guide*, May, p. 34
Clarkson, David. "Spotlight, Philip Taaffe". *Flash Art*, summer, p. 114
White, Edmund. "Philip Taaffe, Al Quasbah, 1991". *Artforum*, summer, pp. 66-67

1992
Smith, Roberta. "Abstraction: A Trend That May Be Coming Back". *The New York Times*, Jan 10, p. C28

1992
Bevan, Roger. "Aldo Rossi Designs Young Art at Hayward". *The Journal of Art Newspaper*, Feb 15, p. 9
Calvo-Platero, Mario. "A Gagosian piace il Bel Paese". *Il Sole 24 Ore*, Feb 23, p. 27
Whitford, Frank. "Schlock of the New, Frank Whitford on Trivial Pursuits at the Hayward". *The London Sunday Times*, Feb 23, p. 14
Welish, Marjorie. "Abstraction, Advocacy of..." *Tema Celeste*, Mar, p. 75-80
Kuspit, Donald. "Fin de Siècle Abstraction: The Ambiguous Re-Turn Inwards". *Tema Celeste*, Mar, pp. 53-55
Johnson, Ken. "Philip Taaffe at Gagosian". *Art in America*, Mar, pp. 115-116
Carrier, David. "Afterlight: Exhibiting Abstract Painting in the Era of Its Belatedness". *Arts Magazine*, Mar, pp. 60-61
Bell, Tiffany. "Les peintures de Kelly aujourd'hui". *Artstudio*, spring, pp. 158-171; 172-175
Casadio, Mariuccia. "Philip Taaffe: Hypnotic Painter". *Interview*, May, pp. 96-101; 129

1991
Kaneda, Shirley. "Philip Taaffe". *Bomb*, spring, pp. 36-41
Smith, Roberta. "A Selection of Work from the 80's at the Whitney". *The New York Times*, Mar 8
Karcher, Eva. "So dealt Go-Go". *Forbes*, (German Edition), Apr 4, pp. 146-148
Kimmelman, Michael. "At the Whitney, A Biennial That's Eager to Please". *The New York Times*, Apr 19, pp. C1, C24
Kaneda, Shirley. "Paintings and its Others, In the Realm of the Feminine". *Arts Magazine*, summer, pp. 58-64
Perkowitz, Sidney. "True Colors". *The Sciences*, May / Jun, pp.26-27
McEvilley, Thomas. "Two Big Shows: Post Modernism and its Discontents". *Artforum*, summer, pp.89-103
Lingemann, Susanne. "Flaute bringt Bewegung ins Kunstmarkt-Karussell". *Art #6*, Jun, pp.22; 103-107
Amelio, Lucio, and Franco Mollina. "The McDonald's of Art". *Tema Celeste*, May / Jun, p. 35
Smith, Roberta. "Works From the 80's With a Certain Optimism". *The New York Times*, Sep 21
Moore, Alan. "Processing Myth: Collins & Milazzo at the Core of the Nouveau Vogue". *Cover Magazine*, Oct
Kuspit, Donald. "The Last Decade". *Artforum*, Dec
Cottingham, Laura. "The Last Decade". *Contemporanea*, Dec 23
Liotta, Christine. "Who Framed Modern Art or the Quantitative Life of Roger Rabbit". *Tema Celeste*, May / Jun 31
Decker, Andrew. "Art A GoGo". *New York Magazine*, Sep 2, pp. 39-44
Kimmelman, Michael. "At Carnegie 1991, Sincerity Edges Out Irony". *The New York Times*, Oct 27, pp. 31, 34
Zinsser, John. "Geometry and its Discontents". *Tema Celeste*, autumn, pp. 72-76
Rosenblum, Robert. "After Abstract Painting". *Tema Celeste*, autumn, p. 80
Cullum, Jerry. "Interview with Collins & Milazzo". *Art Papers*, Sep / Oct, pp. 28-31
Levin. "Conceptual Abstraction". *The Village Voice*, Nov 26
Kazanjian, Dodie. "Cultural Mix Master". *Vogue*, Dec, pp. 239-244; 310
Larson, Kay. "Art". *New York Magazine* 24, No. 47, Dec 2
Kimmelman, Michael. "Art in Review: Philip Taaffe and Gagosian Gallery". *The New York Times*, Dec 20
Smith, Roberta. "Art & Photography". *The New York Times*, Dec 29, p H31

Tuchman, Phyllis. "Philip Taaffe's Art of Inclusion". *New York Newsday*, Jan 2, p. 69
Weinstein, Matthew, "Philip Taaffe at Gagosian Gallery". *Artforum*, Feb, pp. 109-110
Saltz, Jerry. "Re-animator, Philip Taaffe's Necromancer, 1991". *Arts Magazine*, Mar, p. 17

1990
Hayat, Yves J. "The Art Collector, Volume 1". *Galleries Magazine*, 1990, p.121
Dickhoff, Wilfried. "We Are Not Afraid". *Parkett*, No. 26, pp. 64-68; 70-75; 103-107
Perrone, Jeff. "History is in the Making". *Parkett*, No. 26, pp. 80-87
White, Edmund. "A Propos: Philip Taaffe". *Parkett*, No. 26, pp. 91-93; 95-97
Pellizzi, Francesco. "Fragment on Ornament". *Parkett*, No. 26, pp. 98-101
Denson, G. Roger. "Philip of Naples and the Evocative Geometry of History". *Parkett*, No. 26, pp.108-114
Collins, Tricia and Richard Milazzo. "Rene Ricard: Sinking to the Bottom of Discourse". (part 1), *Tema Celeste*, Jul/Aug

1989
Leigh, Christian. "Art on the Edge of a Nervous Breakdown". *Contemporanea*, Jan
Cyphers, Peggy. Review: Philip Taaffe at Pat Hearn/Mary Boone. *Arts*, Sep, p.100
Bankowsky, Jack. "Philip Taaffe at Mary Boone Gallery; Pat Hearn Gallery". *Artforum*, Oct, pp.169-170
McCoy, Pat. "Philip Taaffe: Pat Hearn, Mary Boone". *Flash Art*, Oct, p. 130
Zimmer, William. "Philip Taaffe: Pat Hearn, Mary Boone". *ArtNews*, Oct, pp. 195-196
Morris, Sarah. "Collins & Milazzo". *Flash Art* 149, Nov/Dec, pp. 168-169; 176
Koslow, Francine A. "Collins & Milazzo: Curators or Commodities Brokers". *Contemporanea II*, No. 9, Dec
Vidali, Roberto. "Collins & Milazzo". *Juliet Art Magazine* 45, Dec

1988
Russell, John. "Philip Taaffe". *New York Times*, Jan 3
McCracken, David. "Different Views of a Post-modernist World". *Chicago Tribune*, Apr 15
McEvilley, Thomas. "Marginilia: On Son of Sublime". *Artforum*, May
Woodruff, Mark. "Collins & Milazzo: Doing It Their Way". *Taxi*, Sep
Smith, Roberta. "80's Art with a Passport to West Germany". The New York Times, Oct 2
McEvilley, Thomas. "Marginalia: Fils du Sublime". *Art Press* 130, Nov
Collins, Tricia and Richard Milazzo. "Art at the End of the Social". Translated by Stefan Sandelin.Malmo, Sweden: The Rooseum, Jul-Oct

1987
Nairne, Sandy. "State of the Art: Ideas & Images in the 1980's". London: Chatto & Windus, pp. 223
Heartney, Eleanor. "The Hot New Cool Art: Simulationism". *ArtNews*, Jan, pp. 130-137
Liebmann, Lisa. "M.B.A. Abstractionism". *Flash Art*, Jan/Feb
Kuspit, Donald. "'What It Is' at Tony Shafrazi". *Artscribe*, Jan/Feb, p. 70
Morgan, Stuart. "Frankfurt: 'Prospect 86' at the Kunstverein and Schirn Kunsthalle". *Artscribe*, Jan/Feb
Becker, Robert. "Philip Taaffe". *Interview*, Mar
Smith, Roberta. "Philip Taaffe". *The New York Times*, Mar 27
Indiana, Gary. "Negative Sublime Revisited". *Village Voice*, Apr 7
Brenson, Michael. "Whitney Biennial's New Look". *The New York Times*, Apr 10
Indiana, Gary. "Another Review of the Whitney". *Village Voice*, Apr 28
Levin, Kim. "Minimalisn't". *Village Voice*, Apr 28
Cameron, Dan. "Art and Its Double". *Flash Art*, May, pp. 57-71
Perl, Jed. "Artburn". *Vogue*, May, pp. 308-310; 368
Zimmer, William. "'Post Abstract Abstraction' in Ridgefield". *The New York Times*, Jul 5, p. 18
Glueck, Grace. "What Do You Call Art's Newest Trend: 'Neo-Geo'...Maybe". *The New York Times*, Jul 6
Perrone, Jeff. "Fashion is the Real Thing in Abstraction". *Arts Magazine*, Jul
Smith, Roberta. "Art: 'Generations of Geometry,' an Abstract Show". *The New York Times*, Jul 17
Bonetti, David. "Talking Abstract". *Art in America*, Jul
McGill, Douglas C. "Art People: Neo-Geo's Newest". *The New York Times*, Jul 24
Panicelli, Ida. "Customs: Ida Panicelli on the Whitney". *Artforum*, summer, pp. 11-12
Pincus-Witten, Robert. "Electrostatic Cling". *Artscribe*, Jul
Heartney, Eleanor. "Philip Taaffe at Pat Hearn". *ArtNews*, Sep, p. 206
Collings, Matthew. Interview (part 1): "Collins & Milazzo: Posthumous Meanings," *Artscribe International*, Sep/Oct, pp. 42-49
Collins, Tricia & Richard Milazzo. "Radical Consumption and New Poverty: A Discourse on Irony and Superfluity". *New Observations*, No. 51, Oct
Ottomon, Klaus. "Neo-Geo". Bijutsu Techo, Dec
Collins, Tricia, and Richard Milazzo. "Tropical Codes". *Kunstforum*, Dec 1987-Jan 1988
Wei, Lily. "Talking Abstract". *Art in America*, Dec, pp. 112-123
Collings, Matthew. "Collins & Milazzo: Posthumous Meanings". Interview, pt.II, *Artscribe International*, Sep/Oct

1986
Levin, Kim. "The Unresponsive Eye". *The Village Voice*, Jan 28
Taaffe, Philip. "Sublimity, Now and Forever, Amen". *Arts Magazine*, Mar
Decter, Joshua. "Cult and Decorum". *Arts Magazine*, Mar
Siegel, Jeanne. "Geometry Desurfacing: Ross Bleckner, Alan Belcher, Ellen Carey, Peter Halley, Sherrie Levine, Philip Taaffe, James Welling". *Arts Magazine*, Mar
Silverthorne, Jeanne. "Philip Taaffe at Pat Hearn". Artforum, Apr, p. 108
Perl, Jed. "Art". *The New Criterion* 4, Apr, pp. 57-62
Ottman, Klaus. "Supermannerism". *Flash Art*, Apr, pp. 59-61
Kuspit, Donald. "Young Necrophiliacs, Old Narcissists: Art About the Death of Art". *Artscribe International*, Apr
Pincus-Witten, Robert. "Entries: The Scene That Turned on a Dime". *Arts Magazine*, Apr, pp. 20-21
Foster, Hal. "Signs Taken for Wonders". *Art in America*, Jun, pp. 80-91, 139
Smith, Roberta. "Philip Taaffe at Pat Hearn". *Art in America*, Jun, pp. 125-126
Taylor, Paul. "The Return of (Conceptual) Art". *Parkett*, No. 9, Jun
Cameron, Dan. "Paravision". *Fugura* (Seville, Spain), No. 6
McGill, Douglas C. "The Lower East Side's New Artists". *The New York Times*, Jun 10
"Flash Art Panel: From Criticism to Complicity". *Flash Art*, Jul
Muchnic, Suzanne. "Commodity-Culture Art Rides Again". *Los Angeles Times*, Jul 26
Jones, Alan. "Paravision: An Interview with Tricia Collins and Richard Milazzo". Galleries 14, Aug-Sep, pp. 41-47; 93-94 (106-109 English)
Knight, Christopher. "L.A. Invasion of 'it'". *Los Angeles Herald Examiner*, Aug 10
Relyea, Lane. "Cool Art, Hot Commodities". *L.A. Weekly*, 8, No. 38, Aug 15-21
Westfall, Stephen. "The Synthetic Sublime". *L.A. Weekly*, 8, No. 38, Aug 15-21
Tomkins, Calvin. "The Art World: Between Neo-and Post -". *The New Yorker*, Nov 24
Siebert, Charles. "How a Painting Happens". *Esquire*, Dec, pp. 169-173
Nemeczek, Alfred. "Neo-Geo Weder Trend Nocj Stil". *Art*, Dec
Schjeldahl, Peter. "A Visit to the Salon of Autumn 1986". *Art in America*, Dec, pp. 15-21
Audiello, Massimo. "Philip Taaffe". *Vanity*, Dec

1985
Robinson, Walter. "Philip Taaffe". *Art in America*, Jan 1985
Brenson, Michael. Review: Chi Chi Show. *The New York Times*, Apr 9
Indiana, Gary. "Just an Opinion". *The Village Voice*, Jun 25
Koehler, Jutta. "Ploetzlich ein Begriff". *Koelner Stadtanzeiger*, Jul 2
Indiana, Gary. "The Collins & Milazzo Effect". *The Village Voice*, Jul 2
W.K., "Endphase de Kunst". *Koelner Stadtanzeiger*, Jul 2
Cameron, Dan. "The Other Philip Taaffe". *Arts Magazine*, Oct, p. 18
Kohn, Michael. "Philip Taaffe". *Flash Art*, Nov, pp. 72-73
McCormick, Carlo. "Popometry". *Artforum*, Nov
Evans-Clark, Philip. "Neo-Surrealism, or The Archetype of the Artist as an Ostrich". *Arts Magazine*, Dec
Politi, Giancarlo, and Helena Kontova. "Two Italians in New York". *Flash Art*. Dec

1984
Smith, Roberta. "Art & Its Double". *The Village Voice*, Oct 23, p. 45
Carr, C. "Shock of the Old". *The Village Voice*, Oct 30

1982
Walker, James. "A Sense of Place". *Artscribe*, No. 38, Dec

Authors' Biographies

David Brody

David Brody is an artist and writer living in Brooklyn, N.Y. Born in New York City in 1958, he attended Harvard University, Skowhegan, and CalArts, and currently teaches graduate studies at the Maryland Institute College of Art. His art criticism is published on artcritical.com and he has written for Cabinet Magazine and the Brooklyn Rail. His paintings and wall drawings have been shown at Pierogi Gallery, The Drawing Center, and The Brooklyn Museum, and his digital animations have been shown at MoMA, Museo Nacional Centro de Arte Reina Sofia, Madrid, and the Centre Georges Pompidou.

Enrique Juncosa

Born in Palma de Mallorca, Spain in 1961, Enrique Juncosa is the Director of the Irish Museum of Modern Art in Dublin since 2003. Previously he was Deputy Director of Museo Nacional Centro de Arte Reina Sofia, Madrid, and before that he was Deputy Director of the Valencian Institute of Modern Art (IVAM), Valencia. He was also the curator of the Spanish Pavillion in the Venice Biennale in 2009.

He has curated more than 30 exhibitions since the early 1990s. Most recent ones include Francis Alÿs (2003), Olafur Eliasson (2003), Juan Uslé (2004), Dorothy Cross (2005), Howard Hodgkin (2006), Miroslaw Balka (2007) Miquel Barceló (2008), James Coleman (2009) and Philippe Parreno (2009).

He has also published six books of poetry and two collections of essays, and is the editor of the IMMA journal *Boulevard Magenta*.

Colm Tóibín

Colm Tóibín is the author of six novels, including 'The Master' and 'Brooklyn', and two collections of stories. His work has been translated into thirty languages. He has received honorary doctorates from the University of Ulster and from University College Dublin. He is a regular contributor to the Dublin Review and the New York Review of Books and is a contributing editor at the London Review of Books. He has taught at Stanford University, the University of Texas at Austin and is currently Leonard Milberg Lecturer in Irish Letters at Princeton University. He is a member of the Arts Council.

Photographic Credits

P. 13 Duchamp, Marcel (1887–1968): *Three Standard Stoppages* (3 Stoppages Digitale (1)(A) Etalon). Paris, 1913–14. New York, Museum of Modern Art (MoMA). Wood box 11 ⅛ × 50 ⅞ × 9 in (28.2 × 129.2 × 22.7 cm), with three threads 39 ⅜ in (100 cm), glued to three painted canvas strips 51/4 × 47 ¼ in (13.3 × 120 cm), each mounted on a glass panel 7 ¼ × 49 ⅜ × ¼ in (18.4 × 125.4 × 0.6 cm), three wood slats 2 ½ × 43 × ⅛ in (6.2 × 109.2 × 0.2 cm), shaped along one edge to match the curves of the threads. Katherine S. Dreier Bequest. Acc. n.: 149.1953.a-i.
© 2010. Digital image, The Museum of Modern Art, New York / Scala, Florence

P. 20 Johns, Jasper (b.1930): *Painting Bitten by a Man*, 1961. New York, Digitale (1)(A) Museum of Modern Art (MoMA). Encaustic on canvas mounted on type plate, 9 ½ × 6 ⅞ in (24.1 × 17.5 cm). Gift of Jasper Johns in memory of Kirk Varnedoe, Chief Curator of the Department of Painting and Sculpture, 1989-2001. Acc. n.: 211.2007. © 2011. Digital image, The Museum of Modern Art, New York/Scala, Florence

P. 15 Klee, Paul (1879–1940): *Structural I*, 1924. New York, Metropolitan Museum of Art. Gouache on cardboard, bordered with ink, 11 ¼ × 5 ½ in (28.6 × 14 cm). The Berggruen Klee Collection, 1984 (1984.315.38).
© 2010. Image copyright The Metropolitan Museum of Art/Art Resource/Scala, Florence

P. 19 Joan Miró Spanish, 1893–1983, *Ciphers and Constellations in Love with a Woman*, 1941. Gouache and watercolor with traces of graphite on ivory wove paper, 456 × 380 mm, Gift of Mrs. Gilbert W. Chapman, 1953.338, The Art Institute of Chicago. Photography © The Art Institute of Chicago

Other photo credits:

P. 55 *Composition with Gemstones II*, 2001–02, mixed media on canvas, 158 × 217 cm. Photo Courtesy Cheim & Read, New York

P. 115 Aubrey Mayer: Philip Taaffe, 2009
© Aubrey Mayer

Philanthropy at IMMA

Honorary Patrons

Lochlann & Brenda Quinn
George McClelland
Maurice & Maire Foley
Gerard O'Toole
Eoin & Patricia Mc Gonigal
Brian & Elsa Ranalow

Patrons

Ivor Fitzpatrick
Moya Doherty & John McColgan
Dr. Maureen O'Driscoll-Levy
Bank of Ireland
Joe Christle
Kerlin Gallery
Daniel Caffrey
de Blacam & Meagher
Mark Adams Fine Art
William & Laura Burlington
Lorcan O'Neill
Mairead & Finbar Cahill
Brian McMahon

Benefactors

Frank X. Buckley
Horwath Bastow Charleton
Thomas E. Honan
Smurfit Kappa Group
Bernard Dunleavy
Louis O'Sullivan
Bryan Guinness Charitable Trust
Jane Williams
Margaret Glynn
Cormac O'Malley
Image Now
Red Dog
Ruaidhri O'Boyle
Michael Corrigan & Mary Kilcullen
Ian Whyte
Maurice Collins & Nora Rice
Ruaidhri O'Boyle
Jacqueline & Campbell Bruce

Acknowledgments

Georges Armaos and all at Gagosian Gallery
Rafael Jablonka
Birgit Müller and Jablonka Galerie
Doris Ammann and Thomas Ammann Fine Art, A.G.
Giordano Raffaelli and Studio d'Arte Raffaelli, Trento
Elena Bortolotti and Galerie Ropac, Paris
Colm Tóibín
David Brody
Jonathan Brennan

Philip Taaffe would like to gratefully acknowledge the editorial assistance of Raymond Foye, Donald Kennison, Nathan Smith, Kim Spurlock, Charles Stein, and Peter Lamborn Wilson

Philip Taaffe photographic credits: Rob McKeever, Tom Powel, Steven Sloman, Jean Vong

The Irish Museum of Modern Art wishes to express a special thank you to those who have generously lent their works to the exhibition

Published on the occasion of
Philip Taaffe – Anima Mundi

Irish Museum of Modern Art
23 March – 12 June 2011

Exhibition curated by Enrique Juncosa
Director, Irish Museum of Modern Art

IMMA Exhibition Team
Enrique Juncosa, Director
Seán Kissane, Senior Curator: Head of Exhibitions
Eimear O'Raw, Curatorial Coordinator: Exhibitions
Gale Scanlan, Operations Manager
Cillian Hayes, Technical Crew Supervisor
Edmund Kiely, Technical Supervisor

Catalogue
Editor: Eimear O'Raw
Co-Editor: Raymond Foye
Designed by Herman Lelie and Stefania Bonelli, London
Enrique Juncosa's text: translation from the Spanish by Jonathan Brennan
Produced by fandg.co.uk
Printed by EBS, Italy
Prepared by the Irish Museum of Modern Art, Dublin

First Published in 2011 by
Irish Museum of Modern Art
Áras Nua-Ealaíne na hÉireann
Royal Hospital, Military Road
Kilmainham, Dublin 8
Ireland
Tel +353 1 612 9900 Fax +353 1 612 9999
E-mail info@imma.ie Website www.imma.ie

Available through D.A.P. / Distributed Art Publishers
155 Sixth Avenue, 2nd Floor, New York, N.Y. 10013
Tel +212 627-1999 Fax +212 627-9484

www.philiptaaffe.info

ISBN: 978-1-907020-60-5

Exhibition kindly supported by

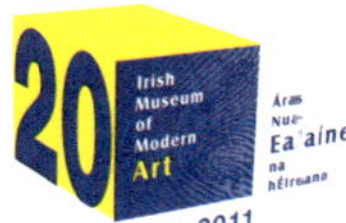

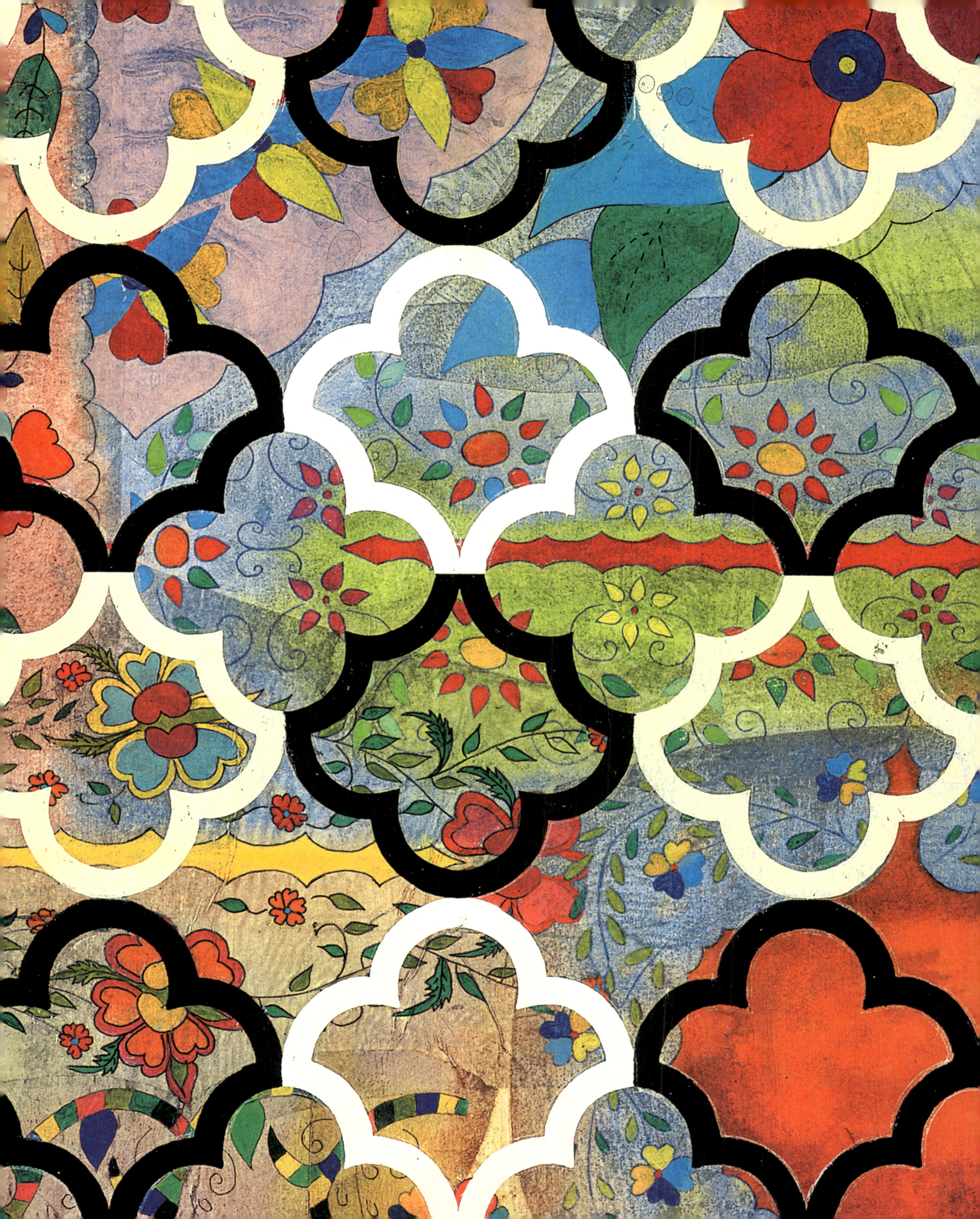

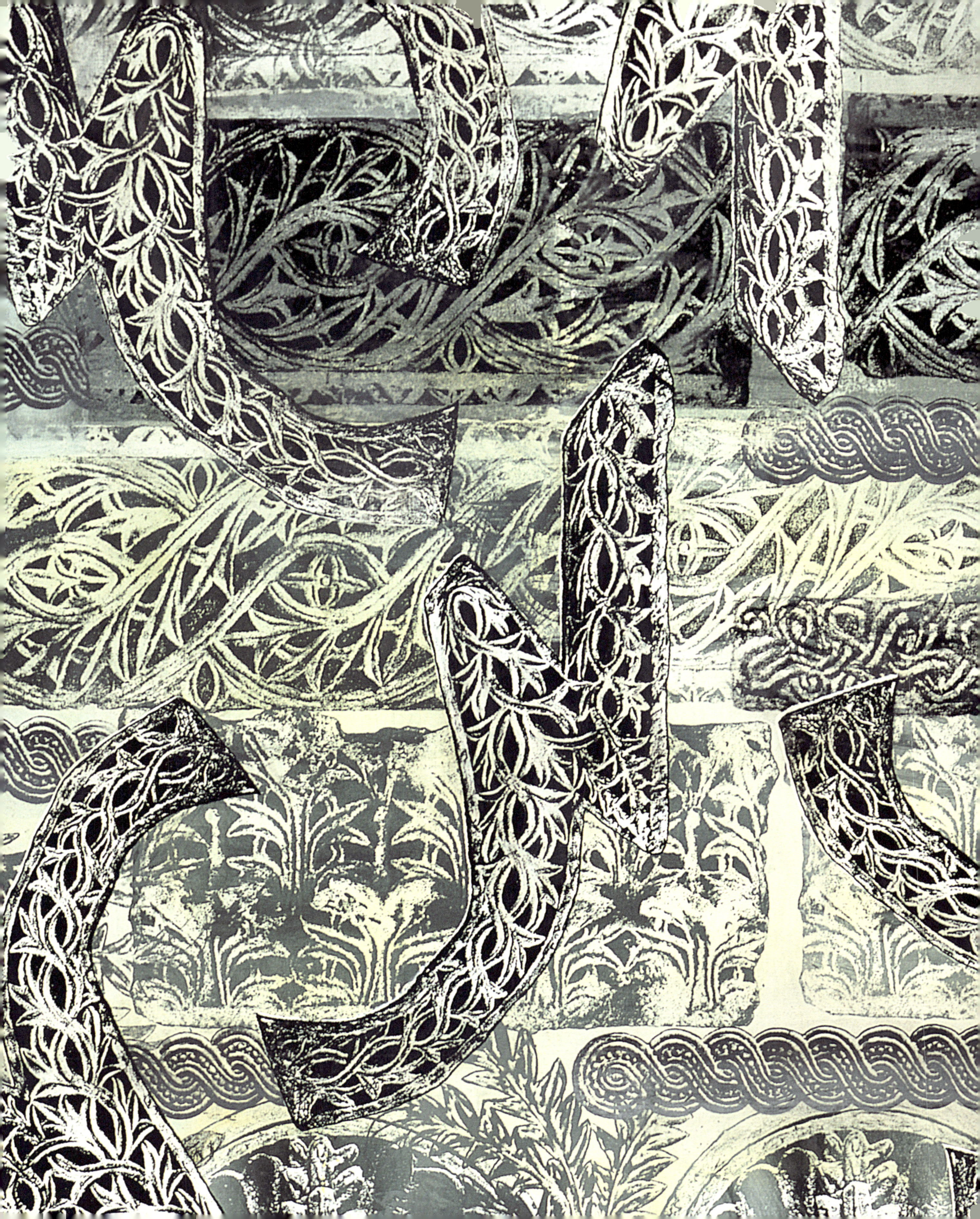

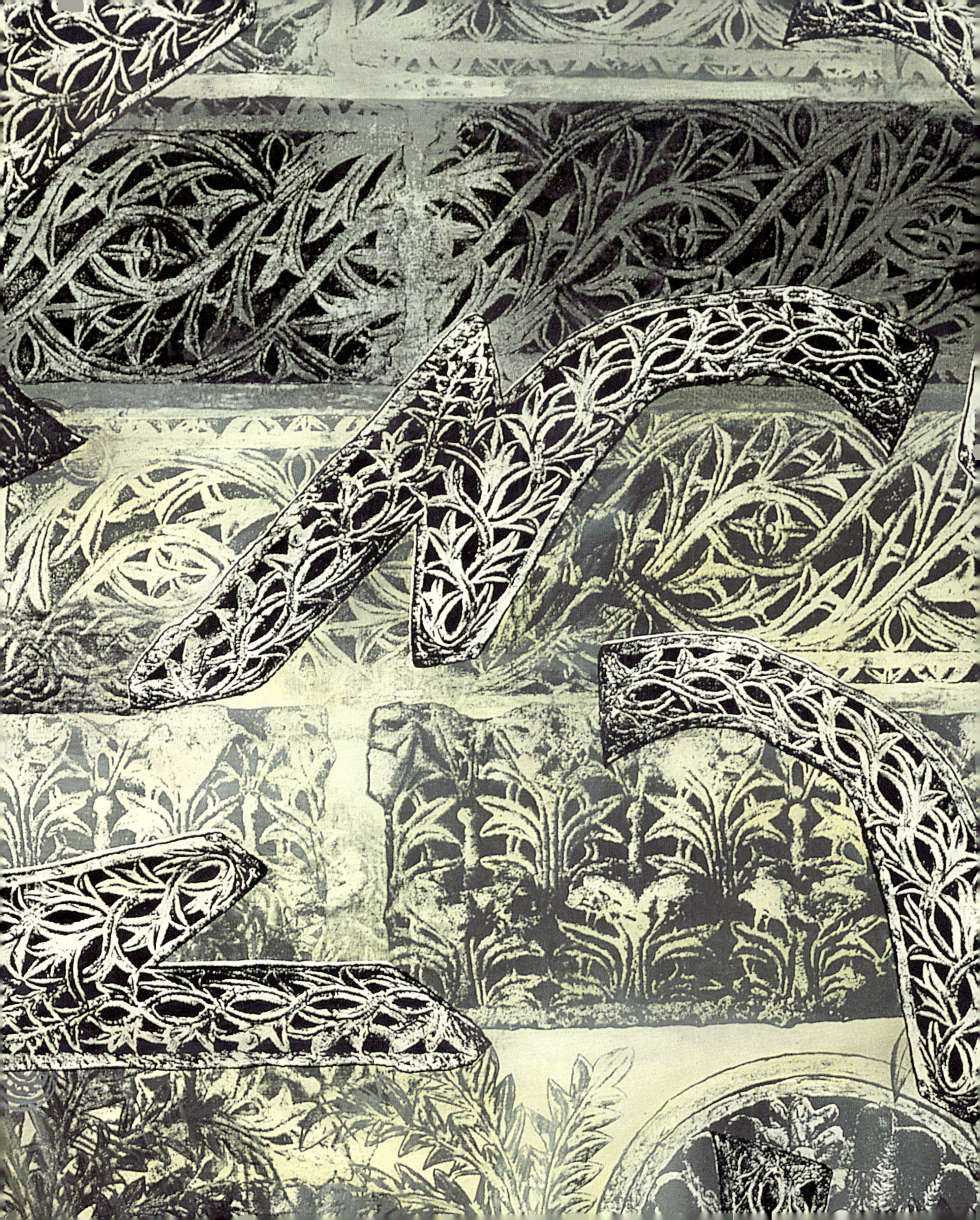

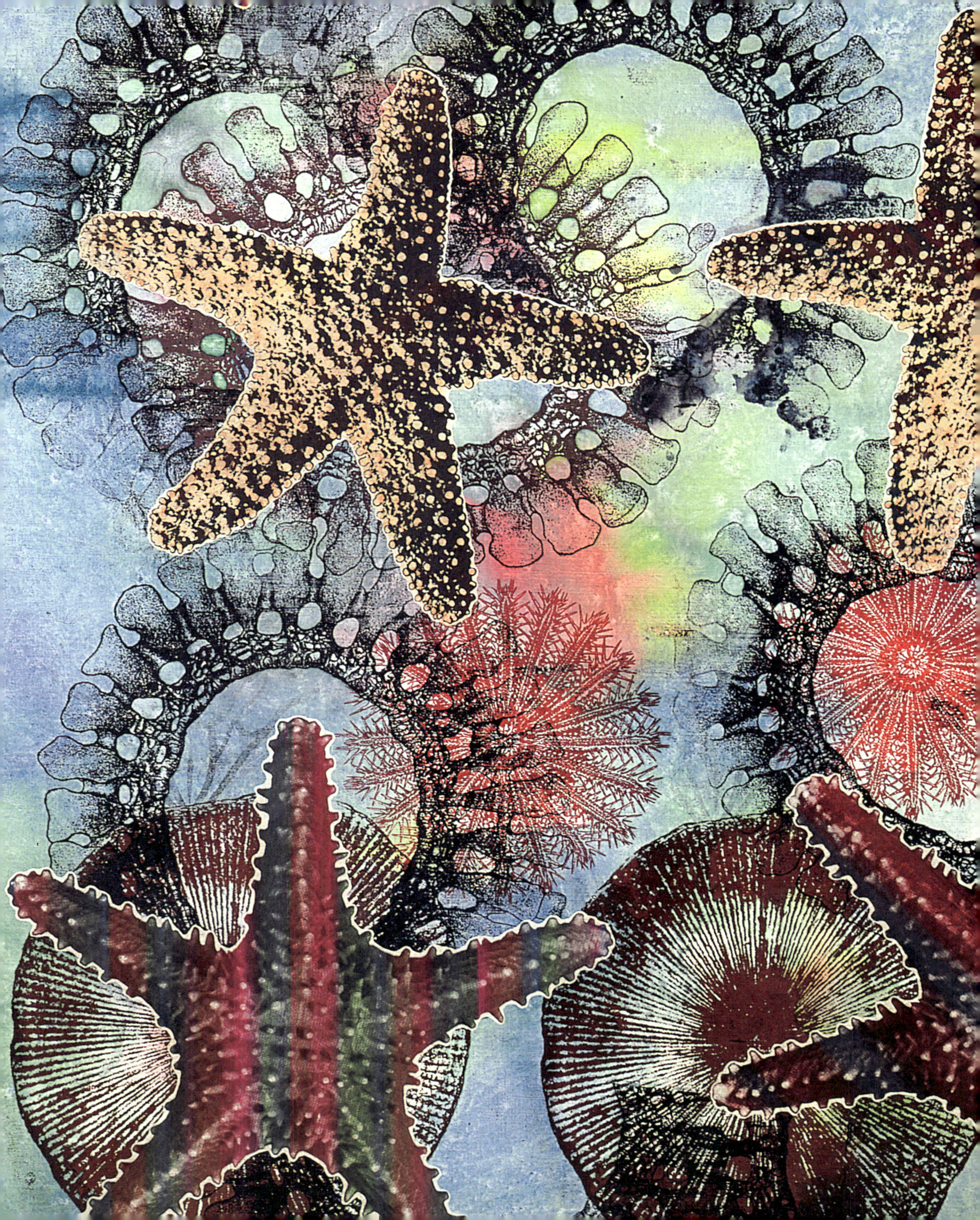